Recursive Block Coding for Image Data Compression

Paul Michael Farrelle

Recursive Block Coding for Image Data Compression

With 90 Figures

Springer-Verlag
New York Berlin Heidelberg
London Paris Tokyo Hong Kong

Paul Michael Farrelle
Optivision, Inc.
Davis, CA 95616
USA

Dedicated
to the memory of
Anil K. Jain (1946–1988)
a truly brilliant man.

Library of Congress Cataloging-in-Publication Data
Farrelle, Paul Michael.
    Recursive block coding for image data compression / Paul Michael Farrelle.
       p.   cm.
    ISBN 0-387-97235-8 (alk. paper)
    1. Image processing—Mathematics.   2. Coding theory.   I. Title.
TA1632.F37   1990
621.36′7—dc20   90-30261

Printed on acid-free paper.

Photocomposed text prepared from the author's Troff file.
Printed and bound by Edwards Brothers, Inc., Ann Arbor, Michigan.
Printed in the United States of America.

9 8 7 6 5 4 3 2 1

ISBN 0-387-97235-8 Springer-Verlag New York Berlin Heidelberg
ISBN 3-540-97235-8 Springer-Verlag Berlin Heidelberg New York

Preface

Image data compression has been the subject of extensive research for the past two decades. It is the results of this research that have provided the basis for the development of efficient image communication and archival systems that are now being introduced at an increasingly rapid rate. This research and development continues as we continually strive to optimize the classical trade off between the amount of compression and the reconstructed image quality. Clearly, as we increase the compression ratio in these controlled quality image coding schemes, then we should expect to see some degradation in the reconstructed image, at least after some point. Depending on the application, the challenge is either to maximize the image quality at a fixed rate, or to minimize the rate required for a given quality.

We have developed a new technique, namely Recursive Block Coding, or RBC, that has its roots in noncausal models for 1d and 2d signals. The underlying theoretical basis provides a multitude of compression algorithms that encompass two source coding, transform coding, quad tree coding, hybrid coding and so on. Since the noncausal models provide a fundamentally different image representation, they lead to new approaches to many existing algorithms and in particular lead to useful approaches for asymmetric, progressive, and adaptive coding techniques.

On the theoretical front, our basic result shows that a random field (i.e., an ensemble of images) can be coded block by block such that the interblock redundancy can be completely removed while the individual blocks are transform coded. For the chosen image models (used commonly in the literature), the optimum (KL) transform for the blocks is shown to be the (fast) discrete sine transform.

On the practical side, the major artifact of *tiling*, a block boundary effect, present in the conventional block by block transform coding techniques has been greatly suppressed. At the same time, the underlying algorithms remain efficient even if the block size is reduced down to 4×4 or 8×8. This would certainly be an important factor in practical, high speed implementations.

This monologue contains not only a theoretical discussion of the algorithms, but also exhaustive simulations and suggested methodologies for ensemble design techniques. Each of the resulting algorithms has been applied to two image ensembles obtained from a total of twelve 512×512 monochrome images, mainly from the USC image database, over a range of image data rates. The results are reported in various ways, namely: subjective descriptions, photographs, mathematical MSE values, and h-plots, a recently proposed graphical representation showing a high level of agreement with image quality as judged subjectively.

PAUL M. FARRELLE

Davis, California
August 1989

Acknowledgments

I would like to express my gratitude to the many people who made this monologue possible. Dr. Anil K. Jain was instrumental to its success because of his keen insight and valuable discussions. Dr. Jorge Sanz, of IBM Research Almaden, was a source of lively discussions, but even more importantly, Jorge was the one who encouraged me to publish this book. I wish to thank Hans J. Dohse, Elizabeth Fenner, and Vivien Braly for their help with the figures. This work was done in the Computer Vision Research Lab. at U. C. Davis and it would not have been as much fun without Iskender Agi, Jim Apffel, Steve Azevedo, Jon Brandt, Ahmed Darwish, Hans Dohse, Sandeep Guliani, David Paglieroni, John Sanders, Brad Van Tighem, Eric Tsujimoto, and Matt Wagner. In this age of computer networks, no lab is an island and I also thank Dr. Ralph Algazi and his programmers: Tom Arons, Richard Rollins, and Jim Stewart from the Signal and Image Processing Laboratory. I would also like to mention three colleagues from British Telecom Research Laboratories: Dr. Norman Kenyon, for introducing me to the image data compression problem, and Dr. Ian Corbett and Dr. John Thompson for their early support which laid the foundations for me to come to U. C. Davis.

Finally I would like to thank Ursula, our daughter Marissa, and my parents for their constant support and encouragement.

Vita

Dr. Paul Michael Farrelle was born in Manchester, England, on April 4, 1959. He entered Jesus College, Cambridge University, England in 1977 and received the B.A. degree (first class honors with distinction) in the Electrical Sciences Tripos in 1980. He was an executive engineer in the picture coding group at British Telecom Research Labs. (BTRL), Martlesham Heath, Ipswich, England from 1980 to 1981 when he was given leave to attend U. C. Davis where he received his M. S. degree in Electrical Engineering in December 1982. After spending another year at BTRL, he returned to U. C. Davis in September 1983 to continue his research and joined the Signal and Image Processing Lab. as a research assistant to Dr. Anil K. Jain. He later helped found the Computer Vision Research Lab (CVRL) which was directed by Dr. Jain and then received his doctorate in March 1988. Since April 1987, he has directed algorithm and software development for image data compression products at Optivision Inc., Davis, California. His research interests include digital signal and image processing, data compression, computer graphics, fast algorithms, and computer architectures.

Publications

Jain, A. K. and P. M. Farrelle, "Recursive block coding," *Proc. 16th Asilomar Conf. Circuits Syst. Comput.*, pp. 431-436, Pacific Grove, CA, Nov. 1982.

Farrelle, P. M., "Recursive block coding techniques for data compression," M. S. Thesis, Signal and Image Processing Laboratory, U. C. Davis, Davis, CA, Dec. 1982.

Farrelle, P. M., "Recursive block coding," *Proc. Colloquium on Transform Techniques in Image Processing*, London, England, May 1983.

Farrelle, P. M. and A. K. Jain, "Recursive block coding," *Proc. International Picture Coding Symposium*, France, 1984.

Jain, A. K., P. M. Farrelle, and V. R. Algazi, "Image Data Compression," in *Digital Image Processing Techniques*, ed. M. Ekstrom, Prentice-Hall, Englewood Cliffs, NJ, 1984.

Farrelle, P. M. and A. K. Jain, "Recursive block coding—a new approach to transform coding," *IEEE Trans. Commun.*, vol. COM-34, pp. 161-179, Feb. 1986.

Farrelle, P. M., S. Srinivasan, and A. K. Jain, "A unified transform architecture," *Proc. ICASSP 86*, pp. 293-296, Tokyo, Japan, April 1986.

Farrelle, P. M. and A. K. Jain, "Recursive block coding with a variable block size," *Proc. International Picture Coding Symposium*, Tokyo, Japan, April 1986.

Farrelle, P. M. and A. K. Jain, "Quad-tree based two source image coding," *MILCOM 86*, pp. 49.2.1-49.2.5, Monterey, CA, Oct. 1986.

Jain, A. K. and P. M. Farrelle, "Recursive block coding techniques for image data compression," *Proc. Symposium on Image Compression*, Center for Telecommunications Research, Columbia University, Oct. 1987.

Jain, A. K., P. M. Farrelle, J. Brandt, and I. A. Agi, "Image data compression: recent advances and future directions," *Proc. 21st Asilomar Conf. Circuits Syst. Comput.*, Pacific Grove, CA, Nov. 1987.

Jain, A. K. and P. M. Farrelle, "Image data compression techniques," *Proc. Indo-U.S. Symposium on Signals and Systems*, Bangalore, India, Jan. 1988.

Farrelle, P. M., "Recursive block coding," Ph. D. Dissertation, Computer Vision Research Laboratory, U. C. Davis, Davis, CA, March 1988.

Farrelle, P. M., D. G. Harrington, and A. K. Jain, "Image data compression in a PC environment," Appl. of Digital Image Processing XI, Andrew G. Tescher, Ed., *Proc. SPIE 974*, pp. 177-186, Dec. 1988.

Farrelle, P. M., "A programmable image compression system," *Proc. International Workshop on Visual Information Processing for Television and Telerobotics*, Williamsburg, VA, May 1989.

Table of Contents

List of Figures

List of Tables

List of Algorithms

1

Introduction

1.1 The Need for Data Compression

Digital image data arises for one of three reasons: the image source is inherently digital; we desire to use digital techniques to process images which may actually be analog; or we desire, or have no choice but to use digital transmission networks or digital storage media. Images arise from broadcast TV, videoconference, satellite, medical, and seismic applications, among others, but whatever their origin they invariably contain an enormous amount of data after digitization. This is achieved by sampling the image, or each image in a sequence, in both the horizontal and vertical directions and then each resulting analog sample is digitized using an analog-to-digital converter (ADC) with equally spaced output levels to form a digital picture element, or pixel. This raw digital representation is called pulse code modulation (PCM) and typical image channels are quantized using 8 bits/pixel.

In some cases the image acquisition process itself performs the sampling and quantization while othertimes the analog, and possibly continuous, signal is digitized externally as a second stage. For example, traditional vidicon cameras used in the television industry produce a one-dimensional (1d) signal which represents an image which has already been sampled in the temporal and vertical directions, while more modern solid state charge couple device (CCD) cameras also sample the image along the scan line in the horizontal direction and so the camera output is already sampled in both directions. The output of a CCD array is a series of analog amplitudes corresponding to the amount of light which hits each pixel. However, the output of the camera may be either analog (RS-170) or digital depending on whether or not the camera contains internal ADCs.

Monochrome (black and white) images contain only one channel while color images contain three channels where each channel contains samples from one component in the color coordinate system which may be the three primary colors (RGB) or the luminance and chrominance signals (YIQ) or (YUV). Satellite image data contains even more channels, for example LANDSAT produces images in seven frequency bands. If we sample at rates comparable to conventional TV image quality then the image may contain $512 \times 512 \times 8 = 2.10 \times 10^6$ bits/channel for a single frame. If we consider color image sequences at frame rates of 30Hz, as in broadcast TV, then if each channel were sampled at the same rate and each pixel were quantized using 8 bits/channel then the data rate would be 188.74×10^6 bits/sec.

It is now easy to appreciate the need for data compression whenever we have a wideband video source signal but only a narrowband communication link or storage medium, e.g. computer networks, telephone links, and magnetic disks or tapes. In particular, the many applications include: single frame image transmission, broadcast TV transmission, videoconferencing, remotely piloted vehicles (RPVs), document archival systems, digital radiology networks, and systems requiring access to large engineering drawing, and image data bases.

There are two main categories of compression: lossy and lossless. Lossless compression may be achieved using open-loop DPCM for example [1, 2] but the attainable compression factor is rather limited at somewhere between 2:1 and 3:1 depending on image statistics. Lossy compression on the other hand can be designed to offer any desired amount of compression at the expense of the quality of the reconstructed image after decompression. The issue now becomes how to achieve a certain compression rate while optimizing the image quality, or vice versa, how to maintain a desired quality while minimizing the data rate. This book addresses these issues but makes no attempt to achieve lossless compression.

1.2   Data Compression Techniques

The various methods available to achieve data compression are [3-5] based on predictive, transform, and vector quantization techniques, with possible hybrid combinations.

Predictive Coding—DPCM

Differential pulse code modulation (DPCM), perhaps the simplest practical data compression algorithm, achieves compression by exploiting local correlation directly in the image spatial domain. Rather than directly encoding the pixel intensity, neighboring pixels are used to form a prediction of its value and it is the prediction error which is encoded. In a highly correlated image, a well chosen predictor will produce a prediction error which is small on the average. This variance reduction is the basis of DPCM based compression schemes. Since the prediction error has a smaller variance than the original image it means that, if we reduce the number of bits available to encode each pixel, then the quantization noise will be less if we use DPCM rather than PCM at the same reduced rate. In our work we will not use DPCM directly but rather in hybrid coding where DPCM is used together with transform coding.

Transform Coding

To obtain a large amount of data compression, up to 50:1 for single frames, we must use transform coding rather than predictive techniques. Transform coding is significantly different from DPCM and achieves compression in the transform or *generalized frequency* domain. For the one dimensional (1d) case, the image is divided into mutually exclusive blocks and typical block sizes are 1×8 and 1×16. Larger block sizes offer better compression, up to a point, at the expense of increased complexity. The block of data is then considered as a vector and is linearly transformed by multiplying it by a transform matrix. The aim is to transform an original vector, which has energy equally distributed among the samples, to a new space where most of the energy is concentrated in only a few coefficients. Data compression can then be achieved by coding only those coefficients that have substantial energy.

A number of transforms have been considered for image coding including the discrete Fourier (DFT) [6], cosine (DCT) [7], sine (DST) [8], Walsh-Hadamard (WHT) [9], Haar (Hr) [10], Slant or Slant Walsh (SWT) [11,12], and Slant-Haar (SHT) [13] transforms. All of these transforms have a fast algorithm and in addition are separable so that a two dimensional (2d) transformation can be achieved by sequentially applying a 1d transformation in each direction.

Karhunen-Lòeve Transform (KLT)

The statistically optimal transform for data compression is the KLT which is determined by the autocorrelation matrix of the source [1, chapter 11]. In particular the rows of the KLT are the eigenvectors of this matrix. Unfortunately this transformation has no fast algorithm in general and this is why tremendous efforts have been made to try and determine a transform which has a fast algorithm and also closely approximates the performance of the KLT. It now seems to be generally accepted that the DCT [7] is the best choice for common image data having high inter-pixel correlation. We shall discuss DCT performance in more detail in chapters four and five.

Hybrid Coding

This coding method was first proposed by Habibi [14] and in our work we extend the method to derive hybrid RBC. Hybrid coding combines the advantages of transform coding and DPCM to produce a technique which performs somewhere between 1d and 2d transform coding but with a system that is only slightly more complex than the 1d transform coder. The basic configuration is a 1d transform coder with a DPCM coder for each active transform coefficient. Instead of encoding the coefficient directly we use a DPCM coder which exploits correlation in the direction orthogonal to the transform coder leading to improved performance at the expense of a few DPCM coders for the active transform coefficients.

Vector Quantization (VQ)

Vector quantization is not a new idea but it has received a great deal of attention recently. It originates from the pioneering work of Shannon [15, 16] who showed that better performance can always be achieved by quantizing the source as a series of vectors rather than scalars, even if the source is memoryless, that is each member of the sequence is independent of the rest. Perhaps the current interest is due to the advent of faster computers and VLSI implementations [17, 18] because, although the decoding stage is particularly simple, the design and encoding stages are very computationally intensive. Despite the computational load, the basic principle of VQ is extremely straightforward. We first divide the image into regions which are typically square blocks, but could be any tessellating shape, and then code these samples collectively. The term *vector* comes from the fact that we code all of the samples in this region (vector) by a single codeword. The codeword is an index into a vector codebook and points to the codebook entry which is closest to the input vector. If the number of codebook entries is less than the total number of possible input vectors then we have achieved some data compression. For example if we consider a vector of length 16 which might be due to a block size of 4×4, 8×2 or 16×1, etc., then if the codebook contains 4096 vectors each codeword is 12 bits long and the average data rate is $12/16 = 0.75$ bits/pixel.

1.3   The Problem—the Tile Effect

Perhaps the limiting factor for image data compression using transform coding or VQ is the so-called *block* or *tile* effect. At sufficiently high rates, the loss of fidelity is a continuous function of the data rate. However there comes a point when any further reduction in the rate produces the *tile effect* and this leads to a huge discontinuity in the perceived fidelity. In a recent paper [19] Miyahara reported subjective results that this artifact is 10 times more objectionable than equal energy random noise. The cause of the problem is that each block of the image is coded independently, that is without reference to the neighboring blocks, and so the distortion introduced by the coding is discontinuous from block to block. The eye picks up the change in luminance at the edges of the blocks, especially in the smooth regions where no such change is expected. Furthermore, the effect is amplified since the regular block structure ensures that these problem areas are all aligned and the resulting image resembles a mosaic constructed from small tiles. In other words we are sensitive not only to the amplitude of errors but also to their structure.

1.4   Our Approach—Two Source Decomposition

We now describe our approach to the problem of limiting the *tile effect*, but first let us describe some previous efforts. Reeve and Lim [20] attacked the problem directly and proposed two techniques to limit the artifact. The first was to overlap the blocks so that the pixels in these overlapping regions are coded in two, or more, blocks. After decoding, any pixel which is coded in more than one block is reconstructed as the average of these values. This seems to work well but it leads to an overhead of 13% for 16×16 blocks and even more for smaller blocks. The second technique uses a normal block structure with no overlap so that there is no overhead and operates by low pass filtering the image along the block boundaries after decoding. However this approach will tend to replace the sharp block structure with a blurred structure which may be more acceptable but is still an artifact.

More recent theoretical work by Nakagawa and Miyahara [21] shows some promise for limiting the artifact although the technique is yet to be confirmed for practical images. In this work the concept of the KLT is generalized to a distortion measure that is position dependent. In this way it is possible to design transforms which will produce a small error at the block boundaries at the expense of those pixels towards the center. This will produce an increased error rate when compared to the traditional KLT design but there is potential for improved visual quality by striving for continuity at the block boundaries.

Work by Meiri and Yudilevich [22] is similar to our approach and both their "pinned sine transform coder" and our "recursive block coder" have their roots in earlier work by Jain [4, 8, 23]. The general scheme is to model the image using stochastic partial differential or difference equations (PDEs) of the form

$$Lx = \epsilon \qquad (1.4.1)$$

where L is a linear differential or difference operator, x is some finite segment of the image, and ϵ is the stochastic error signal which drives the model. When coding a block of the image we separate the observed pixel values into the sum of two sources. The first is the prediction or *boundary response*, $x_b(n)$, which is the solution of $Lx = 0$ subject to the values at the block boundaries. The second is the prediction error or *residual* $y(n)$ where

$$y(n) \overset{\Delta}{=} x(n) - x_b(n) \qquad (1.4.2)$$

which is the component of the pixel value which arises from the stochastic nature of the model and also any deterministic factors such as edges which are not accounted for by the model. The boundaries are coded using PCM for example and the residual is then transform coded using the DST [24].

The reason why this two source decomposition (x_b, y) reduces the *tile effect* is because if we share the boundary values, which are typically one pixel wide, between two neighboring blocks then the boundary response which interpolates the boundary values will be continuous across the transition from one block to the next despite any coding distortion in the boundaries. Furthermore, as shown in section 2.13, the prediction is such that the residuals from adjacent blocks are uncorrelated which means that we do not expect continuity in this component, and since the blocks are also physically separated by the boundary pixel(s), any artifacts due to block coding the residual will not produce such an objectionable *tile effect* in the output which is the superposition of the continuous boundary response and the residual.

Meiri and Yudilevich use a continuous PDE and then approximate the continuous solution for the boundary response while we start with a discrete model and remain in this domain throughout, and as we shall show in chapter two their boundary response is in fact a Coon's patch [25, p. 198] which differs greatly from the solution of the discrete PDE.

Two source coding schemes have been used before as a way to segment the image into stationary or low frequency regions and nonstationarities or edges with the aim of more efficiently coding the individual components rather than the composite signal. These earlier methods were not concerned directly with the *tile effect* but we will briefly mention them here.

The first efforts were made by Schreiber *et. al.* [26, 27] who segment the image into low and high frequency components and then encode the low frequency components but only send the location of the high frequency components which are the transitions between the low frequency regions. The decoder then simulates these high frequency components using *synthetic highs* which are proportional to the Laplacian of a unit step signal.

Yan and Sakrison [28] fit a piecewise linear function to an image scan line (actually the contrast rather than the intensity) and then encode the position and amplitude of the breakpoints to form the first component. The second residual component is the difference between the original and the piecewise linear approximation and this is coded using a full frame 256×256 Fourier transform coder.

1.5   Organization

Having described our approach to solving the specific problem of reducing the *tile effect* we can now describe the layout of this book. In chapter two we introduce the fundamental theory underlying the RBC algorithm. Some of this work is a repeat of material that we have presented earlier but is included here so that this becomes a self contained reference superceding our previous publications. New results include a spatial domain description of the prediction function (surface) which is derived by solving the boundary problems directly rather than resorting to transform domain methods. As a result of this we are able to better understand previous efforts in this field [22] and provide a unifying theory.

In chapter three we turn our attention to the bit allocation problem and review previous results. We then point out some of the shortcomings of earlier approximations and provide some new piecewise closed form equations for the allocation process based on more accurate approximations made by Wang and Jain [29]. We also stress the integer bit allocation algorithm which has been mentioned in past research efforts but has not yet achieved widespread acceptance.

In chapter four we introduce a quantitative error measure [30] and then apply the non-adaptive RBC and DCT coding algorithms to two image ensembles and compare results of computer simulations for 1d, hybrid, and 2d schemes. In chapter five we make the algorithm more flexible by allowing adaptive classification and again compare RBC and DCT coding.

In chapter six we move away from fixed blocks to a new algorithm which is based on a variable block size determined by a quad-tree segmentation. The statistical prediction is replaced by the simpler bilinear form and the residual is then transform coded and various transforms are investigated before determining that the DCT produces the best subjective results. In chapter seven we return to the residual image resulting from the quad-tree segmentation and apply vector quantization instead of transform coding. The various algorithms presented in earlier chapters are then discussed and compared in the concluding chapter.

Finally, the appendices provide supplementary expositions that support the main discussion at various points throughout the book.

2

RBC—The Theory
behind the Algorithms

2.1 Introduction

RBC is based on representing digital images by discrete models and then using these models to derive algorithms for image data compression. In this chapter we will introduce the models and their properties and describe the resulting generic RBC algorithms, in one and two dimensions. In later chapters we will provide variations on the basic theme by allowing for adaptation within the algorithm.

In particular, we discuss modeling in section 2.2 and then in section 2.3 we introduce autoregressive (AR) models which form the basis for the 1d theory. We then derive the 1d theory in sections 2.4 and 2.5 leading to the 1d RBC algorithm in section 2.6. We then study the boundary response in detail in section 2.7.

We turn to 2d image models in sections 2.8 and 2.9 and determine the 2d boundary response in section 2.10. The 2d RBC algorithm is presented in section 2.11 and then an approximate boundary response leads to a simplified algorithm in section 2.12. The chapter then concludes with a discussion of the advantages of RBC in section 2.13.

2.2 Modeling

Models come in two basic types: *deterministic* and *stochastic*, and they are differentiated by whether or not they contain *random variables* (rv's).

As a simple example, consider the deterministic model:

$$x(n) = \alpha x(n-1) ; \quad n = 1, 2, \cdots \qquad (2.2.1)$$

Given an initial value, $x(0)$, this model generates the sequence:

$$x(n) = \alpha^n x(0) ; \quad n = 1, 2, \cdots \qquad (2.2.2)$$

which is completely determined by the initial value of the sequence.

We can modify the deterministic model to form the simple stochastic model:

$$x(n) = \alpha x(n-1) + e(n) \; ; \quad n = 1, 2, \; \cdots \qquad (2.2.3)$$

where $e(n)$ is a sequence of independent identically distributed (iid) rv's.

Given the initial value, $x(0)$, this model generates the sequence:

$$x(n) = \alpha^n x(0) + \{\alpha^{n-1}e(1) + \alpha^{n-2}e(2) + \; \cdots$$
$$\cdots \; + \alpha e(n-1) + e(n)\} \; ; \quad n = 1, 2, \; \cdots \qquad (2.2.4)$$

which is no longer completely determined by the initial value of the sequence. Moreover it is not even determined by all the past values since for each n there is an uncertainty, or *innovation* $e(n)$, which is independent of the previous values of the sequence.

We refer to the set of all possible sequences and their law of generation, the model, as the *process*. In this work, when deriving 1d algorithms, we have assumed that the original process is AR. We will first discuss the prediction properties of AR models and then use these to develop the noncausal decomposition of AR processes into two mutually uncorrelated processes which forms the basis for RBC.

2.3 Autoregressive Models

AR models arise when we use a *causal* minimum variance representation (MVR) for a stochastic sequence [1 (chapter 6),31, 32]. That is, we write the current value of the sequence as the sum of a causal prediction and the resulting prediction error, viz.,

$$\boxed{x(n) = \bar{x}(n) + \epsilon(n)} \qquad (2.3.1)$$

where the predictor, $\bar{x}(n)$, is chosen to minimize the mean square value of the prediction error, $\epsilon(n)$, and we define this minimum as

$$\sigma^2 \triangleq \min_{\bar{x}(n)}\{E[\epsilon^2(n)]\} \; . \qquad (2.3.2)$$

The predictor is the conditional mean, viz.,

$$\bar{x}(n) = E[x(n) \mid x(n-l) \; ; \; l = 1,2, \; \cdots] \qquad (2.3.3)$$

which will, in general, be a nonlinear combination of the past values. However, if the $x(n)$ process is Gaussian, or *normal*, then the predictor will in fact be linear. In any case, we choose to limit ourselves to linear predictors from now on so when we refer to an MVR it should be understood that we intend a *linear* MVR.

After imposing the linear constraint, $\bar{x}(n)$ becomes the predictor which is a weighted sum of past values of the sequence, viz.,

$$\bar{x}(n) = \sum_{l=1}^{\infty} h(l)x(n-l)$$ (2.3.4)

where the prediction coefficients $h(1), h(2), \ldots$ are found by minimizing the prediction mean square error (MSE). The result requires solving a set of *normal equations* [31] that arise from the orthogonality condition

$$E[\epsilon(n)x(n-l)] = 0 ; \quad l = 1, 2, \cdots .$$ (2.3.5)

We will not pursue the derivation here, just noting that the coefficients are a function of the correlation function of the sequence $x(n)$. We now use the orthogonality condition to determine the prediction error correlation function. In words, (2.3.5) states that the prediction error is uncorrelated with the past values of the sequence. Furthermore, it is seen from (2.3.1) that each past value is itself the sum of previous values and a past prediction error, consequently the current prediction error is uncorrelated with past prediction errors and its correlation function is

$$r_\epsilon(l) \triangleq E[\epsilon(n)\epsilon(n-l)] = \sigma^2\delta(l)$$ (2.3.6)

where $\delta(l)$, the Kronecker delta function, takes the value of one when $l = 0$ but is otherwise always zero.

The spectral density function (SDF), or simply the power spectrum, of a random sequence $x(n)$ with correlation function $r_x(l)$ is defined as

$$S_x(z) \triangleq \sum_{l=-\infty}^{\infty} r_x(l)z^{-l} = S_x(z^{-1}); \quad z = e^{j\omega} .$$ (2.3.7)

So applying this definition to $r_\epsilon(l)$ we see that the prediction error is a *white* noise sequence with constant SDF

$$S_\epsilon(z) = \sigma^2 ; \quad z = e^{j\omega} .$$ (2.3.8)

The causal MVR is a linear difference equation and we can use discrete linear system theory to relate the power spectra of $\epsilon(n)$ and $x(n)$ which are the input and output of a linear system, called the *realization filter* (RF), with transfer function $\dfrac{1}{H(z)}$ as shown in Fig. 2.3.1(b). In particular we have [33, p. 347]

$$S_x(z) = \frac{S_\epsilon(z)}{H(z)H(z^{-1})} = \frac{\sigma^2}{H(z)H(z^{-1})} ; \quad z = e^{j\omega} .$$ (2.3.9)

where

$$H(z) \triangleq 1 - \sum_{l=1}^{\infty} h(l)z^{-l}$$ (2.3.10)

is the transfer function of the *prediction error filter* (PEF).

It should be noted that the causal MVR is an all pole model and therefore if the SDF of the sequence $x(n)$ is all pole with a finite number of poles, then the predictor will also be of finite order. However, if the SDF contains zeros, then we will not be able to find a finite number of parameters $h(l)$ for a white noise driven system (Fig. 2.3.1 (b)) whose output actually matches the power spectrum of $x(n)$. Conversely we will not be able to find a PEF such that the output of Fig. 2.3.1(a) is a white noise sequence. In other words, there will be no finite causal MVR which will generate the required SDF, but it is always possible to approximate such a SDF to an arbitrary accuracy by increasing the filter order, p [31, 34].

We define the output of the pth-order causal RF, when driven by white noise, as a pth-order Markov sequence and the corresponding MVR is a pth-order AR model.

Random sequences, including speech signals and 1d scan lines of images, are often modeled by the pth-order AR process

$$x(n) = \sum_{l=1}^{p} h(l)x(n-l) + \epsilon(n)$$

(2.3.11)

where $h(1),...,h(p)$ are the autoregression constants, $\epsilon(n)$ is a sequence of iid rv's with zero mean and variance σ^2, and, as noted above, the orthogonality condition ensures that $\epsilon(n)$ and $x(m)$ are statistically uncorrelated if $n > m$.

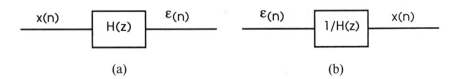

(a)   (b)

FIGURE 2.3.1. Linear system representation for a causal MVR. (a) Prediction Error Filter (PEF); (b) Realization Filter (RF).

The model generates an all pole SDF for $x(n)$, so in practice the order p is chosen so that the model spectrum is sufficiently close to that of the real data.

The stationarity of the sequence $x(n)$ is determined by [35, p. 222] the location of the zeros of the PEF, $H_p(z)$,

$$H_p(z) \triangleq 1 - h(1)z^{-1} - \cdots - h(p)z^{-p} \qquad (2.3.12)$$

and if they are all within the unit circle, then the AR process is asymptotically stationary.

Example—1st-order AR process

For the simple, but often used, 1st-order AR process, the defining equation is simply

$$x(n) = h(1)x(n-1) + \epsilon(n), \qquad (2.3.13)$$

which is stationary if $|h(1)| < 1$. Assuming stationarity, we consider the correlation function, $r_x(l)$,

$$r_x(l) \triangleq E[x(n)x(n+l)]$$
$$= h(1)E[x(n)x(n+l-1)] + E[x(n)\epsilon(n+l)] . \qquad (2.3.14)$$

Now since $x(n)$ and $\epsilon(n+l)$ are uncorrelated the second term is zero and

$$r_x(l) = h(1)r_x(l-1) = \sigma_x^2[h(1)]^{|l|}. \qquad (2.3.15)$$

So the AR coefficient, $h(1)$, is the one step correlation coefficient, ρ, and we can restate the equations as:

$$x(n) = \rho x(n-1) + \epsilon(n), \qquad (2.3.16)$$

$$r_x(l) = \sigma_x^2 \rho^{|l|}. \qquad (2.3.17)$$

We can also relate the variance of the AR sequence $x(n)$ to that of the driving sequence, $\epsilon(n)$, via

$$\sigma^2 = E[\epsilon^2(n)] = E\left\{[x(n) - \rho x(n-1)]^2\right\} = \sigma_x^2(1-\rho^2) . \quad (2.3.18)$$

Hence

$$\sigma_x^2 = \frac{\sigma^2}{1-\rho^2} . \qquad (2.3.19)$$

2.4 Noncausal Models

In the previous section we limited ourselves to causal PEFs. In some applications causality is a physical limitation. For example, if we wish to model the stock market we can only use previous observations to predict what will happen tomorrow or next month.

However, in data compression applications we can impose some delay in the system and use "future" values to help us encode the current values, so long as we transmit or store the "future" values for decoding. Furthermore in two or more dimensions, causality is no longer an intrinsic constraint. In practice causality is often enforced due to some fixed scanning pattern which generates a 1d sequence from the multi-dimensional data. This is the case with conventional TV cameras where the camera tube is scanned from left to right and top to bottom 30 times per second to give a 1d signal representation of 3d moving images.

In this section we will derive noncausal models by removing the causality constraint which, for our image coding application, is equivalent to assuming that we are able to buffer some portion of the image for processing.

We define a noncausal linear MVR where the prediction estimate depends on future as well as past values of $x(n)$, i.e.,

$$x(n) = \sum_{l \neq 0} a(l)x(n-l) + e(n) \qquad (2.4.1)$$

where $e(n)$ is the noncausal prediction error sequence, whose statistics are as yet unknown. The prediction coefficients $a(l)$ are again chosen to minimize the prediction MSE. These prediction coefficients are obtained by solving a related set of *normal equations* similar to the causal design. In the *z-transform* domain the solution becomes [31, 32]

$$A(z) = \frac{\beta^2}{S_x(z)} ; \quad z = e^{j\omega} \qquad (2.4.2)$$

where $A(z)$ is the PEF

$$A(z) = - \sum_{l=-\infty}^{\infty} a(l)z^{-l}; \quad a(0) \triangleq -1, \qquad (2.4.3)$$

β^2 is the minimized value of the prediction error, and $S_x(z)$ is the SDF of the sequence $x(n)$.

We may also interpret the noncausal MVR as a system with input $e(n)$, output $x(n)$ and transfer function $\dfrac{1}{A(z)}$. Hence the input and output SDFs are related by

$$S_x(z) = \frac{S_e(z)}{A(z)A(z^{-1})} . \qquad (2.4.4)$$

Substituting for $S_x(z)$ from (2.4.2) we obtain the prediction error SDF as

$$S_e(z) = \beta^2 A(z^{-1}) = \beta^2 A(z) \qquad (2.4.5)$$

with corresponding covariance function

$$r_e(l) = \beta^2 \left\{ \delta(l) - \sum_{m=1}^{\infty} a(m)(\delta(l-m) + \delta(l+m)) \right\}. \qquad (2.4.6)$$

In particular, if $x(n)$ is an AR process, then it has been shown earlier [31] that if we define $h(0) \triangleq -1$ then we can determine the noncausal MVR parameters for a pth-order AR process as

$$a(l) = \begin{cases} \dfrac{-\sum_{m=0}^{p-l} h(m)h(l+m)}{\sum_{m=0}^{p} h^2(m)} & ; 1 \le |l| \le p, \\[20pt] 0 & ; \text{otherwise,} \end{cases} \qquad (2.4.7)$$

and

$$\beta^2 = \frac{\sigma^2}{\sum_{m=0}^{p} h^2(m)}. \qquad (2.4.8)$$

Thus the noncausal MVR for a pth-order AR process is

$$x(n) = \sum_{l=1}^{p} a(l)[x(n-l) + x(n+l)] + e(n) \qquad (2.4.9)$$

and the correlation function of the prediction error sequence is

$$r_e(l) = E[e(n)e(n-l)]$$
$$= \beta^2 \left\{ \delta(l) - \sum_{m=1}^{p} a(m)(\delta(l-m) + \delta(l+m)) \right\} \qquad (2.4.10)$$

so $e(n)$ is a *colored* noise sequence unlike its causal counterpart $\epsilon(n)$ which is white.

Example—noncausal MVR for a 1st-order AR sequence

For a 1st-order AR sequence, with correlation coefficient ρ, the above equations simplify to

$$a(1) = \frac{\rho}{(1+\rho^2)}, \qquad (2.4.11)$$

$$x(n) = \frac{\rho}{(1+\rho^2)}[x(n-1) + x(n+1)] + e(n), \qquad (2.4.12)$$

$$\beta^2 = E[e^2(n)] = \frac{\sigma^2}{(1+\rho^2)} = \sigma_x^2 \left[\frac{1-\rho^2}{1+\rho^2} \right].$$

2.5 Two Source Decomposition

We are now ready to derive the 1d RBC algorithm for pth-order Markov sequences. We have already shown how to derive the noncausal PEF coefficients for such a process in the preceding section. However, so far we have assumed an infinite sequence and ignored the boundary effects.

Now let us consider a finite segment of the pth-order Markov sequence of length $(N+2p)$, say, then (2.4.9) becomes

$$
\begin{bmatrix} e(1) \\ \cdot \\ \cdot \\ \cdot \\ e(N) \end{bmatrix}
+
\begin{bmatrix}
a(1)x(0)+a(2)x(-1)+\cdots+a(p)x(-p+1) \\
a(2)x(0)+\cdots+a(p)x(-p+2) \\
\cdot \\
a(p)x(0) \\
0 \\
\cdot \\
0 \\
a(p)x(N+1) \\
\cdot \\
a(2)x(N+1)+\cdots+a(p)x(N+p-1) \\
a(1)x(N+1)+a(2)x(N+2)+\cdots+a(p)x(N+p)
\end{bmatrix}
\qquad (2.5.1)
$$

If $\mathbf{x}$ and $\mathbf{e}$ are defined as $N \times 1$ vectors of components $x(1), \ldots, x(N)$ and $e(1), \ldots, e(N)$ respectively, then (2.5.1) can be written in vector form as

$$\boxed{\mathbf{Tx} = \mathbf{e} + \mathbf{b}_f} \tag{2.5.2}$$

where $\mathbf{T}$ is a symmetric $N \times N$ banded Toeplitz matrix with p sub-diagonals, and $\mathbf{b}_f$, the $N \times 1$ *filtered boundary* vector, contains only $2p$ non-zero terms which depend on the boundary values consisting of the *initial* values

$$\mathbf{x}_i \triangleq [x(-p+1), \ldots, x(0)]^T \tag{2.5.3}$$

and the *terminal* values

$$\mathbf{x}_t \triangleq [x(N+1), \ldots, x(N+p)]^T \tag{2.5.4}$$

where the superscript T denotes transposition. In particular, we can write $\mathbf{b}_f$ in vector form as

$$\mathbf{b}_f = \mathbf{Fb} \tag{2.5.5}$$

where

$$\mathbf{b} \triangleq \begin{bmatrix} \mathbf{x}_i \\ \cdots \\ \mathbf{x}_t \end{bmatrix}, \tag{2.5.6}$$

$$\mathbf{F} \triangleq \begin{bmatrix} \mathbf{f} & \mathbf{0} \\ \mathbf{0} & \mathbf{0} \\ \mathbf{0} & \mathbf{f}^T \end{bmatrix}, \tag{2.5.7}$$

and

$$\mathbf{f} \triangleq \begin{bmatrix} a(p) & . & . & a(2) & a(1) \\ & & & & a(2) \\ & & & & . \\ & \mathbf{0} & & & . \\ & & & & . \\ & & & & a(p) \end{bmatrix}. \tag{2.5.8}$$

Note that $\mathbf{b}$ is a $2p \times 1$ vector, $\mathbf{f}$ is a $p \times p$ matrix and $\mathbf{F}$ is an $N \times 2p$ matrix.

The vector equation (2.5.2) leads directly to a two source decomposition of $\mathbf{x}$, viz.,

$$\boxed{\mathbf{x} = \mathbf{x}_b + \mathbf{y}}$$

(2.5.9)

where

$$\boxed{\begin{aligned} \mathbf{x}_b &\triangleq \mathbf{T}^{-1}\mathbf{b}_f = (\mathbf{T}^{-1}\mathbf{F})\mathbf{b}\;, \\ \mathbf{y} &\triangleq \mathbf{x} - \mathbf{x}_b = \mathbf{T}^{-1}\mathbf{e}\;. \end{aligned}}$$

(2.5.10)

We now have $\mathbf{x}$ as the sum of two processes: $\mathbf{x}_b$ and $\mathbf{y}$. The first, $\mathbf{x}_b$, is the solution of the difference equation (2.4.9) in the absence of the driving term $\mathbf{e}$, viz.,

$$x(n) - \sum_{l=1}^{p} a(l)[x(n-l) + x(n+l)] = 0\;; \quad n = 1, \ldots, N \qquad (2.5.11)$$

given the boundary conditions, $\mathbf{x}_i$ and $\mathbf{x}_t$. This is a deterministic boundary value problem and so we call $\mathbf{x}_b$ the boundary response. If we subtract $\mathbf{x}_b$ from $\mathbf{x}$ then we are left with $\mathbf{y}$ which we therefore call the residual. Another way of thinking about these two processes is to consider $\mathbf{x}_b$ as the (vector) prediction of $\mathbf{x}$ based on the boundary values $\mathbf{x}_i$ and $\mathbf{x}_t$ and then $\mathbf{y}$ is the (vector) prediction error.

The mutual correlation between the two components is

$$\mathbf{R}_{yx_b} \triangleq E[\mathbf{y}\mathbf{x}_b^{T}]$$

(2.5.12)

which may be expressed, using (2.5.10), as

$$\mathbf{R}_{yx_b} = \mathbf{T}^{-1}E[\mathbf{e}\mathbf{b}_f^{T}]\mathbf{T}^{-1}\;.$$

(2.5.13)

Now the mean square prediction in (2.4.1) guarantees that $\mathbf{e}$ is uncorrelated with both $\mathbf{x}_i$ and $\mathbf{x}_t$, hence $\mathbf{e}$ is also orthogonal to $\mathbf{b}_f$ which is a linear combination of the elements in $\mathbf{x}_i$ and $\mathbf{x}_t$, and we have

$$E[\mathbf{e}\mathbf{b}_f^{T}] = \mathbf{0}\;.$$

(2.5.14)

Substituting into (2.5.13), we conclude that $\mathbf{y}$ and $\mathbf{x}_b$ are uncorrelated since

$$\boxed{\mathbf{R}_{yx_b} = \mathbf{0}}$$

(2.5.15)

and we have decomposed $\mathbf{x}$ into two orthogonal processes.

The autocorrelation matrix of the residual process is given by

$$\mathbf{R}_y = E[\mathbf{y}\mathbf{y}^{T}] = \mathbf{T}^{-1}E[\mathbf{e}\mathbf{e}^{T}]\mathbf{T}^{-1}$$

(2.5.16)

and (2.4.10) in vector form, becomes

$$\mathbf{R}_e = E[\mathbf{e}\mathbf{e}^{T}] = \beta^{2}\mathbf{T}$$

(2.5.17)

therefore,

$$\mathbf{R}_y = \beta^2 \mathbf{T}^{-1}. \tag{2.5.18}$$

In summary then, a vector $\mathbf{x}$ of N elements of a pth-order AR process can be written as

$$\mathbf{x} = \mathbf{x}_b + \mathbf{y} \tag{2.5.19}$$

where

(i) $\mathbf{y}$ and $\mathbf{x}_b$ are orthogonal,

(ii) $\mathbf{x}_b$ depends on $2p$ boundary elements outside the sequence $\{x(n); \ 1 \le n \le N\}$, and

(iii) the covariance of $\mathbf{y}$ is $\beta^2 \mathbf{T}^{-1}$, where $\mathbf{T}$ is a banded Toeplitz matrix determined by the noncausal MVR prediction error filter $A(z)$.

This representation has been used by Jain [8, 31] to develop the so-called fast KL transform algorithm for 1st-order Markov processes. That algorithm is a special case of the more general recursive block coding introduced here.

2.6   The 1d RBC Algorithm

In RBC the boundary variables are shared by adjacent blocks so the p boundary values denoted as $\mathbf{x}_t$ for block $(K-1)$ become $\mathbf{x}_i$ for block K as shown in Fig. 2.6.1. This is achieved by introducing a delay of duration 1 block, or $(N+p)$ samples, for the boundary values.

The resulting 1d RBC algorithm is shown in block diagram form in Fig. 2.6.2. It is assumed that the KL transforms, or their approximations, for the residual process and the boundary response are known or have been suitably chosen and that they are $\mathbf{A}$ and $\mathbf{B}$ respectively.

In the algorithm description we introduce the notation $\mathbf{x}^*$ to mean the reproduced value of $\mathbf{x}$ where the difference, if any, is due to the encoding process. This is necessary because we must design a coder whose predictor uses values available to the decoder in the absence of channel errors. If we did not do this then the encoder and decoder would lose track of

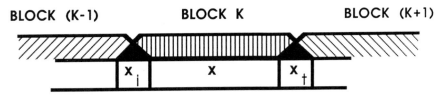

FIGURE 2.6.1.   Boundary variables for 1d RBC.

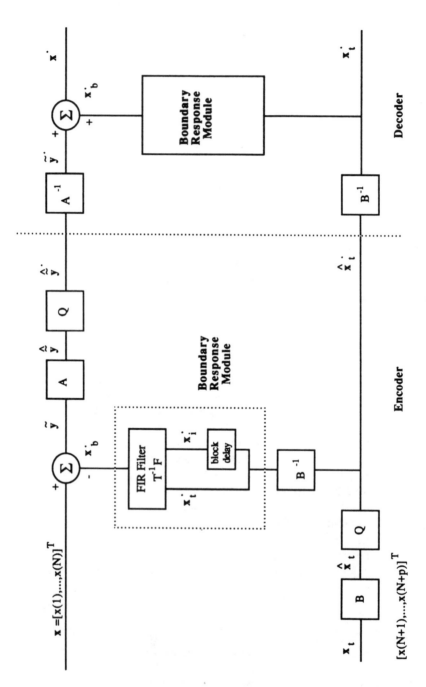

Fig. 2.6.2. 1d RBC algorithm for a pth-order Markov process.

ALGORITHM 2.6.1. 1d RBC for a pth-order Markov Process (see Fig. 2.6.2).

Algorithm 2.6.1
(1) Recalling that the above discussion refers to zero mean processes, the global mean is subtracted from each data sample before coding, and it is added back in by the decoder.
(2) The new boundary vector $\mathbf{x}_l$ is transformed using $\mathbf{B}$, quantized and transmitted or stored depending on whether this is a communication or a database entry device. It is then inverse transformed to form $\mathbf{x}_l^*$.
(3) The vector $\mathbf{x}_i^*$, the same as $\mathbf{x}_l^*$ from the previous block, and the current $\mathbf{x}_l^*$ are passed through the noncausal FIR filter $\mathbf{T}^{-1}\mathbf{F}$ according to (2.5.10) to produce $\mathbf{x}_b^*$, the quantized boundary response, which is also available at the decoder in the absence of channel errors.
(4) The residual process $\tilde{\mathbf{y}}$ is obtained by subtracting $\mathbf{x}_b^*$ from the original data vector $\mathbf{x}$ again using (2.5.10) and then transformed using $\mathbf{A}$, quantized, and transmitted or stored.
(5) The inverse process at the decoder produces the reconstructed values $\mathbf{x}^*$ and $\mathbf{x}_i^*$.

each other and the coding error would be increased. Consequently the boundary vector $\mathbf{x}_l$ with components $\{x(N+1),...,x(N+p)\}$ is encoded and then decoded before being used to form the boundary response. Whenever we use quantized boundary variables, the resulting residual $\tilde{\mathbf{y}}$, is different from the $\mathbf{y}$ that we have been referring to in the theoretical derivation. However, if the boundary quantization error is small then $\tilde{\mathbf{y}} \approx \mathbf{y}$.

2.7 Boundary Response for First Order AR Models

In the particular case $p = 1$ which is of great interest in 1d image coding, the prediction has a closed form solution which is particularly simple for small blocks and high correlation coefficient, ρ. When $p = 1$ the equations in section 2.5 become simplified and in particular:

(a)   the symmetric Toeplitz matrix, T, becomes tridiagonal with a first row $[1, -a(1), 0, ..., 0]$;

(b)   **f** becomes the scalar $a(1)$;

(c)   and $\mathbf{b}_f$ becomes $a(1)[x(0), 0, ..., 0, x(N+1)]^T$ with only two non-zero entries.

In this case, the prediction, or boundary response, is the solution of the simple difference equation

$$x(n) = a(1)(x(n-1) + x(n+1)) ; \quad n = 1, 2, ..., N \quad (2.7.1)$$

subject to the boundary conditions $x(0)$ and $x(N+1)$.

Transform Domain Solution

We could solve this equation by transform methods since the DST Ψ, defined as

$$\boxed{\Psi(i,j) \triangleq \sqrt{\frac{2}{N+1}} \sin \frac{ij\pi}{N+1} ; \quad 1 \le i,j \le N} \qquad (2.7.2)$$

diagonalizes the tridiagonal Toeplitz matrix **T** as shown in Appendix B. Hence, if we transform the original equation

$$\mathbf{Tx}_b = \mathbf{b}_f \qquad (2.7.3)$$

we obtain

$$\mathbf{\Psi T}(\mathbf{\Psi\Psi})\mathbf{x}_b = \mathbf{\Psi b}_f \qquad (2.7.4)$$

where we have made use of the fact that the DST is its own inverse, i.e. $\mathbf{\Psi\Psi} = \mathbf{I}$, the identity matrix. If we use $\hat{\ }$ to denote transformation then we have

$$\Lambda\hat{\mathbf{x}}_b = \hat{\mathbf{b}}_f \qquad (2.7.5)$$

where Λ is a diagonal matrix of eigenvalues $\{\lambda(k)\}$ given by

$$\lambda(k) = 1 - 2a(1) \cos \frac{k\pi}{N+1} ; \quad k = 1, ..., N . \qquad (2.7.6)$$

We can now interpret the boundary response in the DST domain as

$$\hat{x}_b(k) = \frac{\hat{b}_f(k)}{\lambda(k)} ; \quad k = 1, ..., N , \qquad (2.7.7)$$

and we have a series expansion for the boundary response

$$x_b(n) = \sum_{k=1}^{N} \hat{x}_b(k) \Psi(n,k) . \qquad (2.7.8)$$

It should be noted that since $\mathbf{b}_f$ has only two non-zero entries, the first and last, its DST is simply a linear combination of the first and last DST basis vectors, viz.,

$$\hat{\mathbf{b}}_f = a(1)x(0)\Psi_1 + a(1)x(N+1)\Psi_N \qquad (2.7.9)$$

where

$$\Psi_k \triangleq [\Psi(1,k), \ \Psi(2,k), \ \ldots, \ \Psi(N,k)]^T \qquad (2.7.10)$$

is the kth column of the DST matrix. Therefore

$$\hat{x}_b(k) = a(1)x(0)\frac{\Psi_1(k)}{\lambda(k)} + a(1)x(N+1)\frac{\Psi_N(k)}{\lambda(k)} \qquad (2.7.11)$$

and although it is shown in section 6 of Appendix B that the DST of each of the components of $\hat{\mathbf{x}}_b$ is a $\sinh(.)$ function, it is instructive to solve the difference equation (2.7.1) directly without resorting to transform techniques.

Spatial Domain Solution

We can rewrite (2.7.1) in the following form

$$x(n-1) - 2x(n) + x(n+1) = t^2 x(n) \qquad (2.7.12)$$

where

$$t^2 = \frac{1}{a(1)} - 2 . \qquad (2.7.13)$$

which is the standard difference equation (A.3.2) in Appendix A and the solution is given in (A.3.11) as

$$x(n) = x(0)\frac{\sinh(N+1-n)\theta}{\sinh(N+1)\theta} + x(N+1)\frac{\sinh n\theta}{\sinh(N+1)\theta} . \qquad (2.7.14)$$

So the boundary response for a 1st-order AR model is the weighted sum of the two boundary points, $x(0)$ and $x(N+1)$, where the weighting function is a hyperbolic sine. This is shown in Fig. 2.7.1 where the individual components from each boundary point are shown together with their sum which is the prediction. The argument θ is determined implicitly by (A.3.7) as

$$\cosh\theta = 1 + \frac{t^2}{2} = \frac{1}{2a(1)} = \frac{1+\rho^2}{2\rho} , \qquad (2.7.15)$$

where we have used (2.4.11) to substitute for $a(1)$. If we divide numerator and denominator by ρ, we get

$$\cosh\theta = \frac{e^\theta + e^{-\theta}}{2} = \frac{\rho^{-1} + \rho}{2} , \qquad (2.7.16)$$

hence,

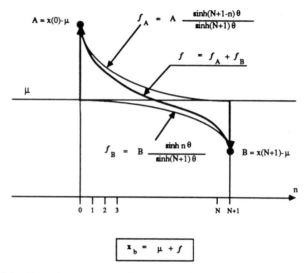

FIGURE 2.7.1. Boundary response for a 1st-order Markov process.

$$e^{\theta} = \frac{1}{\rho} \; ; \qquad \theta = \ln\frac{1}{\rho} \, . \tag{2.7.17}$$

When there is high correlation ($\rho \approx 1$), $\theta \approx 0$ and we have

$$\frac{1}{\rho} = e^{\theta} = 1 + \theta + \frac{\theta^2}{2!} + \cdots \approx 1 + \theta \tag{2.7.18}$$

but

$$\frac{1}{\rho} = \frac{1}{1 - (1-\rho)} \approx 1 + (1-\rho) \tag{2.7.19}$$

hence

$$\theta \approx 1 - \rho. \tag{2.7.20}$$

The maximum argument for the sinh(.) function in (2.7.14) is $(N+1)\theta$ and therefore if $(N+1)(1-\rho)$ is small we can approximate the sinh(.) functions by linear functions since $\sinh x \approx x$ for small x. In fact the maximum percentage error in this approximation is 2.7% for $(N+1)(1-\rho) \le 0.4$ as shown in Fig. 2.7.2 and we effectively have linear interpolation, viz.,

$$x(n) = (1 - w)x(0) + w\, x(N+1) \tag{2.7.21}$$

where

$$w = \frac{n}{N+1} \, . \tag{2.7.22}$$

Since the predictor is linear there is no longer any need to subtract the mean from the data samples before coding since a) subtracting the mean, interpolating, then adding it back in is equivalent to b) simply linearly interpolating the original data samples as shown in Fig. 2.7.3.

The maximum allowable block sizes for approximations within 3% and 6% are tabulated below for various values of ρ.

TABLE 2.7.1. Maximum block size as a function of ρ.

ρ	.80	.85	.90	.91	.92	.93	.94	.95	.96	.97	.98	.99
3 %	1	1	3	3	4	4	5	7	9	12	19	39
6 %	2	3	5	5	6	7	9	11	14	19	29	59

Simple Algorithm for 1st-Order AR Models

This leads to a much simpler algorithm for RBC coding highly correlated 1st-order Markov sequences. The block diagram is shown in Fig. 2.7.4 and the differences from the general algorithm of Fig. 2.6.2 are listed below.

(i)   The terminal vector $\mathbf{x}_t$ becomes the scalar $x(N+1)$.

(ii)   The transform $\mathbf{B}$ is removed leaving a simple scalar quantizer.

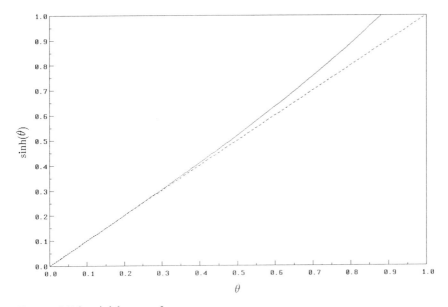

FIGURE 2.7.2. sinhθ versus θ.

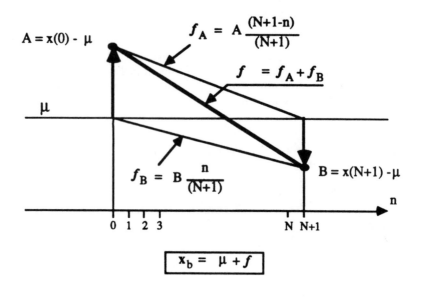

$$x_b = \mu + f$$

(a)

$$x_b = f$$

(b)

FIGURE 2.7.3. Linear boundary response: (a) removing the mean first; (b) linear interpolation with original samples.

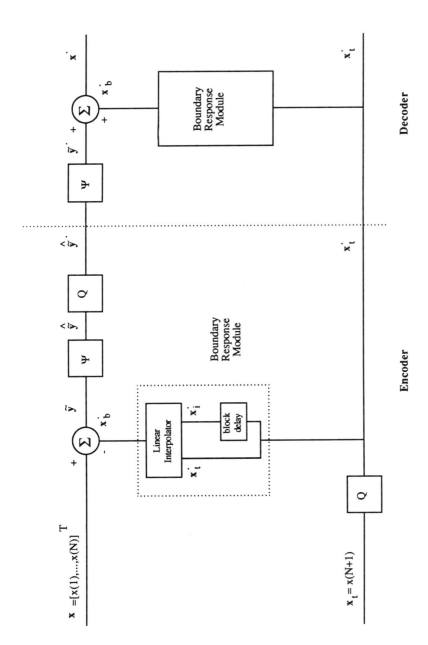

Fig. 2.7.4.   1d RBC algorithm for a highly correlated 1st-order Markov process.

(iii) The FIR filter is replaced by a simple linear interpolator.

If $(N+1) = 2^r$ then the linear interpolator can be efficiently implemented using only shift and add operations. This is done by replacing the mid-point, $x(\dfrac{N+1}{2})$, by the average of the end-points $x(0)$ and $x(N+1)$. We then have two identical problems with end-points $\{x(0), x(\dfrac{N+1}{2})\}$ and $\{x(\dfrac{N+1}{2}), x(N+1)\}$. This process is continued until the intensity of each pixel 1, 2,..., N has been evaluated.

Further simplifications arise since the KLT **A** for the residual of a 1st-order Markov process is the DST. This is because we have from (2.5.18)

$$\mathbf{R}_y \triangleq E[\mathbf{y}\mathbf{y}^T] = \beta^2 \mathbf{T}^{-1}$$

and in the DST domain we have

$$\mathbf{R}_{\hat{y}} \triangleq E[\hat{\mathbf{y}}\hat{\mathbf{y}}^T] = E[\mathbf{\Psi}\mathbf{y}\mathbf{y}^T\mathbf{\Psi}] = \mathbf{\Psi}\,\mathbf{R}_y\,\mathbf{\Psi} = \beta^2\Lambda^{-1} \qquad (2.7.23)$$

a diagonal matrix, and so by definition $\mathbf{\Psi}$ is the KLT for the residual process **y**.

If we were to code a 1st-order Markov process using traditional transform coding then it is known that the KLT does not have a fast algorithm [36]. However, we have just shown that RBC of a 1st-order Markov process produces a residual whose KL transform is the DST which has a fast algorithm [8, 37] and that is why this algorithm has also

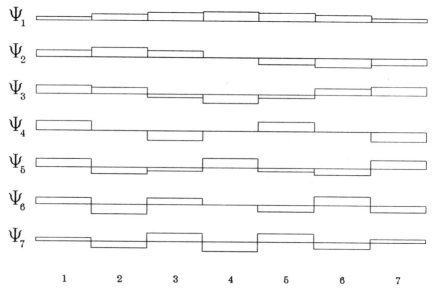

FIGURE 2.7.5. DST basis vectors for $N = 7$.

been called *fast KLT coding* [8]. It should be noted that the original DST algorithm proposed by Yip and Rao was subsequently shown by Wang [38] to be invalid for $N \geq 7$ and so either a double length FFT algorithm [8] or Wang's own algorithm [39] should be used to implement the DST.

It is known [40, 41], and discussed in more detail in section 6.6, that the DST is not as good a transform for data compression of natural images as the DCT which closely approximates the KLT for highly correlated 1st-order Markov processes [42]. On the contrary, the residual image for such a source is optimally encoded using the DST. The underlying reason why this is so may be grasped intuitively by studying the DST basis vectors shown in Fig. 2.7.5 for $N = 7$. The low order basis vectors have little energy at the edges of the block but large values at the center. This allows the DST to compensate for the poorer prediction at the center of the blocks while the prediction is good at the extremes close to the two boundary points and small DST values are quite sufficient. In other words, the prediction and DST work well together performing complementary functions.

We now conclude the 1d discussion with a description of the simplified algorithm when $p = 1$.

ALGORITHM 2.7.1. 1d RBC when $p = 1$ (see Fig. 2.7.4).

Algorithm 2.7.1
(1) The new boundary value $x(N+1)$ is quantized and transmitted or stored as $x^{\bullet}(N+1)$ depending on the application.
(2) The value $x^{\bullet}(0)$, the same as $x^{\bullet}(N+1)$ from the previous block, and the current $x^{\bullet}(N+1)$ are linearly interpolated to produce $\mathbf{x}_b^{\bullet}$, the quantized boundary response, which is also available at the decoder in the absence of channel errors.
(3) The residual process $\tilde{\mathbf{y}}$ is obtained by subtracting $\mathbf{x}_b^{\bullet}$ from the original data vector $\mathbf{x}$ using (2.5.10) and then transformed using the DST, quantized, and transmitted or stored.
(4) The inverse process at the decoder produces the reconstructed values $\mathbf{x}^{\bullet}$ and $x^{\bullet}(N+1)$.

2.8 2d Minimum Variance Models

We will now extend the 1d results to 2d minimum variance models and then consider their application to images.

Let $x(i,j)$ be any zero-mean, stationary random field and let $\bar{x}(i,j)$ be the optimum linear mean square estimate of $x(i,j)$ based on all samples of the field other than $x(i,j)$ itself; viz.,

$$\bar{x}(i,j) = \sum_{k,l \neq (0,0)} \sum a(k,l)x(i-k,j-l) . \qquad (2.8.1)$$

The noncausal *linear* MVR is then

$$x(i,j) = \bar{x}(i,j) + e(i,j). \qquad (2.8.2)$$

The prediction coefficients are obtained, as before, by minimizing the mean square prediction error to obtain the 2d extension of (2.4.2) as

$$A(z_1,z_2) = \frac{\beta^2}{S_x(z_1,z_2)} . \qquad (2.8.3)$$

As noted before, the SDF is defined on the unit circle $z = e^{j\omega}$, and equating coefficients on each side of the equation we obtain

$$\boxed{a(k,l) = -\frac{c(k,l)}{c(0,0)}} \qquad (2.8.4)$$

where

$$c(k,l) = \frac{1}{4\pi^2} \int\limits_{-\pi}^{\pi} \int\limits_{-\pi}^{\pi} S_x^{-1}(\omega_1,\omega_2) \, exp\,[j\,(k\omega_1 + l\omega_2)] \, d\omega_1 \, d\omega_2 \qquad (2.8.5)$$

and the minimized prediction error is given by

$$\beta^2 = E[e^2(i,j)] = \frac{1}{c(0,0)} . \qquad (2.8.6)$$

As in the 1d case, the prediction error field $e(i,j)$ is zero-mean but not white and its covariance function is given by

$$r_e(k,l) = -\beta^2 a(k,l) . \qquad (2.8.7)$$

In practice, the Fourier series may be truncated to obtain a finite-order (approximate) noncausal MVR, provided that the reciprocal SDF has a uniformly convergent Fourier series [34].

2.9 Examples of 2d Noncausal Image Models

Noncausal representations are boundary value problems in both coordinates and, as discussed in [23, 43], they correspond to the elliptic class of partial differential equations (PDEs). For example the discrete approximation of a Helmholtz PDE gives the so-called *NC1 model*

$$x(i,j) = \alpha \left[x(i-1,j) + x(i+1,j) + x(i,j-1) + x(i,j+1) \right] + e(i,j) \qquad (2.9.1)$$

where $|\alpha| < \dfrac{1}{4}$ and $e(i,j)$ is a zero-mean random field whose covariance function is given by

$$r_e(k,l) = \beta^2 \begin{cases} 1 & , (k,l) = (0,0) \\ -\alpha_1 & , (k,l) = (\pm 1,0) \text{ or } (0, \pm 1) \\ 0 & , \text{ otherwise} \end{cases} \qquad (2.9.2)$$

The SDFs for $e(i,j)$ and $x(i,j)$ are then obtained as

$$S_e(z_1,z_2) = \beta^2 \left\{ 1 - \alpha_1(z_1 + z_1^{-1} + z_2 + z_2^{-1}) \right\}, \qquad (2.9.3)$$

$$S_x(z_1,z_2) = \frac{S_e(z_1,z_2)}{\left\{ 1 - \alpha(z_1 + z_1^{-1} + z_2 + z_2^{-1}) \right\}^2} . \qquad (2.9.4)$$

For this model to be a minimum variance (all pole) model we require, from (2.8.3), that

$$S_x(z_1,z_2) = \frac{\beta^2}{A(z_1,z_2)} \qquad (2.9.5)$$

where

$$A(z_1,z_2) = 1 - \alpha(z_1 + z_1^{-1} + z_2 + z_2^{-1}) . \qquad (2.9.6)$$

This clearly requires $\alpha = \alpha_1$ to allow a pole-zero cancellation. However, the choice $\alpha \neq \alpha_1$ generally gives a better covariance fit [23]. Hence (2.9.1) may be considered as a noncausal autoregressive moving average (ARMA) model which contains both poles and zeros. In fact, the values

$$\alpha \approx 0.2496; \quad \alpha_1 \approx 0.95\,\alpha \qquad (2.9.7)$$

have been found to provide a good fit to the covariance function of certain images [23, 43].

Other noncausal models including the one which realizes the separable covariance model

$$r_x(k,\ l) = \rho_1^{|k|}\rho_2^{|l|}; \quad \rho_1 \approx \rho_2 \approx 0.95, \quad\quad (2.9.8)$$

are available [23, 29, 43] and are applicable to the coding algorithm considered here. However, in this book we have used the NC1 model to derive the 2d RBC algorithm.

The NC1 Model

When we consider an N x N data block $\mathbf{X}$ of the image represented by the NC1 model, then (2.9.1) becomes

$$\mathbf{QX} + \mathbf{XQ} = \mathbf{E} + \alpha\mathbf{B} \quad\quad (2.9.9)$$

where $\mathbf{Q}$ is a symmetric, N x N, tridiagonal Toeplitz matrix, viz.,

$$\mathbf{Q} \triangleq \begin{bmatrix} 1/2 & -\alpha & & & \\ -\alpha & & & 0 & \\ & & & & \\ & 0 & & & -\alpha \\ & & & -\alpha & 1/2 \end{bmatrix}, \quad\quad (2.9.10)$$

$\mathbf{E}$ is an N x N matrix with elements $e(i,\ j)$, and $\mathbf{B}$ is an N x N matrix which depends only on the four boundary vectors: $\mathbf{b}_1 = [x(0,1),\ \ldots,$ $x(0,N)]^T$, $\mathbf{b}_2 = [x(1,0),\ \ldots,\ x(N,0)]^T$, $\mathbf{b}_3 = [x(N+1,1),\ \ldots,$ $x(N+1,N)]^T$, and $\mathbf{b}_4 = [x(1,N+1),\ \ldots,\ x(N,N+1)]^T$ shown in Fig. 2.9.1.

In particular

$$\mathbf{B} = \mathbf{B}_1 + \mathbf{B}_2 \quad\quad (2.9.11)$$

where

$$\mathbf{B}_1 = [\mathbf{b}_1\ \mathbf{0} \cdots \mathbf{0}\ \mathbf{b}_3]^T \quad\quad (2.9.12)$$

$$\mathbf{B}_2 = [\mathbf{b}_2\ \mathbf{0} \cdots \mathbf{0}\ \mathbf{b}_4]\ . \quad\quad (2.9.13)$$

Two Source Decomposition

The analysis is somewhat simplified when we column scan the N x N matrices to obtain N^2 x 1 vectors. So if we let lower case letters denote the vectors corresponding to the matrices in (2.9.9) we have

$$\boxed{\mathbf{Px} = \mathbf{e} + \alpha\mathbf{b}} \quad\quad (2.9.14)$$

where

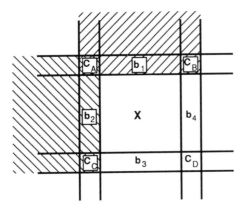

FIGURE 2.9.1. Corner and boundary variables for 2d RBC.

$$\mathbf{P} \triangleq (\mathbf{I} \otimes \mathbf{Q} + \mathbf{Q} \otimes \mathbf{I}) \tag{2.9.15}$$

and $\otimes$ is the Kronecker product [44, p. 236]. We now have an equation which is of the same form as (2.5.2) from which we derived the 1d RBC algorithm and we again have the two source decomposition, viz.,

$$\boxed{\mathbf{x} = \mathbf{x}_b + \mathbf{y}} \tag{2.9.16}$$

where

$$\boxed{\begin{aligned} \mathbf{x}_b &\triangleq \alpha \mathbf{P}^{-1} \mathbf{b}; \\[1em] \mathbf{y} &\triangleq \mathbf{x} - \mathbf{x}_b = \mathbf{P}^{-1} \mathbf{e}. \end{aligned}} \tag{2.9.17}$$

or in matrix notation

$$\mathbf{Q}\mathbf{X}_b + \mathbf{X}_b\mathbf{Q} = \alpha\mathbf{B}; \quad \mathbf{Q}\mathbf{Y} + \mathbf{Y}\mathbf{Q} = \mathbf{E}. \tag{2.9.18}$$

We have now represented the original process $\mathbf{X}$, as the sum of a boundary response $\mathbf{X}_b$, and a residual process, $\mathbf{Y}$. We will form the boundary response by solving (2.9.18) and then subtract this from the original data to get the residual. To transform the residual using its KL transform requires knowledge of the autocorrelation matrix $\mathbf{R}_y$. We first relate $\mathbf{R}_y$ to $\mathbf{R}_e$ using (2.9.17) to give

$$\mathbf{R}_y = E[\mathbf{P}^{-1}\mathbf{e}(\mathbf{P}^{-1}\mathbf{e})^T] = \mathbf{P}^{-1}\mathbf{R}_e\mathbf{P}^{-1} \tag{2.9.19}$$

since $\mathbf{P}^{-1}$ is symmetric. We then substitute for $\mathbf{R}_e$ using (2.9.2) to give

$$\mathbf{R}_e = \beta^2(\mathbf{I} \otimes \mathbf{Q}_1 + \mathbf{Q}_1 \otimes \mathbf{I}) = \beta^2\mathbf{P}_1. \tag{2.9.20}$$

where $\mathbf{Q}_1$ is similar to $\mathbf{Q}$ except that α_1 replaces α and similarly $\mathbf{P}_1$ is defined as $\mathbf{P}$ with $\mathbf{Q}$ replaced by $\mathbf{Q}_1$. Substituting into (2.9.19) then gives

$$\mathbf{R}_y = \beta^2 \, \mathbf{P}^{-1}\mathbf{P}_1\mathbf{P}^{-1}. \tag{2.9.21}$$

Now since Ψ diagonalizes $\mathbf{Q}$ (and $\mathbf{Q}_1$) we can show that $\Psi \otimes \Psi$ diagonalizes $\mathbf{P}$ (and $\mathbf{P}_1$) as follows:

$$
\begin{aligned}
(\Psi \otimes \Psi)\mathbf{P}(\Psi \otimes \Psi) &= (\Psi \otimes \Psi)(\mathbf{I} \otimes \mathbf{Q} + \mathbf{Q} \otimes \mathbf{I})(\Psi \otimes \Psi) \\
&= (\Psi\mathbf{I}\Psi) \otimes (\Psi\mathbf{Q}\Psi) + (\Psi\mathbf{Q}\Psi) \otimes (\Psi\mathbf{I}\Psi) \\
&= \mathbf{I} \otimes \Lambda + \Lambda \otimes \mathbf{I} \\
&= \mathbf{L}, \quad \text{say} \tag{2.9.22}
\end{aligned}
$$

where Λ and $\mathbf{L}$ are diagonal matrices.

Therefore transforming (2.9.21) by $(\Psi \otimes \Psi)$ we get the autocorrelation matrix in the DST domain as

$$\mathbf{R}_{\hat{y}} = \beta^2 \, \mathbf{L}^{-1}\mathbf{L}_1\mathbf{L}^{-1} \tag{2.9.23}$$

which is diagonal and therefore $(\Psi \otimes \Psi)$ is the KL transform of $\mathbf{y}$. Equivalently Ψ is the KL transform of $\mathbf{Y}$ and as with 1d RBC of a 1st-order Markov process, the KL transform of the residual process is the DST.

We now consider how to form the boundary response which will in turn provide the residual via simple subtraction.

2.10   2d Boundary Response via Transform Methods

The 2d boundary response $\mathbf{X}_b$ is the solution of the partial difference equation

$$x(i,j) = \alpha \left[x(i-1,j) + x(i+1,j) + x(i,j-1) + x(i,j+1) \right] \tag{2.10.1}$$

subject to $x(i, 0)$, $x(i, N+1)$, $x(0, j)$, and $x(N+1, j)$; $i,j = 1,...,N$: the boundary conditions.

Transform Domain Solution

Again we can solve this equation by transform methods since Ψ diagonalizes $\mathbf{Q}$. Equation (2.9.18) is a restatement of (2.10.1) in matrix notation, viz.,

$$\mathbf{Q}\mathbf{X}_b + \mathbf{X}_b\mathbf{Q} = \alpha\mathbf{B} .$$

Taking the 2d DST of this equation leads to

$$
\begin{aligned}
\alpha\Psi\mathbf{B}\Psi &= \Psi\mathbf{Q}\mathbf{X}_b\Psi + \Psi\mathbf{X}_b\mathbf{Q}\Psi \\
\alpha\hat{\mathbf{B}} &= \Psi\mathbf{Q}(\Psi\Psi)\mathbf{X}_b\Psi + \Psi\mathbf{X}_b(\Psi\Psi)\mathbf{Q}\Psi \\
\alpha\hat{\mathbf{B}} &= \Lambda\hat{\mathbf{X}}_b + \hat{\mathbf{X}}_b\Lambda \tag{2.10.2}
\end{aligned}
$$

where we have again used the fact that Ψ is its own inverse. Λ is a diagonal eigenvalue matrix with elements

$$\lambda(k) = \frac{1}{2} - 2\alpha \cos \frac{k\pi}{(N+1)} ; \qquad k = 1, ..., N \qquad (2.10.3)$$

which are similar to the eigenvalues introduced in (2.7.6) but are different because although the matrices $\mathbf{Q}$ and $\mathbf{T}$ are both symmetric, tridiagonal, and Toeplitz they have different entries, viz. $[-\alpha, \frac{1}{2}, -\alpha]$ and $[-a(1), 1, -a(1)]$ respectively. If we consider a single element of the matrix $\mathbf{B}$, we have

$$\boxed{\hat{x}_b(p,q) = \frac{\alpha\, \hat{b}(p,q)}{[\lambda(p) + \lambda(q)]} .} \qquad (2.10.4)$$

This provides a fast algorithm for finding the boundary response using the DST.

Since α is positive and close to 0.25 the eigenvalues are positive and increase with index k. Consequently the low-order coefficients of $\hat{\mathbf{B}}$ are boosted while the high-order elements are attenuated and the boundary response is a low pass filtered version of $\mathbf{B}$ in the DST domain. For highly correlated images $\alpha \approx 0.25$ and we will always use $\alpha = 0.25$ for 2d RBC in the following experiments.

2.11   The 2d RBC Algorithm

As in the 1d case, the boundary variables are shared by adjacent blocks as shown in Fig. 2.9.1 and so, neglecting the first row and column of the image, only one corner, C_D, and two boundaries $\mathbf{b}_3$, $\mathbf{b}_4$, are coded with each block. The resulting 2d RBC algorithm is shown in Fig. 2.11.1 and the individual blocks of the diagram are described below.

Note that since $\alpha = 0.25$ there is no need to remove the global mean prior to coding following an argument similar to the one presented in section 2.7, and illustrated in Fig. 2.7.3, for 1d coding.

ALGORITHM 2.10.1.   2d Boundary Response via the DST.

Algorithm 2.10.1
(1) form $\mathbf{B}$ from the four boundaries $\mathbf{b}_1$, $\mathbf{b}_2$, $\mathbf{b}_3$, and $\mathbf{b}_4$ according to (2.9.11);
(2) transform $\mathbf{B}$ using the 2d DST;
(3) weight each coefficient according to (2.10.4); and
(4) inverse transformation provides $\mathbf{X}_b$.

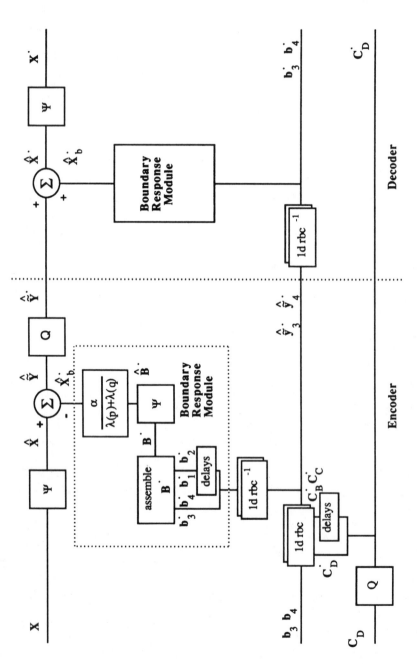

Fig. 2.11.1   Original 2d RBC algorithm

ALGORITHM 2.11.1. 2d RBC.

Algorithm 2.11.1

(1) The new corner point, C_D, is quantized and stored or transmitted depending on the application.

(2) The boundaries are coded using 1d RBC (algorithm 2.7.1).

(3) The boundaries must then be decoded so that the encoder and decoder have the same boundary points to form the 2d boundary response.

(4) The two stored boundaries, $\mathbf{b_1^*}$ and $\mathbf{b_2^*}$, are then used together with $\mathbf{b_3^*}$ and $\mathbf{b_4^*}$ to form the matrix, $\mathbf{B^*}$.

(5) Using algorithm 2.10.1 with $\alpha = 0.25$ and without the inverse transformation, $\mathbf{B^*}$ provides the boundary response, $\mathbf{X_b^*}$, in the DST domain.

(6) The data core, $\mathbf{X}$, is then transformed using the 2d DST and the transformed boundary response is subtracted to give the transformed residual $\tilde{\mathbf{Y}}$ where $\tilde{\ }$ again denotes perturbation due to boundaries which are imperfect due to quantization error.

(7) Finally, the transformed residual is quantized and transmitted or stored.

2.12 Approximate Boundary Response

The transform domain representation of (2.10.4) does not give much insight into the functional form of the boundary response, and we will now solve the difference equation directly in the spatial domain. As a result of the insight gained by this approach we will be able to simplify the 2d RBC algorithm which we have just described by proposing an approximation to the boundary response.

Spatial Domain Solution

We rewrite (2.10.1), to facilitate an analogy with the canonical equation (A.5.2) in Appendix A, as

$$x(i-1,j)+x(i+1,j)-4x(i,j)+x(i,j-1)+x(i,j+1) = t^2 x(i,j) \quad (2.12.1)$$

where

$$t^2 = \frac{1}{\alpha} - 4 , \quad (2.12.2)$$

and the solution is given in (A.5.16) as the sum of four functions, one for the boundary on each side of the square region. If we consider the case for the boundary $\mathbf{b}_4$ at $j = (N+1)$ we have from (A.5.9)

$$x_b(i,j) = \sum_{p=1}^{N} c_p \frac{\sinh j\omega_p}{\sinh (N+1)\omega_p} \sin \frac{p\pi i}{N+1} \qquad (2.12.3)$$

and by setting $j = (N+1)$ it is clear that c_p is proportional to the pth DST coefficient of $\mathbf{b}_4$, viz.,

$$c_p = \sqrt{\frac{2}{N+1}} \, \hat{b}_4(p) \qquad (2.12.4)$$

and ω_p is determined via (A.5.12) as

$$\cosh \omega_p = 2 + \frac{t^2}{2} - \cos \frac{p\pi}{N+1}$$

$$= \frac{1}{2\alpha} - \cos \frac{p\pi}{N+1} . \qquad (2.12.5)$$

The angles $\pi\theta_p \triangleq \dfrac{p\pi}{N+1}$ and ω_p are tabulated below for the case $N = 7$, $\alpha = 0.25$.

Unlike the 1d case in section 2.7 where we were able to derive a simple closed form solution for the boundary response, in 2d we are left with a series solution. However it does provide some physical insight into the interpolation problem since it states that each DST harmonic $b_4(p)$, of the boundary values decays as a sinh(.) function but the rate of decay depends on p, via ω_p, increasing rapidly for higher harmonics. The decay functions for the amplitude of each harmonic are plotted in Fig. 2.12.1.

The term $\left\{ c_p \dfrac{\sinh j\omega_p}{\sinh(N+1)\omega_p} \right\}$ is proportional to the amplitude of the pth DST harmonic (in the i direction) as a function of j and there is no obvious simple function which will describe this effect for general boundary conditions. For example, if $b_4(i) = A \sin \dfrac{i\pi}{N+1}$ then c_p is zero for all p except $p = 1$ and the rate of decay is controlled by $\omega_1 = .3878$ for $N = 7$. Similarly if $b_4(i) = A \sin \dfrac{Ni\pi}{N+1}$ then only $c_N \neq 0$ and the rate is now controlled by $\omega_N = 1.7354 > 4 \omega_1$ for $N = 7$.

TABLE 2.12.1. $\pi\theta_p$ and ω_p for $N = 7$.

p	1	2	3	4	5	6	7
$\pi\theta_p$	.3927	.7854	1.1781	1.5708	1.9635	2.3562	2.7489
ω_p	.3878	.7478	1.0607	1.3170	1.5141	1.6530	1.7354

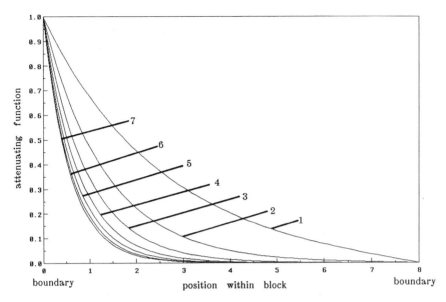

FIGURE 2.12.1. Attenuating functions for each harmonic, $N = 7$.

If we transform (2.12.3) in the j direction, using the DST of a sinh(.) function which is given in (B.6.2) in Appendix B, we get

$$
\begin{aligned}
\hat{x}_b(p,q) &= \sqrt{\frac{2}{N+1}} \; \frac{\hat{b}_4(p) \sin \dfrac{Nq\pi}{N+1}}{2\left(\cosh \omega_p - \cos \dfrac{q\pi}{N+1}\right)} \\[2ex]
&= \alpha \sqrt{\frac{2}{N+1}} \; \frac{\hat{b}_4(p) \sin \dfrac{Nq\pi}{N+1}}{\left(1 - 2\alpha \cos \dfrac{p\pi}{N+1} - 2\alpha \cos \dfrac{q\pi}{N+1}\right)} \\[2ex]
&= \alpha \sqrt{\frac{2}{N+1}} \; \frac{\hat{b}_4(p) \sin \dfrac{Nq\pi}{N+1}}{[\lambda(p) + \lambda(q)]}
\end{aligned}
\qquad (2.12.6)
$$

where we have used (2.12.5) to substitute for ω_p and $\lambda(p)$ is defined in (2.10.3). Note that we have derived (2.10.4) for the boundary conditions $\mathbf{b}_1 = \mathbf{b}_2 = \mathbf{b}_3 = 0$ and $\mathbf{b}_4$ is arbitrary since then $\hat{b}(p,q) = \hat{b}_4(p) \, \Psi_N(q)$.

If we impose a constraint on the form of $\mathbf{b}_4$ and now assume that the corner point $C_B \triangleq x(N+1, N+1)$ equals A, all other corner points are zero, and the boundary $\mathbf{b}_4$ is merely the 1d boundary response due to C_B, viz.,

$$b_4(i) = A \frac{\sinh i\theta}{\sinh(N+1)\theta} \tag{2.12.7}$$

where $\cosh\theta = \dfrac{1+\rho^2}{2\rho}$ and then from (B.6.2) we have

$$\hat{b}_4(p) = A \sqrt{\frac{2}{N+1}} \frac{\sin \dfrac{Np\pi}{N+1}}{2(\cosh\theta - \cos\dfrac{p\pi}{N+1})} \tag{2.12.8}$$

and (2.12.6) becomes

$$\hat{x}_b(p,q) = \frac{\alpha A}{N+1} \frac{\sin \dfrac{Np\pi}{N+1}\sin \dfrac{Nq\pi}{N+1}}{[\lambda(p)+\lambda(q)][\cosh\theta - \cos\dfrac{p\pi}{N+1}]} . \tag{2.12.9}$$

Even in the limit as $\alpha \to \dfrac{1}{4}$, $\theta \to 0$, and the boundary $b_4(i) \to \dfrac{A\,i}{N+1}$, a straight line, this response is

$$\hat{x}_b(p,q) \to$$

$$\frac{A}{2(N+1)} \frac{\sin \dfrac{Np\pi}{N+1}\sin \dfrac{Nq\pi}{N+1}}{[2 - \cos\dfrac{p\pi}{N+1} - \cos\dfrac{q\pi}{N+1}][1 - \cos\dfrac{p\pi}{N+1}]} . \tag{2.12.10}$$

which is not a simple surface as shown in Fig. 2.12.2.

However, if we consider two boundaries at a time, then their combined effect is indeed a greatly simplified surface. The effect of the second boundary b_3 is that of b_4 when rotated about the line $i = j$ as shown in Fig. 2.12.3.

To obtain the combined response we simply add the RHS of (2.12.9) to itself with p and q interchanged to obtain

$$\hat{x}_b(p,q) = \frac{\alpha A}{N+1} \frac{\sin \dfrac{Np\pi}{N+1}\sin \dfrac{Nq\pi}{N+1}}{[\lambda(p)+\lambda(q)]}$$

$$\left\{ \frac{1}{(\cosh\theta - \cos\dfrac{p\pi}{N+1})} + \frac{1}{(\cosh\theta - \cos\dfrac{q\pi}{N+1})} \right\} . \tag{2.12.11}$$

If $\cosh\theta = \dfrac{1}{4\alpha}$ then the last term which is a sum of fractions becomes

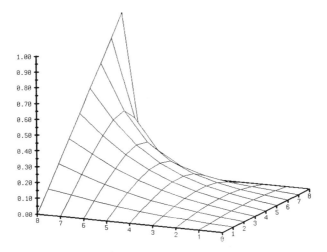

FIGURE 2.12.2. 2d boundary response to a boundary of amplitude $\dfrac{i}{N+1}$.

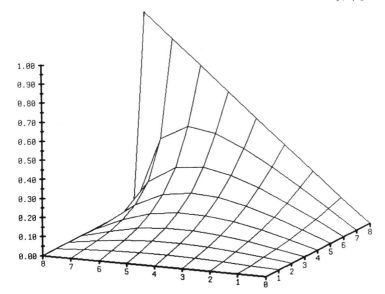

FIGURE 2.12.3. 2d boundary response to a boundary of amplitude $\dfrac{j}{N+1}$.

$$2\alpha \left\{ \frac{1}{\lambda(p)} + \frac{1}{\lambda(q)} \right\} = \frac{2\alpha\,[\lambda(p) + \lambda(q)]}{\lambda(p)\,\lambda(q)} \qquad (2.12.12)$$

and $[\lambda(p) + \lambda(q)]$ cancels in (2.12.11) to give

$$\hat{x}_b(p,q) = \frac{2A\alpha^2}{N+1} \frac{\sin\dfrac{Np\pi}{N+1}\sin\dfrac{Nq\pi}{N+1}}{\lambda(p)\,\lambda(q)}$$

$$= \frac{2A}{N+1} \frac{\sin\dfrac{Np\pi}{N+1}}{2(\cosh\theta - \cos\dfrac{p\pi}{N+1})} \frac{\sin\dfrac{Nq\pi}{N+1}}{2(\cosh\theta - \cos\dfrac{q\pi}{N+1})}. \qquad (2.12.13)$$

By observation this is the 2d DST of

$$\boxed{x_b(i,j) = A\,\frac{\sinh\theta i\,\sinh\theta j}{\sinh^2(N+1)\theta}} \qquad (2.12.14)$$

where $\cosh\theta = \dfrac{1}{4\alpha} \approx 1$ and this may be interpreted as the corner response due to the corner value of A at $(N+1,N+1)$. In the extreme cases when $i=N+1$ and $j=N+1$ this bisinh(.) function becomes the sinh(.) boundary response function, $\dfrac{A\,\sinh\theta k}{\sinh(N+1)\theta}$; $k=i$ or j, for 1d RBC which we derived in (2.7.14). For highly correlated images, $\theta \approx 0$, and after we make the small angle approximation then the corner response, $x_c(i,j)$ say, becomes bilinear, viz.,

$$\boxed{x_c(i,j) = A\,\frac{ij}{(N+1)^2}} \qquad (2.12.15)$$

as shown in Fig. 2.12.4.

Of course we must sum the effects of all four corners to get the total corner response, viz.,

$$x_c(i,j) = \frac{Aij + B(N+1-i)j + C\,i(N+1-j) + D(N+1-i)(N+1-j)}{(N+1)^2}$$

$$(2.12.16)$$

where A, B, C, and D are the corner values.

The Alternative 2d RBC Algorithm

This analysis provides an alternative way to form $\mathbf{X}_b$ via

$$\mathbf{X}_b = \mathbf{X}_c + \mathbf{X}_r \qquad (2.12.17)$$

where $\mathbf{X}_c$ is the bilinear corner response and $\mathbf{X}_r$ is the additional response due to the 1d boundary residuals. This in turn leads to a three source decomposition, viz.,

$$\mathbf{X} = \mathbf{X}_c + \mathbf{X}_r + \mathbf{Y} \qquad (2.12.18)$$

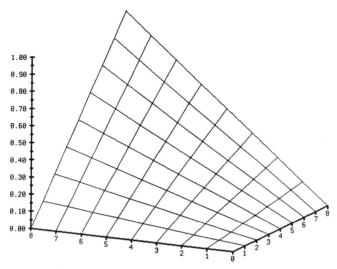

FIGURE 2.12.4. Corner response: the corner value leads to a linear boundary prediction during 1d coding. These linear boundaries then have a 2d boundary response as shown in Figs. 2.12.2 and 2.12.3 which then sum to give a bilinear corner response.

where $\mathbf{Y}$ is the 2d RBC residual as before. Since the 1d boundary response has already been accounted for in $\mathbf{X}_c$ we replace $\mathbf{b}_k$ by the corresponding residual signal $\mathbf{y}_k$ in (2.12.3) and (2.12.4) to form

$$
\mathbf{X}_r(i,j) = \sqrt{\frac{2}{N+1}} \left\{ \sum_{k=1}^{N} \frac{\hat{y}_2^{\bullet}(k)\sinh(N+1-j)\omega_k + \hat{y}_4^{\bullet}(k)\sinh j\omega_k}{\sinh(N+1)\omega_k} \sin\frac{k\pi i}{N+1} \right.
$$
$$
\left. + \frac{\hat{y}_1^{\bullet}(k)\sinh(N+1-i)\omega_k + \hat{y}_3^{\bullet}(k)\sinh i\omega_k}{\sinh(N+1)\omega_k} \sin\frac{k\pi j}{N+1} \right\} \qquad (2.12.19)
$$

where we have used the quantized values which are also available at the decoder. So $\mathbf{X}_r$ is a series expansion in k and each term is the weighted sum of four subimages which are $90°$ rotations of each other and the fundamental pattern is $\sqrt{\dfrac{2}{N+1}} \left\{ \dfrac{\sinh i\omega_k}{\sinh(N+1)\omega_k} \sin\dfrac{k\pi j}{N+1} \right\}$ where ω_k is determined by (2.12.5) and listed in Table 2.12.1 for $N=7$.

An advantage of this technique is that, unlike algorithm 2.10.1, we do not have to inverse transform the boundaries after quantization although if we were to use this representation to evaluate the boundary response instead of using the DST as described in algorithm 2.10.1, then the number of computations would probably still be greater. However, since the

ALGORITHM 2.12.1. Alternative 2d RBC Algorithm (see Fig. 2.12.5).

Algorithm 2.12.1
(1) We first quantize the corner point C_D and transmit or store it, again depending on the application.
(2) We then form the bilinear corner response, $\mathbf{X}_c$, and subtract it from the core data, $\mathbf{X}$.
(3) The 1d boundaries are coded using 1d RBC (algorithm 2.7.1) as before.
(4) Those 1d boundary residual quantized coefficients which are to be used in the approximation are now used as an index into the stored patterns to obtain the residual boundary response, $\mathbf{X}_r$, which is also subtracted from the core data $\mathbf{X}$ in the spatial domain.
(5) The resulting residual $\mathbf{Y}$, is 2d transform coded using the DST and the quantized coefficients are then either transmitted or stored.

higher harmonics are severely attenuated and contribute little to the boundary response we may approximate the exact interpolating function by only retaining a small number of the harmonics and setting the rest to zero. Furthermore, since the harmonics of the boundary residuals are quantized with a relatively small number of bits then we can store the separable 2d $\left\{ \sin(.)\ \sinh(.) \right\}$ functions for this small number of allowed values and use table look-up to form $\mathbf{X}_r$. So to obtain the residual boundary response for a given block we would use the 1d boundary residual quantized coefficients, $\hat{y}_1^{\bullet}(k), \ldots, \hat{y}_4^{\bullet}(k)$, as an index into the look-up table (LUT) and sum the four corresponding patterns.

Preliminary experiments suggest that keeping just the first residual coefficient is sufficient, at least when $N = 7$.

The prediction errors, or residual energies, when only the first k boundary residual coefficients are used to form the core predictions are given in Table 2.12.2. When $k = 0$ we have only the corner response $\mathbf{X}_c$, when $k = 7$ we have the full RBC boundary response, and in between is an approximation. The results are presented for two of the images, shown in Fig. 4.2.1, which we shall be coding in later chapters: lenna and the baboon. Lenna contains large regions which are separated by clear boundaries so that the 1d RBC residual contains mainly low frequencies, while the baboon is quite different with much higher frequencies present in both the original and the 1d residuals. In either case there is a dramatic reduction in the prediction error when we include the

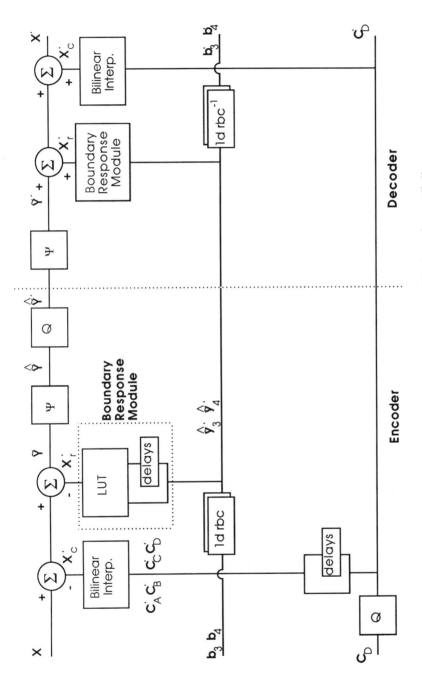

Fig. 2.12.5 2d RBC algorithm using spatial domain prediction

TABLE 2.12.2. Mean residual energy for different approximations to the 2d RBC boundary response.

image	number of residual coefficients							
	0(bilinear)	1	2	3	4	5	6	7(RBC)
lenna	337	153	141	138	137	137	137	136
baboon	1095	629	598	584	577	574	572	570

additional response due to the first residual coefficient together with the bilinear corner response. As we add in the effect of the higher residual harmonics the extra reduction in the prediction error is less significant and the difference between the approximation using only one residual coefficient and the full 2d RBC boundary response is rather small at 12.5% for lenna and 10.3% for the baboon. This is clearly seen in Fig. 2.12.6 which shows (a) the bilinear corner response; (b) the approximate boundary response keeping only the first residual coefficient; and (c) the complete 2d RBC boundary response.

This is a very significant result because, by replacing the previously proposed [24] core prediction filter, which requires a full 2d DST, with a simple approximation which uses only LUTs, the objection that RBC is much more complicated than DCT coding is made invalid.

Other interpolating functions which do not depend on the NC1 model could be used either because they have been used in similar applications before or their simplicity recommends them. We will briefly consider some of these and compare the resulting boundary response images.

Bilinear Patches

This corresponds to just the corner response $\mathbf{X}_c$ and although extremely simple makes no use of the available boundary values and as expected performs well only in those smooth regions where information is preserved when we subsample by $(N+1)$ in both directions.

Coon's Patches

Coon's patches [25, p. 198] are formed from linear blending functions as with bilinear patches, but use all of the boundary values. The surface may be expressed in a number of ways but the most relevant to this discussion is to consider it as the sum of three parts. The first is the bilinear corner response $\mathbf{X}_c$, and the remaining two are linear interpolations of the boundary residuals $\{\mathbf{y}_2, \mathbf{y}_4\}$ and $\{\mathbf{y}_1, \mathbf{y}_3\}$. That is for each pair of opposite boundaries the residual is linearly interpolated, viz.

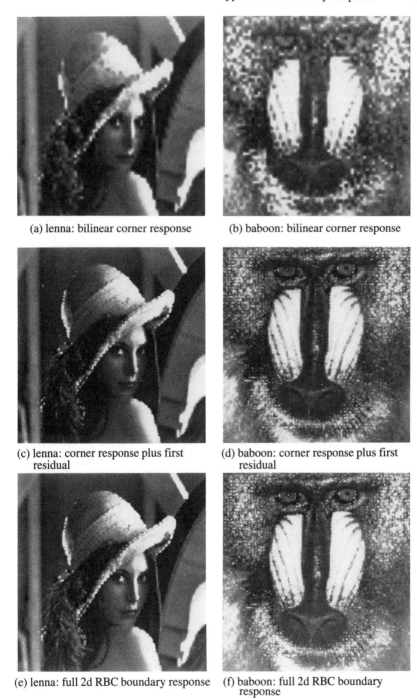

(a) lenna: bilinear corner response   (b) baboon: bilinear corner response

(c) lenna: corner response plus first   (d) baboon: corner response plus first
    residual   residual

(e) lenna: full 2d RBC boundary response   (f) baboon: full 2d RBC boundary
                                                 response

Fig. 2.12.6   The corner response (a),(b) and approximate 2d RBC boundary
               response (c),(d) for N=7.

$$X_{Coon's}(i,j) = X_C(i,j) + \frac{(N+1-i)y_2(j) + i\, y_4(j)}{N+1}$$

$$+ \frac{(N+1-j)y_3(i) + j\, y_1(i)}{N+1} . \qquad (2.12.20)$$

This corresponds to setting $\sinh i\omega_p = i\omega_p$ in (2.12.3) which is clearly over optimistic especially for the higher harmonics as clearly illustrated in Fig. 2.12.1. Consequently, as one might expect, Coon's patches tend to over emphasize the high frequencies and give a high contrast interpolation. For blocks containing edges, while the prediction is better than with bilinear patches it is worse than RBC prediction. Furthermore there is a background texture resembling a coarse linen which is caused by the boosted high frequencies.

Examples of the Coon's interpolating function when $N=7$ and $N=15$ are shown in Fig. 2.12.7 for lenna and Fig. 2.12.8 for the baboon. The overemphasis of high frequencies is clearly illustrated with the baboon which contains high frequency boundary residual coefficients.

Although they do not refer to their approximation as a Coon's surface, this is the approximation made by Meiri and Yudilevich [22] when they approximate the continuous Helmholtz equation. They argue the validity of the corner response but choose this linear approximation for the residual boundary response simply because it does not involve the model parameter and is straightforward.

Bicubic Patches

We can fit piecewise bicubic patches through the corner points to form the boundary response instead of using bilinear patches in the hope that the prediction will be improved at the considerable expense of additional computation. However this interpolating function also does not make use of the boundary values and the resulting prediction is still much worse than the RBC prediction as seen in Fig. 2.12.7 and Fig. 2.12.8. In fact the bicubic predictor tends to produce some overshoot and the prediction MSE, or mean residual energy, is increased when compared to the simpler bilinear patches.

The mean residual energies for the different interpolating functions, when applied to lenna and the baboon with the corner points spaced every 8 and every 16 pixels, are given in Table 2.12.3. Note that perfect corner points and boundary values were used to form the predictions although in practice they would be coded approximations. Furthermore, when computing the mean residual energy the input and output images were simply subtracted without distinguishing between those points used to form the prediction, which are perfectly interpolated, and the predicted values.

(a) 2d RBC boundary response, N=7   (b) 2d RBC boundary response, N=15

(c) Coon's interpolating function, N=7   (d) Coon's interpolating function, N=15

(e) Bicubic interpolating function, N=7   (f) Bicubic interpolating function, N=15

Fig. 2.12.7   Block prediction for lenna using different interpolating functions
when N=7 and N=15.

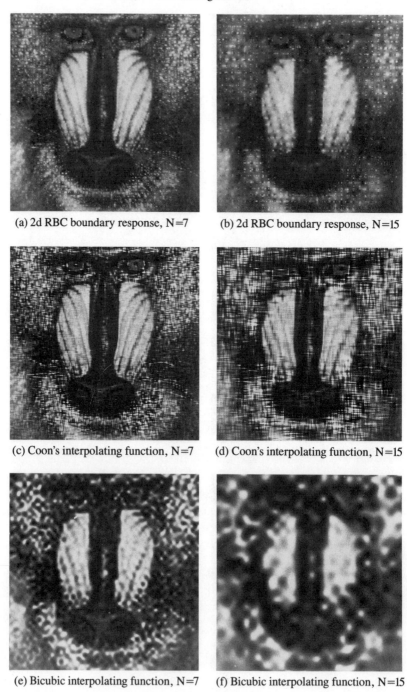

(a) 2d RBC boundary response, N=7   (b) 2d RBC boundary response, N=15

(c) Coon's interpolating function, N=7   (d) Coon's interpolating function, N=15

(e) Bicubic interpolating function, N=7   (f) Bicubic interpolating function, N=15

Fig. 2.12.8   Block prediction for the baboon using different interpolating
functions when N=7 and N=15.

TABLE 2.12.3. Mean residual energy for alternative interpolating functions.

image	$N+1$	interpolating function					
		1d RBC	cubic	2d RBC	Coon's	bilinear	bicubic
lenna	8	308	334	136	194	337	365
	16	646	729	303	449	651	743
baboon	8	843	965	570	1016	1095	1321
	16	1219	1389	785	1563	1373	1675

2.13   Advantages of RBC

In this section we will discuss the improved performance: reduced MSE and improved subjective image quality, which is made possible with RBC.

Removing Interblock Redundancy

If we consider the 1d residual autocorrelation function we have

$$\mathbf{R}_e = \beta^2 \mathbf{T} \qquad (2.13.1)$$

so that the autocorrelation function is $(2p+1)$ units wide and $r_e(p+n) = r_e(-p-n) = 0$ and hence $e(k)$ is uncorrelated with $e(k+p+n)$ and $e(k-p-n)$ where n is a positive integer. Consequently the residuals in a given block are uncorrelated with all of the residuals in all other blocks since the minimum separation for two residuals which are not in the same block is $p+1$ pixels.

On the contrary, for traditional block coding, such as DCT or VQ, there is correlation between adjacent blocks of data. For example, when images are modeled as 1st-order AR processes, $r_x(l) = \sigma_x^2 \rho^{|l|}$ as shown in (2.3.17) and then the correlation between two pixels i and j in adjacent blocks is $r_x(i,j) = \sigma_x^2 \rho^{N-i+j}$; $i,j = 1,...,N$. None of this interblock redundancy is exploited in the coding process and consequently RBC can provide higher compression at the same rate since the representation removes all interblock redundancy.

This same argument applies equally well to 2d RBC.

Reducing the Tile Effect

In traditional block coding algorithms, including VQ and DCT coding, neighboring blocks are coded independently. As we have just noted this results in a reduced efficiency when compared to RBC but RBC has the further advantage of reducing the tile effect.

To appreciate this we must first explain the origin of the tile effect. When each block is coded it is distorted relative to the original block and the distortion level increases for higher compression ratios. So we can think of a complete compression/expansion system as a noisy transmission system where the noise is correlated within a block but uncorrelated between blocks. This results in discontinuities at the block edges which become *fault lines* as each block is randomly thrust up or down. It is this fracturing of the image surface along a regular grid which causes the tile effect and it is most clearly visible when the block edge lies in smooth regions where the adjacent blocks were originally highly correlated.

With RBC the same thing happens to the residual which is block coded using the DST. However it is not so noticeable because, as we have just seen, all adjacent blocks are uncorrelated in this residual domain. To return to the original domain the residual is added to a boundary response, which is continuous from block to block, and so the tile effect is reduced in the output image.

3

Bit Allocation and Quantization for Transform Coding

3.1 Introduction

The most important part of a transform coding scheme is undoubtedly the bit allocation and quantization. True, there are *good* and *bad* transforms, there is straight transform coding and there is RBC, but whichever choice you make for the overall algorithm it will only be as good as the quantization scheme allows. In other words, a good transform and bad quantizer may well perform worse than a bad transform with a very good quantizer—but what do we mean by *good* and *bad*?

The choice of transform is usually made under the constraint that it has a fast algorithm to reduce the computational burden while it approximates the statistically optimal Karhunen-Lòeve transform which, as we shall show, is the transform that diagonalizes the autocorrelation matrix. For typical images and highly correlated 1st-order Markov processes the DCT is the transform of choice, and would be considered a *good* transform. On the other hand, given the same data source, the WHT does not approximate the KL transform as well as the DCT and so this would be an example of an *inferior* transform, although it does have the merit of very simple evaluation. Similarly, for RBC of typical images, the DST is a *good* choice while the DCT would be a *bad* choice.

When we consider quantization for transform and RBC coding, the problem is first to select the quantizers and then to distribute a certain number of bits between the various transform domain coefficients, and also the boundaries in the case of RBC, to maximize the fidelity of the reconstructed images.

There are a number of ways to get this design wrong. We could choose the wrong quantizer, set the dynamic range too small or too large, or allocate the bits inefficiently. Any of these problems could lead to a lower fidelity than picking an *inferior* transform, but quantizing efficiently.

In the following sections we will consider the design process for the quantization of transform coefficients for DCT and RBC coding. In section 3.2 we will discuss the choice of a fidelity criterion and the corresponding optimal transform and quantization scheme. In section 3.3 we will turn to the bit allocation problem and after stating the theoretical solution, which has no closed-form solution in general, we will study a number of approximate solutions proposed previously. We will also develop a new general approximation based on the results of Wang and Jain [29]. In section 3.4 we will incorporate the constraint that each coefficient be assigned an integral number of bits, and provide an exact integer programming solution to the constrained optimization problem. In section 3.5 we will show a simple modification to allow a reconstruction level at zero which can visually enhance non adaptive zonal coding schemes. In section 3.6 we will discuss the importance of the choice of the quantizer rate-distortion function to conclude our study of bit allocation.

In section 3.7 we will turn our attention to quantization in RBC and derive the corresponding integer bit allocation algorithms for both 1d and 2d coding.

In section 3.8 we will discuss the design process for an image ensemble rather than a single image and provide some background material for color coding in section 3.9.

3.2   Choice of Transform and Quantizer

We consider the general source encoding scheme shown in Fig. 3.2.1 which uses transform techniques to exploit the correlation in the spatial domain. We show a 1d transform coding example to fix the notation but the results hold in the general case of two and more dimensions. The input vector is $\mathbf{x}$, the encoding transform is $\mathbf{A}$, and the transformed vector is $\hat{\mathbf{x}} \triangleq \mathbf{Ax}$.

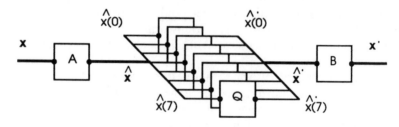

FIGURE 3.2.1. General source encoding scheme: transform coding.

Fidelity Criterion

In order to make any progress we must decide on some fidelity criterion to drive the design process. The traditional fidelity measure is the average MS distortion D, between the input $x(n)$ and the reconstructed output $x^{\bullet}(n)$ from the cascaded encoder and decoder. D is defined as

$$D \triangleq E\left\{[x(n) - x^{\bullet}(n)]^2\right\} \qquad (3.2.1)$$

where the expectation is the average over all of the image pixels. This distortion measure is independent of the specific encoding process, but if we consider any block processing, where the block size is N, then it is convenient to rewrite (3.2.1) as

$$D = E\left\{\frac{1}{N}\sum_{n=1}^{N}[x(n) - x^{\bullet}(n)]^2\right\} \qquad (3.2.2)$$

where the expectation is now the average over all of the image blocks. In vector notation this is

$$D = E\left\{\frac{1}{N}[\mathbf{x} - \mathbf{x}^{\bullet}]^T[\mathbf{x} - \mathbf{x}^{\bullet}]\right\}$$

$$= \frac{1}{N}E\left\{|\mathbf{x} - \mathbf{x}^{\bullet}|^2\right\} \qquad (3.2.3)$$

where $|.|^2$ is the Euclidean norm in N-space.

There have been attempts to include the human visual properties into the fidelity measure [45] and this leads to a weighted MS distortion. However we will consider the unweighted MS distortion as our fidelity criterion in the following discussion.

Transform Domain Distortion

For this particular case of block processing we can express D in terms of the MS distortion in the transform domain where the distortion in the kth coefficient is defined as

$$d_k \triangleq E\left\{[\hat{x}(k) - \hat{x}^{\bullet}(k)]^2\right\} \qquad (3.2.4)$$

Now for any unitary transform $\mathbf{A}$, we have $\mathbf{A}^{-1} = \mathbf{A}^T$, so $\mathbf{x} = \mathbf{A}^T\hat{\mathbf{x}}$ and if, as we shall soon show, $\mathbf{B} = \mathbf{A}^T$, then $\mathbf{x}^{\bullet} = \mathbf{A}^T\hat{\mathbf{x}}^{\bullet}$ and (3.2.3) may be rewritten as

$$D = \frac{1}{N}E\left\{|\mathbf{A}^T[\hat{\mathbf{x}} - \hat{\mathbf{x}}^{\bullet}]|^2\right\}$$

$$= \frac{1}{N}E\left\{[\hat{\mathbf{x}} - \hat{\mathbf{x}}^{\bullet}]^T\mathbf{A}\,\mathbf{A}^T[\hat{\mathbf{x}} - \hat{\mathbf{x}}^{\bullet}]\right\}$$

$$= \frac{1}{N}E\left\{[\hat{\mathbf{x}} - \hat{\mathbf{x}}^{\bullet}]^T[\hat{\mathbf{x}} - \hat{\mathbf{x}}^{\bullet}]\right\}$$

$$= \frac{1}{N}E\left\{|\hat{\mathbf{x}} - \hat{\mathbf{x}}^{\bullet}|^2\right\}. \qquad (3.2.5)$$

Comparing this with (3.2.3), we see that for any unitary transform $\mathbf{A}$ with $\mathbf{B} = \mathbf{A}^T$, the distortion in the transform and spatial domains are equal, and this is Parseval's relation. So if we maximize the fidelity in the transform domain then we will have an encoding scheme which is also optimal when viewed from the spatial domain.

Optimal Transformation and Quantization

Huang and Schultheiss [46] were the first to tackle the problem of determining the encoding transform $\mathbf{A}$, the decoding transform $\mathbf{B}$, and the transform encoders to minimize D. They actually minimized the distortion in each channel d_k, separately rather than the overall average, D. The optimal MS quantization problem for a scalar had been solved independently by Max [47] and Lloyd [48] and the resultant quantizer, the Lloyd-Max quantizer, is used to encode each transform coefficient. Under the assumption that the encoders are Lloyd-Max quantizers, the optimal choice of transform $\mathbf{A}$ is the matrix of eigenvectors of the correlation matrix of $\mathbf{x}$ which we call the KL transform. Then the decoding transform $\mathbf{B}$ is $\mathbf{A}^{-1}(= \mathbf{A}^T)$.

More recently Segall [49] has shown that the Lloyd-Max quantization scheme is indeed the best quantization method to minimize the MSE averaged over all components, as well as optimizing for each coefficient independently.

So in summary, the optimal MS distortion transform coding scheme is characterized by:

(a) $\mathbf{A}$ is the KL transform, $\mathbf{B} = \mathbf{A}^T$,

(b)   Lloyd-Max quantizers for each coefficient.

Transform

If we assume a 1st-order Markov model for one-dimensional image scan lines, then the KL transform [36] has no fast algorithm and so the computational complexity is $O(N^2)$. However it has been demonstrated [7] that for a highly correlated Markov source the DCT

$$C(i,j) \triangleq \begin{cases} \dfrac{1}{\sqrt{N}} & i = 1, \; 1 \le j \le N \\[2ex] \sqrt{\dfrac{2}{N}} \; \cos\dfrac{(2j+1)i\pi}{2N} & 2 \le i \le N, \; 1 \le j \le N \end{cases} \tag{3.2.6}$$

which does have a fast algorithm [50] closely approximates the performance of the KL transform. Since image correlation is typically 0.95 or higher, then this is a good approximation and the DCT has become the standard transform for both 1d and 2d coding.

In RBC, as we have shown in chapter 2, the DST is the true KL transform and not an approximation.

Amplitude Probability Density Function

We must select an appropriate probability density function (pdf) and variance for the coefficient amplitudes since the Lloyd-Max quantizers are tabulated for a unity variance signal with a particular pdf.

It was originally argued by Chen and Smith [51] that the DCT coefficients would have a Gaussian distribution based on the central limit theorem. However it has been shown more recently by Reininger and Gibson [52] that the coefficients are better modeled using a Laplacian or gamma density, while Eggerton and Srinath [45] claim that a truncated Cauchy density function provides a better fit to the DCT coefficient histogram than either a Gaussian or Laplacian distribution. Yuan and Yu [53] have considered the WHT and concluded that the best model for the ac coefficients is Laplacian.

In this work we have used a Laplacian distribution to model the DCT ac transform coefficients and a Gaussian model for the dc coefficient, while all of the DST transform coefficients of the RBC residuals are fitted by a Laplacian pdf. Note that for a positive image the dc coefficient is a positive quantity but here we are assuming a zero mean image where the dc coefficient for each block has a Gaussian distribution centered about zero. This is achieved by subtracting the mean, or 128 in our case, from each pixel before coding and then adding it back in at the decoder. Alternatively, after transforming the original image, the dc coefficient can be adjusted by subtracting $N\mu$ for 2d coding or $\sqrt{N}\mu$ for 1d coding to provide a zero mean sequence for quantization. As before this must be added back at the decoder.

Coefficient Variances

We must estimate or measure the coefficient variances σ_k^2, which are defined as

$$\sigma_k^2 \triangleq \sigma_{\hat{x}}^2(k) = E[\hat{x}^2(k)], \qquad (3.2.7)$$

and then scale the tables, or equivalently the data, by the standard deviation σ_k.

The remaining problem is the bit allocation, that is how should we assign a fixed number of bits to the N coefficients so that the spatial domain fidelity is maximized.

3.3   Bit Allocation

Even if $\mathbf{A}$ is only an approximation to the KL transform it will decorrelate the input to some degree (perfectly when $\mathbf{A}$ is the KLT) and then the transform domain variances σ_k^2 will be unequal. In other words, in the transform domain there will be coefficients with larger variances and these will contain more information than those with lower variances, on the average. Note however that the average information is the same in both domains [54] since no information is lost or gained by a linear invertible transformation.

It seems intuitive that we should not allocate the same number of bits to each channel, rather we should allocate more bits to those coefficients which carry the informational burden and indeed this is necessary to maximize performance. Before we can discuss the optimal bit allocation, we must introduce the concept of a rate-distortion function.

Rate-Distortion Functions

Quantizer distortion increases linearly with input variance and so (3.2.5) may be rewritten as

$$D = \frac{1}{N} \sum_{k=1}^{N} \sigma_k^2 \, f(n_k) \qquad (3.3.1)$$

where $f(n)$ denotes the MS distortion that would be achieved by an n-bit quantizer if its input were a unity variance random variable, and n_k is the number of bits allocated to quantize the kth transform coefficient, $\hat{x}(k)$. We also refer to $f(.)$ as the quantizer rate-distortion (rd) function and it depends both on the quantizer and the pdf describing the source to be quantized and unfortunately there is no closed-form expression for $f(.)$ in general.

Optimal Bit Allocation

We can obtain the optimal bit allocation to minimize (3.3.1) for an rd function which, as shown in Fig. 3.3.1, is strictly convex and has a continuous first derivative $f'(.)$ such that $f'(\infty) = 0$. The proof is given in [49] and is based on the Lagrangian multiplier technique, but we simply state the result here.

At an average rate of p bits/pixel, the bit allocation is

$$n_k = \begin{cases} h\left[\dfrac{\theta f'(0)}{\sigma_k^2}\right] & \text{if} \quad 0 < \theta < \sigma_k^2 \\ \\ 0 & \text{if} \quad \theta \geq \sigma_k^2 \end{cases} \qquad (3.3.2)$$

where $h(.)$ is the inverse function of $f'(.)$, and θ is the root of the constraining equation:

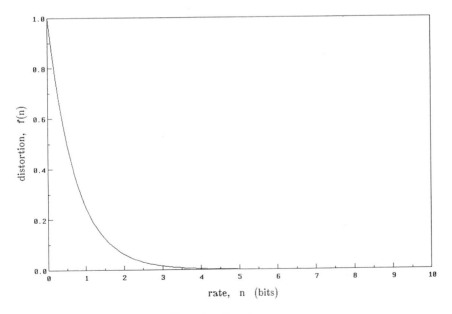

FIGURE 3.3.1. Shannon rate-distortion function.

$$\sum_{k:\sigma_k^2 \ge \theta} n_k = \sum_{k:\sigma_k^2 \ge \theta} h\left[\frac{\theta f'(0)}{\sigma_k^2}\right] = Np. \tag{3.3.3}$$

The minimized distortion is then

$$D_{\min} = \sum_{k:\sigma_k^2 > \theta} \sigma_k^2 f(n_k) + \sum_{k:\sigma_k^2 \le \theta} \sigma_k^2. \tag{3.3.4}$$

We can interpret these equations by noting that θ acts as a threshold and if $\sigma_k^2 < \theta$, no bits are allocated to channel k and the distortion in this channel will then be σ_k^2. This is why (3.3.2) and (3.3.4) differentiate between the two cases, $\sigma_k^2 > \theta$, and $\sigma_k^2 \le \theta$. Equation (3.3.2) seems rather complicated, but it simply states that n_k is chosen such that

$$f'(n_k) = \frac{\theta}{\sigma_k^2} f'(0). \tag{3.3.5}$$

Now as we can see from Fig. 3.3.1, $f'(n)$ is negative and decreases in magnitude as n increases. Consequently when $\theta = \sigma_k^2$, $n_k = 0$, and as σ_k^2 increases above θ the slope becomes less and less and so the number of allocated bits increases. Equation (3.3.4) simply states that the distortion in each channel is either σ_k^2 or $[\sigma_k^2 f(n_k)]$ depending on the relative magnitudes of σ_k^2 and θ.

There is no closed-form expression for $f(.)$, and hence $h(.)$, in general but there is one special case of theoretical importance, the Shannon rd function, which we will consider below.

Shannon Rate Distortion Function

The Shannon rd function is the performance curve of an *ideal* optimal block encoder for a memoryless Gaussian source [35, p. 99]. We use the qualifier *ideal* since it cannot be realized in practice but is the theoretical limit approached for an arbitrarily complex encoder. It can also be shown that the Shannon rd function provides an upper bound on the *ideal* rd functions for a memoryless source with an arbitrary pdf [35, p. 101]. In other words a Gaussian source is the most difficult source to encode. It is interesting to note that this *ideal* relationship is reversed with the practical Lloyd-Max quantizers as shown in Fig. 3.6.1 where the distortion in coding a Laplacian source is greater than for a Gaussian source at the same rate!

The rd function for the Shannon quantizer, unlike the rd function for practical quantizers, has a closed-form expression, viz.,

$$f(n) = 2^{-2n}, \tag{3.3.6}$$

making it very tractable since we have

$$f'(n) = -(2\ln 2)2^{-2n}, \tag{3.3.7}$$

and

$$h(x) = \frac{1}{2} \log_2 \frac{-2 \ln 2}{x}, \qquad (3.3.8)$$

and then the bit allocation is given by

$$\boxed{n_k = n_k(\theta) = \max(0, \tfrac{1}{2} \log_2 \frac{\sigma_k^2}{\theta})}, \qquad (3.3.9)$$

where θ is determined such that the average rate $= p$. Note that if $\sigma_k^2 > \theta$ for all k, then using (3.3.6) and (3.3.9) we see that

$$d_k = \sigma_k^2 f(n_k) = \theta. \qquad (3.3.10)$$

That is the Shannon quantizer bit allocation is such that if all $\sigma_k^2 > \theta$ the distortion is θ, a constant independent of σ_k^2, for each channel. The minimized distortion at the rate p is given by

$$D_{\min} = \frac{1}{N} \sum_{k=1}^{N} \min(\theta, \sigma_k^2). \qquad (3.3.11)$$

Approximations

As noted earlier there is no closed-form expression for $f(.)$, and hence $h(.)$, in general and so there have been a number of suggested approximations to these functions. The simplest result in explicit, but approximate, bit allocations while others are piecewise approximations leading to iterative solutions. We will consider some of these below.

Huang and Schultheiss

Huang and Schultheiss [46] proposed a bit allocation which approximates the optimal allocation for Gaussian coefficients based on an observation made by Max [47] that the rate-distortion function is of the form

$$f(n_k) = K(n_k)2^{-2n_k} \qquad (3.3.12)$$

where n_k is the number of bits allocated to the kth Lloyd-Max quantizer and $K(n_k)$ is a function varying only slowly with n_k. Huang and Schultheiss approximated $K(n_k)$ by K, a constant, and derived

$$\boxed{n_k = p + \frac{1}{2 \ln 2} \left\{ \ln \sigma_k^2 - \frac{1}{N} \sum_{k=1}^{N} \ln \sigma_k^2 \right\}} \qquad (3.3.13)$$

where p is the average desired bit rate per sample. Note that when the transform domain coefficient variances σ_k^2 are equal this reduces to

$n_k = p$, the average rate, and all of the coefficients are quantized in exactly the same way, as one would expect.

Wintz and Kurtenbach

Wintz and Kurtenbach [55] suggested

$$n_k = p + \frac{2}{\ln 10} \left\{ \ln \sigma_k^2 - \frac{1}{N} \sum_{k=1}^{N} \ln \sigma_k^2 \right\} \qquad (3.3.14)$$

based on an approximation to the rd function for optimal *uniform* quantization of a Gaussian rv [56] rather than the optimal *nonuniform* Lloyd-Max quantizer assumed for (3.3.13). Note however that the result is very similar to (3.3.13) only differing in the scale factors $\dfrac{2}{\ln 10} \approx .87$ and $\dfrac{1}{2 \ln 2} \approx .72$. This similarity is to be expected since the rd functions for the optimal uniform and optimal nonuniform (Lloyd-Max) quantizers are themselves similar for a Gaussian source.

Segall

Segall was perhaps the first to use a piecewise approximation for the numerical results obtained by Max. He used the asymptotic approximation given by Wood [57] for $n > 5$ and added his own approximation for $n \leq 5$ to obtain

$$n_k(\theta) = \begin{cases} \dfrac{1}{1.78} \log_2 \dfrac{1.46 \, \sigma_k^2}{\theta} , & 0.083 \, \sigma_k^2 \geq \theta > 0 \\[2mm] \dfrac{1}{1.57} \log_2 \dfrac{\sigma_k^2}{\theta} , & \sigma_k^2 > \theta > 0.083 \, \sigma_k^2 \\[2mm] 0 , & \theta \geq \sigma_k^2 \end{cases} \qquad (3.3.15)$$

where θ solves

$$\sum_{k=1}^{N} n_k(\theta) = Np. \qquad (3.3.16)$$

Unlike the two preceding examples this is not an explicit expression for n_k until we solve (3.3.16) for θ. However this is a simple iterative process where we start with θ small, say, and then as we increase θ, each n_k decreases until we find a sum which is close enough to Np. The bit allocation is then found directly from (3.3.15) by substituting the value of θ.

It should be noted that this is a more accurate approximation to the same problem addressed by Huang and Schultheiss, that is the Lloyd-Max quantization of N samples each with a Gaussian pdf.

Wang and Jain

Wang and Jain [29] extended the numerical results reported by Max for Gaussian sources [47], and by Paez and Glisson for Laplacian sources [58] using their own numerical algorithm and they tabulated quantizers for Gaussian and Laplacian sources with N levels where $N = 2, 3,..., 35, 36, 64, 128, 256, 512$. They compared their results with those of Max to check the correctness of their algorithm, however they did not mention the discrepancy between their results and those of Paez and Glisson. A more recent paper by Adams and Giesler [59] points out that Paez and Glisson's results are in error and reports new quantizers which we find to be in agreement with those of Wang and Jain, who seem to have been unaware of this work.

Wang and Jain also fitted piecewise exponential curves to their numerical values for $f(.)$ which they tabulate in Table A.9.I, and $h(.)$ which is completely determined by $f(.)$ is given in Table A.9.II. These approximations are extensive and include the Lloyd-Max quantizers and optimal uniform quantizers for Gaussian and Laplacian distributions for $1 \le 2^n \le 512$. For example the approximation for the Lloyd-Max quantizer of a Laplacian source is

$$f(n) = \begin{cases} 2^{-1.1711n}, & 1 \le 2^n < 5 \\ 2.0851 \; 2^{-1.7645n}, & 5 \le 2^n < 36 \\ 3.6308 \; 2^{-1.9572n}, & 36 \le 2^n \le 512 \end{cases} . \qquad (3.3.17)$$

It is a simple exercise to derive bit allocations using the piecewise approximations and a technique similar to the one presented by Segall. However Wang and Jain chose to use the Shannon rd function for their bit allocation since it has a simple closed-form solution.

General Approximation For Piecewise Exponentials

We will derive approximate bit allocations for the general framework of piecewise exponentials adopted by Wang and Jain, viz.,

$$f(n) = \alpha \, 2^{-\beta n}; \qquad a \le 2^n < b \qquad (3.3.18)$$

with α and β changing at $2^n = 5$ and $2^n = 36$ to give an approximation consisting of three curves pieced together. Let us denote the pairs (α, β) as (α_i, β_i), where $i = 0, 1, 2$ to distinguish between the three curve segments and then consider the general case where $f(.)$ is fitted by a piecewise exponential curve and obtain the resulting approximate bit allocation.

Differentiating (3.3.18) we get

$$f'(n) = -(\alpha_i\beta_i \ln 2)2^{-\beta_i n}; \quad \log_2 a_i \leq n < \log_2 b_i \quad (3.3.19)$$

and hence $h(.)$ which is the inverse of $f'(.)$ is

$$h(x) = \frac{1}{\beta_i} \log_2 \frac{-\alpha_i\beta_i \ln 2}{x}; \quad a_i^{-\beta_i} \geq \frac{x}{-\alpha_i\beta_i \ln 2} > b_i^{-\beta_i} \quad (3.3.20)$$

where the range on x is determined by the extent of $f'(.)$, that is $f'(\log_2 a_i) \leq x < f'(\log_2 b_i)$. Substituting into (3.3.2) we then solve for the approximate bit allocation as

$$n_k = h\left[\frac{\theta f'(0)}{\sigma_k^2}\right]$$

$$= h\left[\frac{-\alpha_0\beta_0\theta \ln 2}{\sigma_k^2}\right]$$

and so,

$$n_k = \frac{1}{\beta_i} \log_2 \frac{\alpha_i\beta_i\sigma_k^2}{\alpha_0\beta_0\theta}; \quad \frac{\alpha_i\beta_i}{\alpha_0\beta_0}a_i^{-\beta_i} \geq \frac{\theta}{\sigma_k^2} > \frac{\alpha_i\beta_i}{\alpha_0\beta_0}b_i^{-\beta_i} \quad (3.3.21)$$

It should be noted that although the approximation could be chosen to ensure that $f(.)$ is continuous by selecting

$$\alpha_i\tau^{-\beta_i} = \alpha_{i+1}\tau^{-\beta_{i+1}} \quad (3.3.22)$$

where τ is the transition which equals b_i and a_{i+1}, or we could guarantee that the derivative, $f'(.)$, be continuous by choosing

$$\alpha_i\beta_i\tau^{-\beta_i} = \alpha_{i+1}\beta_{i+1}\tau^{-\beta_{i+1}}. \quad (3.3.23)$$

However we cannot guarantee both since this would require

$$\beta_i = \beta_{i+1} \quad (3.3.24)$$

since

$$f'(n) = -(\beta_i \ln 2)f(n). \quad (3.3.25)$$

Consequently the range on θ for the bit allocation formula in (3.3.21) will not piece together since this requires both $f(n)$ and $f'(n)$ be continuous which is not possible as we have just seen. As a result the ranges will either overlap or be disjoint and we will have to decide on some intermediate value to be the transition for $\frac{\theta}{\sigma_k^2}$.

TABLE 3.3.1. Parameters for piecewise bit allocation.

i	a_i	b_i	α_i	β_i	$\dfrac{\alpha_i\beta_i}{\alpha_0\beta_0}$	$\dfrac{\alpha_i\beta_i}{\alpha_0\beta_0}a_i^{-\beta_i}$	$\dfrac{\alpha_i\beta_i}{\alpha_0\beta_0}b_i^{-\beta_i}$
0	1	5	1	1.1711	1	1	0.1519
1	5	36	2.0851	1.7645	3.1416	0.1836	0.005624
2	36	512	3.6308	1.9572	6.0680	0.005461	0.00003023

As a specific example we will consider approximate bit allocation for the Lloyd-Max quantization of a Laplacian source, based on (3.3.17). The parameters are presented above in Table 3.3.1.

When we substitute these values into (3.3.21) we obtain:

$$n_k(\theta) = \begin{cases} \dfrac{1}{1.9572}\log_2 \dfrac{6.07\,\sigma_k^2}{\theta}\,, & 0.0056\,\sigma_k^2 \geq \theta > 0.000030\,\sigma_k^2 \\[2ex] \dfrac{1}{1.7645}\log_2 \dfrac{3.14\,\sigma_k^2}{\theta}\,, & 0.17\,\sigma_k^2 \geq \theta > 0.0056\,\sigma_k^2 \\[2ex] \dfrac{1}{1.1711}\log_2 \dfrac{\sigma_k^2}{\theta}\,, & \sigma_k^2 > \theta > 0.17\,\sigma_k^2 \\[2ex] 0\,, & \theta \geq \sigma_k^2 \end{cases} \qquad (3.3.26)$$

where θ solves $\displaystyle\sum_{k=1}^{N} n_k(\theta) = Np$.

The Integral Constraint

In all of the bit allocations considered so far, the resulting n_k are not integers and must be rounded to the nearest integer if we are to use a whole number of bits for each coefficient, or at the very least they must be adjusted so that 2^{n_k}, the number of levels, is an integer. If after this adjustment $\dfrac{1}{N}\displaystyle\sum_{k=1}^{N} n_k \neq p$ then we must adjust some of the n_k further, under the same constraint that the number of bits, or levels, be integral until the desired rate p is achieved. This can be done arbitrarily or by estimating the distortion for each of the perturbed allocations and choosing the best.

3.4   Integer Bit Allocation

If we limit ourselves to the case where we are to encode each channel separately, that is the n_k are integers, then it is quite straightforward to solve the bit allocation problem directly based on an algorithm due to Fox [60]. This was noted by Segall and adopted by Wang and Jain for their bit allocation. However despite the simplicity of the algorithm, many authors continue to treat n_k as a continuous variable and assume the Shannon rd function because of its simplicity (although they use Lloyd-Max quantizers for the encoding) and then adjust the resulting allocation until the integral and average rate constraints are met.

In order to describe the algorithm, let us assume that we have Np bits to allocate to the N transform coefficients to obtain an average rate of p bits/pixel, and we have already allocated n of the bits. We now wish to allocate the next bit in such a way that we get maximum benefit in terms of reduced distortion. If we assume a Shannon quantizer (we will consider a general rd function below) then the distortion associated with coefficient k is

$$d_k = \sigma_k^2 f(n_k) = \frac{\sigma_k^2}{2^{2n_k}} \tag{3.4.1}$$

and if we increase n_k to $(n_k + 1)$ then

$$d_k \leftarrow \sigma_k^2 f(n_k + 1) = \frac{\sigma_k^2}{2^{2(n_k+1)}} = \frac{d_k}{4}. \tag{3.4.2}$$

Clearly the maximum returns are obtained when the next bit is allotted to the coefficient with maximum distortion and the overall reduction in the average distortion is then $\dfrac{3 \max(d_k)}{4N}$. This leads to the following integer bit allocation algorithm, Algorithm 3.4.1.

General Integer Bit Allocation

More generally, the next bit should be allocated to the coefficient which gives the maximum return

$$\Delta_k \triangleq \sigma_k^2 [f(n_k) - f(n_k + 1)] \tag{3.4.3}$$

and the overall reduction in the average distortion is then $\dfrac{1}{N} \max(\Delta_k)$. Note that this does not necessarily correspond to the coefficient with maximum distortion as with the Shannon rd function, and so we must check the distortion reduction that we would obtain for each coefficient if we were to increase by one the number of bits allocated to that channel, and then find the maximum value. The number of evaluations can be reduced somewhat by noting that if two or more coefficients have each been allocated n bits so far, then we only need to consider the coefficient with maximum variance. This is because $[f(n) - f(n+1)]$ will be the same for each and therefore, from (3.4.3), only the coefficient with the

ALGORITHM 3.4.1. Shannon Integer Bit Allocation.

Algorithm 3.4.1

(1) initialize:
$$n_k = 0, \quad d_k = \sigma_k^2; \quad k = 1, \ldots, N$$

$$total\_bits = 0, \quad R = 0.0$$

$$D = \frac{1}{N} \sum_{k=1}^{N} d_k$$

(2) while there are bits to allocate ($total\_bits < Np$)
begin

    (3) find the index, k^*, for maximum distortion

$$d_{k^*} = \max_{k}(d_k)$$

    (4) allocate the next bit to the k^*th coefficient

        (4a) $n_{k^*} \leftarrow (n_{k^*} + 1)$
        (4b) $d_{k^*} \leftarrow d_{k^*}/4$

    (5) $total\_bits \leftarrow (total\_bits + 1)$

$$R \leftarrow R + \frac{1}{N}$$

$$D \leftarrow D - \frac{3d_{k^*}}{4N}$$

end

---

largest variance in this set may possibly provide the overall maximum distortion reduction. This is Algorithm 3.4.2.

Comments

Algorithm 3.4.2 is slightly more complicated than Algorithm 3.4.1 since we must now compute the distortion reduction rather than infer it from the current distortion. Although there is no closed-form solution for the rd function in general, we only need the values at integral values of n and these are tabulated with the quantizer characteristics so we can use these values directly or use the piecewise exponential approximation [29] to generate them as needed if we do not want to store all of the values.

A significant advantage of this algorithm is that it produces the correct allocation in one pass with no *ad hoc* adjustments which is extremely

ALGORITHM 3.4.2. General Integer Bit Allocation.

Algorithm 3.4.2

(1) initialize:
$$n_k = 0, \quad d_k = \sigma_k^2; \quad k = 1,...,N$$

$$total\_bits = 0, \quad R = 0.0$$

$$D = \frac{1}{N}\sum_{k=1}^{N} d_k$$

(2) while there are bits to allocate ($total\_bits < Np$)
begin

    (3) find the index, k^*, for maximum return

$$\Delta_{k^*} = \max_{k}(\Delta_k)$$

    (4) allocate the next bit to the k^*th coefficient

        (4a) $n_{k^*} \leftarrow (n_{k^*} + 1)$
        (4b) $d_{k^*} \leftarrow d_{k^*} - \Delta_{k^*}$

    (5) $total\_bits \leftarrow (total\_bits + 1)$

$$R \leftarrow R + \frac{1}{N}$$

$$D \leftarrow D - \frac{\Delta_{k^*}}{N}$$

    end

---

important if we want the allocations to be generated automatically. Furthermore, while calculating the bit allocation for the average rate p, the algorithm generates all of the bit allocations for the lower rates $\dfrac{r}{N}$, where $r = 1, 2,..., Np$. For example Fig. 3.4.1 shows the allocations at rates up to 3 bits per pixel for 1d DCT coding with a block size of 8.

3.5   Zero Level Quantizers

Conventionally, as indicated in the previous section, each coefficient is allocated a whole number of bits: 1, 2, 3 etc. This corresponds to an

BIT ALLOCATION FOR TRADITIONAL TRANSFORM CODING

Image

input file: lenna.grn block size: 8

Quantizers

first (DC) coefficient: Lloyd-Max, Gaussian pdf
remaining (AC) coefficients: Lloyd-Max, Laplacian pdf

Variances

20071.11	1467.81	452.58	189.39	91.19	48.13	27.68	19.64

Final Distortions (average: 10.39)

12.92	6.76	7.08	10.07	4.85	9.49	12.29	19.64

Bit Allocations

distortion	rate	bit allocation							
1171.20	0.125	1	.	.	.	.	.	.	.
598.63	0.250	2	.	.	.	.	.	.	.
372.67	0.375	3	.	.	.	.	.	.	.
270.67	0.500	3	1	.	.	.	.	.	.
209.18	0.625	4	1	.	.	.	.	.	.
163.88	0.750	4	2	.	.	.	.	.	.
132.43	0.875	4	2	1	.	.	.	.	.
106.01	1.000	4	3	1	.	.	.	.	.
88.68	1.125	5	3	1	.	.	.	.	.
74.71	1.250	5	3	2	.	.	.	.	.
61.55	1.375	5	3	2	1	.	.	.	.
53.40	1.500	5	3	3	1	.	.	.	.
46.52	1.625	5	4	3	1	.	.	.	.
40.18	1.750	5	4	3	1	1	.	.	.
34.34	1.875	5	4	3	2	1	.	.	.
29.16	2.000	6	4	3	2	1	.	.	.
25.75	2.125	6	4	3	3	1	.	.	.
22.40	2.250	6	4	3	3	1	1	.	.
19.59	2.375	6	4	3	3	2	1	.	.
17.47	2.500	6	4	4	3	2	1	.	.
15.44	2.625	6	5	4	3	2	1	.	.
13.52	2.750	6	5	4	3	2	1	1	.
11.87	2.875	6	5	4	3	3	1	1	.
10.39	3.000	6	5	4	3	3	2	1	.

FIGURE 3.4.1. 1d DCT bit allocations for lenna with Lloyd-Max quantizers.

even number of levels: 2, 4, 8 etc. symmetrically placed about the origin and so there is no reconstruction level at zero. This can be a problem in a non-adaptive zonal scheme, where each block is coded in the same way, because without a zero code word the basis image corresponding to each active coefficient is present, to a greater or lesser degree, in every block.

In regions of low activity where there are no high frequencies present in the original image, the quantization process will introduce false components in the output image. The magnitude of these components will be the inner level of the quantizers used for these high frequency coefficients. Typically this will produce visible high frequency noise, or graininess, in the smooth regions.

We found that a simple solution to this problem is to sacrifice one level from each quantizer to guarantee a reconstruction level at zero. This immediately removes the noise from the smooth regions which are now also smooth at the output.

Note that one bit quantizers are not allowed with this approach, while 2-bit quantizers become 3-level quantizers etc. The odd level quantizers can be coded with the original number of bits in a non-optimal scheme, or common coefficients from a number of adjacent blocks can be coded together to improve efficiency. For example if a single 3-level quantizer is coded with 2 bits, the efficiency is $(\log_2 3)/2 = 79\%$ while 5 such quantizers permit $3^5 = 243 < 256$ states and can therefore be collectively coded with 8 bits and then the efficiency becomes $(\log_2 243)/8 = 99\%$. In the following discussion two rates, maximum and minimum, are used and the maximum rate would be 2 bits for the example of a 3-level quantizer, while the minimum rate would be $\log_2 3 = 1.58$ bits.

The level allocations are obtained from the bit allocations by deleting any one bit quantizers, calculating the maximum rate defined above, and then selecting the maximum rate closest to the desired rate. For example, if we desire a rate of 1.5 bits/pixel then, using Fig. 3.4.1, the conventional bit allocation for 1d DCT is

$$\boxed{\begin{array}{cccccccc} 5 & 3 & 3 & 1 & . & . & . & . \end{array}} \qquad (3.5.1)$$

However, if we consider the conventional allocation at a higher rate of 1.625 bits/pixel we see that the corresponding level allocation is

$$\boxed{\begin{array}{cccccccc} 31 & 15 & 7 & . & . & . & . & . \end{array}} \qquad (3.5.2)$$

which could be coded at a maximum rate of $12/8 = 1.50$ bits and a minimum rate of 1.46 bits/pixel so the maximum is equal to the desired rate.

3.6   Choice of RD Function for Bit Allocation

When we allocate bits to encode a block of samples we should use the distortion function corresponding to the specific quantizer which will be used. So, if we wish to minimize the overall average MS distortion using a practical quantizer, then we should use the optimal MS (i.e. Lloyd-Max) quantizer distortion function for the assumed sample statistics.

However, if we were not to use the integer bit allocation algorithm, then we would need to approximate the actual rd function probably with a piecewise approximation which would lead to a rather complex bit allocation similar to the one we derived in (3.3.26). It is perhaps for this reason that workers in the past have chosen to use the theoretical rate-distortion bound, $f(n) = 2^{-2n}$, instead of the practical quantizer characteristics to determine the bit allocation.

In particular, Chen and Smith in their much referenced paper [51] used the Shannon bound for their calculations, without reservation or apology. Another possible reason why this has not been questioned by more researchers, is an implicit belief that this approximation would be close enough, quite probably leading to the same allocation. This is plausible since the incremental allocation of a whole bit doubles the number of levels in the quantizer, that is the division of resources is very coarse. We will now investigate the validity of this assumption.

If we consider the theoretical Shannon rd function, we see that whenever we increase the number of bits by one, then the distortion decreases by a factor of four, wherever we are on the curve. This is shown in Fig. 3.6.1 where the logarithm of the distortion is plotted against the rate and the Shannon rd curve is linear. The log rd plots for the practical Lloyd-Max quantizers for Gaussian and Laplacian pdf's are also shown in Fig. 3.6.1 and they are not linear although their slope tends towards that of the Shannon rd curve in the limit as the rate increases without bound.

However, in practical coding schemes the number of bits allocated to the coefficients is quite small and we are operating in the neighborhood of the origin where the performance differs markedly from the Shannon rd function. It is clear from Fig. 3.6.1 that the distortion reduction per bit for the practical quantizers is much less than 4:1 when the rate is 1 or 2 bits. Consequently, if we use the Shannon rd function to derive the bit allocation, then we will expect to see more 1-bit and 2-bit quantizers than with the practical rd functions which are not quite so optimistic about their benefit.

Shannon versus Lloyd-Max

As an example, we show two sets of bit allocations for DCT coding at average rates of 1,2 and 3 bits/pixel in Fig. 3.6.2.

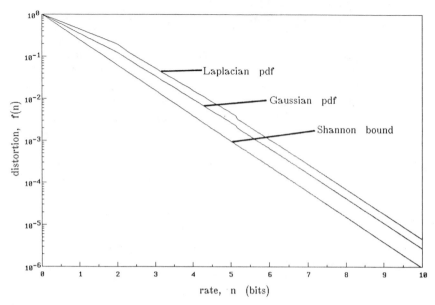

FIGURE 3.6.1. Rate-distortion plots for Lloyd-Max quantizers.

BIT ALLOCATIONS UNDER DIFFERENT ASSUMPTIONS

Image

input file: lenna.grn
block size: 8

Bit Allocations

rate	quantizer	bit allocation							
1	Shannon	4	2	1	1	.	.	.	.
	Lloyd-Max	4	3	1	.	.	.	.	.
2	Shannon	5	3	3	2	1	1	1	.
	Lloyd-Max	6	4	3	2	1	.	.	.
3	Shannon	6	4	4	3	2	2	2	1
	Lloyd-Max	6	5	4	3	3	2	1	.

FIGURE 3.6.2. 1d DCT bit allocations for lenna with Shannon & Lloyd-Max quantizers.

They were each derived using the same set of variances and the integer bit allocation except that for the first the Shannon rd function was used (Algorithm 3.4.1), while for the second, we used the rd function for Lloyd-Max quantization of a Gaussian dc, and Laplacian ac, coefficients

(Algorithm 3.4.2). We found that the MS error performance is always improved by using the practical quantizer distortion function in the bit allocation process while visually, the Shannon design leads to slightly more noise in the output than the Lloyd-Max design. Our observations are supported by Tzou [61] who also uses the integer bit allocation algorithm with the practical quantizer rd function (Algorithm 3.4.2).

Since it is not much more involved to use the practical quantizer characteristics, we will always use Algorithm 3.4.2 to determine the bit allocation for DCT coding and use the piecewise exponentials provided by Wang and Jain to approximate the rd function for Lloyd-Max quantization of: a Gaussian pdf for the dc and a Laplacian pdf for the ac coefficients. The piecewise exponentials are also available in [1].

3.7   RBC Rate Distortion Analysis

Quantization in RBC is somewhat more involved than with traditional transform coding because the boundary distortion and residual distortion are directly coupled. As we shall see, the introduction of distortion in the boundary values leads to an increased variance of each residual coefficient in the transform domain and consequently we cannot minimize the overall distortion by treating each channel independently. We will now derive the equations which show how the increased residual distortion is related to the boundary distortion for both 1d and 2d RBC. We will then use these to derive the corresponding bit allocation algorithms.

1d RBC Rate-Distortion Analysis

We will limit ourselves to the 1st-order Markov case which we will use for image coding. We have from (2.5.9) that, in the absence of any distortion,

$$\mathbf{y} = \mathbf{x} - \mathbf{x}_b. \tag{3.7.1}$$

But in the practical algorithm shown in Fig. 2.7.4 we see that using the quantized boundaries leads to a perturbed residual, $\tilde{\mathbf{y}}$, viz.,

$$\tilde{\mathbf{y}} = \mathbf{x} - \mathbf{x}_b^* \tag{3.7.2}$$

and by comparing these two equations, we see that

$$\tilde{\mathbf{y}} = \mathbf{y} + (\mathbf{x}_b - \mathbf{x}_b^*) = \mathbf{y} + \delta\mathbf{x}_b \tag{3.7.3}$$

where we have introduced the notation $\delta\mathbf{x}$ to denote the quantization, or coding, error in $\mathbf{x}$. If we transform (3.7.3) we will see how the quantization distortion in the boundary variables affects each residual coefficient, viz.,

$$\tilde{\hat{y}} = \hat{y} + \Psi \delta x_b. \tag{3.7.4}$$

Now using (2.7.5), the boundary response in the transform domain is

$$\hat{x}_b = a(1)\Lambda^{-1}\hat{b} \tag{3.7.5}$$

where

$$a(1) = \frac{\rho}{1 + \rho^2}. \tag{3.7.6}$$

Consequently we have

$$\Psi \delta x_b = a(1)\Lambda^{-1}\Psi \delta b \tag{3.7.7}$$

and substituting into (3.7.4) this leads to

$$\tilde{\hat{y}}(k) = \hat{y}(k) + \frac{a(1)}{\lambda(k)}\left[\delta x(0)\Psi(k, 1) + \delta x(N+1)\Psi(k,N)\right]. \tag{3.7.8}$$

Now, due to a property of the noncausal decomposition, y and x_b are orthogonal, which in turn implies orthogonality of $\hat{y}$ and δx_b. If we also assume independent coding distortion in $x(0)$ and $x(N+1)$ then squaring and taking expectations gives

$$\sigma_{\tilde{y}}^2(k) = \sigma_{\hat{y}}^2(k) + 2\frac{a^2(1)}{\lambda^2(k)}\Psi^2(k, 1) E\left\{[\delta x(0)]^2\right\} \tag{3.7.9}$$

where we have made use of the fact that $\Psi^2(k, 1) = \Psi^2(k,N)$. We can write this more compactly as

$$\boxed{\sigma_{\tilde{y}}^2(k) = \sigma_{\hat{y}}^2(k) + w(k)d_b} \tag{3.7.10}$$

where the weight $w(k)$ is defined as

$$w(k) \triangleq 2\frac{a^2(1)}{\lambda^2(k)}\Psi^2(k, 1); \quad \lambda(k) = 1 - 2a(1)\cos\frac{k\pi}{N+1}, \tag{3.7.11}$$

and the boundary distortion, d_b, is

$$d_b \triangleq E\left\{[\delta x(0)]^2\right\} = E\left\{[\delta x(N+1)]^2\right\}. \tag{3.7.12}$$

We have already shown that the boundary response is greatly simplified as $\rho \to 1$ and becomes a straight line in the limit. This is the interpolating function which we shall use in our experiments and so we must modify (3.7.11) to reflect the linear boundary response by setting $\rho = 1$ and then $a(1) = \frac{1}{2}$, $\lambda(k) = 1 - \cos\frac{k\pi}{N+1}$, and the weighting function becomes

$$w(k) = \frac{\Psi^2(k, 1)}{2\lambda^2(k)} = \frac{1}{N+1} \cot^2 \frac{k\pi}{2(N+1)}.$$ (3.7.13)

The weighting function is plotted in Fig. 3.7.1 for the case $N = 15$ and as can be seen the boundary distortion leads to the largest variance increases in the lower DST coefficients, as one might expect, since the linear interpolating function is itself a low frequency function.

Since the quantizer distortion is proportional to the sample variance and we now have the variances of the residual transform domain coefficients as a function of the boundary distortion, we can derive the bit allocation algorithm, which is a modification of Algorithm 3.4.2, the general integer bit allocation algorithm.

We must first compute the necessary statistics, so during the design stage we compute the variance of the boundary variable, σ_b^2, and the residual coefficients, $\sigma_{\tilde{y}}^2(k)$. We measure σ_b^2 directly and $\sigma_{\tilde{y}}^2(k)$, the variance of each coefficient of the transformed residual block, is found as follows. We form the boundary response using the original boundary values and subtract this from the interior values to form the unperturbed residual **y**, which is then transformed and the variance of each coefficient, $\sigma_{\tilde{y}}^2(k)$, is measured.

The bit allocation algorithm is based on testing two hypotheses at each iteration. The first hypothesis is that we should allocate the bit to the boundary variable and the second is that the maximum return would be

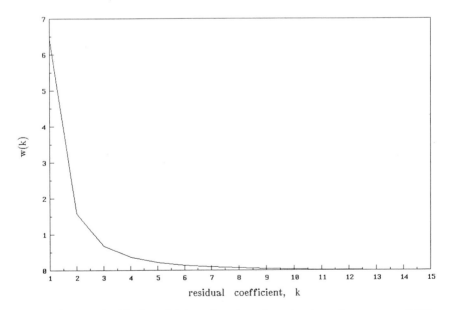

FIGURE 3.7.1. Residual weighting function for the boundary error, RBC ($N = 15$).

achieved by giving this bit to one of the residual coefficients. Note that if we allocate the next bit to the boundary variable, $n_b \to n_b + 1$, there are two sources of return. The first is the reduction in the distortion of the boundary itself

$$\epsilon_b \triangleq [d_b(n_b) - d_b(n_b + 1)], \tag{3.7.14}$$

where

$$d_b(n_b) = \sigma_b^2 f(n_b). \tag{3.7.15}$$

There is also the reduction in the distortion of each residual coefficient, ϵ_k^b, and so the overall return is

$$\Delta_b \triangleq \epsilon_b + \sum_{k=1}^{N} \epsilon_k^b, \tag{3.7.16}$$

where, from (3.7.10),

$$\epsilon_k^b \triangleq \epsilon_b w(k) f(n_k) \tag{3.7.17}$$

is the return in the kth coefficient due to the reduced boundary distortion.

If we allocate the next bit to one of the residual coefficients, then the return is

$$\Delta_k = \epsilon_k \triangleq d_k(n_k) - d_k(n_k + 1); \quad k = 1, \dots, N \tag{3.7.18}$$

where

$$d_k(n_k) = \sigma_{\tilde{y}}^2(k) f(n_k) = [\sigma_{\tilde{y}}^2(k) + w(k)d_b] f(n_k). \tag{3.7.19}$$

The resulting algorithm 3.7.1, which is given below, consists of computing (3.7.16) and (3.7.18) at each iteration and finding the largest value. The next bit is then allocated either to the boundary if Δ_b is the maximum or to the residual coefficient with maximum return otherwise.

2d RBC Rate-Distortion Analysis

The bit allocation for 2d RBC is analogous to the 1d case but we now have four different alternatives to test when we allocate each bit: should we allocate this bit to the corner, the row boundary, the column boundary or the core residual? Before we can answer this question we must find how the boundary distortion contributes to the variance of the core residual coefficients.

Now $\tilde{Y}$ is related to Y by

$$\tilde{Y} = Y + \delta X_b \tag{3.7.20}$$

which is directly analogous to (3.7.3) for the 1d case. Again as in the 1d analysis, we transform this equation to find how the boundary distortion is distributed between the individual core residual coefficients, viz.,

ALGORITHM 3.7.1. 1d RBC Bit Allocation.

Algorithm 3.7.1

(1) initialize:

$$n_b = 0, \quad d_b = \sigma_b^2$$

$$n_k = 0, \quad d_k = \sigma_y^2(k) + w(k)d_b; \quad k = 1,\ldots,N$$

$$total\_bits = 0, \quad R = 0.0$$

$$D = \frac{1}{N+1}\left[d_b + \sum_{k=1}^{N} d_k \right]$$

(2) while there are bits to allocate ($total\_bits < (N+1)p$)

begin

(3) compute the returns Δ_k and the boundary return Δ_b

(4) find the index, k^*, for maximum residual return

$$\Delta_{k^*} = \max_k(\Delta_k)$$

(5) allocate the next bit to obtain the maximum return

if $\Delta_b > \Delta_{k^*}$

(5a) $\Delta^* = \Delta_b$
(5b) $n_b \leftarrow (n_b + 1)$
(5c) $d_b \leftarrow d_b - \epsilon_b$
(5d) $d_k \leftarrow d_k - \epsilon_k^b; \quad k = 1,\ldots,N$

else

(5a) $\Delta^* = \Delta_{k^*}$
(5b) $n_{k^*} \leftarrow (n_{k^*} + 1)$
(5c) $d_{k^*} \leftarrow (d_{k^*} - \Delta_{k^*})$

(6) $total\_bits \leftarrow (total\_bits + 1)$

$$R \leftarrow R + \frac{1}{N+1}$$

$$D \leftarrow D - \frac{\Delta^*}{N+1}$$

end

$$\hat{\tilde{y}}(p,q) = \hat{y}(p,q) + \delta\hat{x}_b(p,q) \qquad (3.7.21)$$

$$= \hat{y}(p,q) + \frac{\alpha\,\delta\hat{b}(p,q)}{[\lambda(p) + \lambda(q)]}; \quad \lambda(i) = \tfrac{1}{2} - 2\alpha\cos\frac{i\pi}{N+1},$$

where we have used (2.10.4), and since δb is sparse, $\delta\hat{b}(p,q)$ can be expressed as

$$\delta\hat{b}(p,q) = \delta\hat{b}_2(p)\Psi(1,q) + \delta\hat{b}_4(p)\Psi(N,q) \qquad (3.7.22)$$
$$+ \delta\hat{b}_1(q)\Psi(1,p) + \delta\hat{b}_3(q)\Psi(N,p).$$

Squaring and taking expectations we have

$$\sigma_{\tilde{y}}^2(p,q) = \sigma_{\hat{y}}^2(p,q) \qquad (3.7.23)$$
$$+ \frac{2\alpha^2}{[\lambda(p) + \lambda(q)]^2}\left[\Psi^2(q,1)d_{col,p} + \Psi^2(p,1)d_{row,q}\right]$$

where we have assumed that $\mathbf{Y}$ and $\mathbf{X}_b$ are orthogonal, which implies that $\mathbf{Y}$ and $\delta\mathbf{X}_b$ will also be uncorrelated. We have further assumed that the distortion in each of the four boundaries is mutually uncorrelated and that the distortion in row boundary, $\mathbf{b}_1$, equals that in $\mathbf{b}_3$, and can be expressed as

$$d_{row,q} = E\left\{[\delta x(0,q)]^2\right\} = E\left\{[\delta x(N+1,q)]^2\right\} \qquad (3.7.24)$$

$$= [\sigma_{row}^2(q) + w(q)d_{cnr}]f(n_{row,q}),$$

since the rows (and columns) are coded using 1d RBC (see (3.7.19)) and similarly for the columns $\mathbf{b}_2$ and $\mathbf{b}_4$ the distortion is

$$d_{col,p} = E\left\{[\delta x(p,0)]^2\right\} = E\left\{[\delta x(p,N+1)]^2\right\} \qquad (3.7.25)$$

$$= [\sigma_{col}^2(p) + w(p)d_{cnr}]f(n_{col,p}).$$

Note that the row and column distortions are not necessarily the same, despite the symmetric model, because in practice the image row and column variances can be different.

Again we can define weighting functions and write this more compactly as

$$\boxed{\sigma_{\tilde{y}}^2(p,q) = \sigma_{\hat{y}}^2(p,q) + w_1(p,q)\left[w_2(q)d_{col,p} + w_2(p)d_{row,q}\right]} \qquad (3.7.26)$$

where the weight $w_1(p,q)$ is defined as

$$w_1(p,q) \triangleq \frac{2\alpha^2}{[\lambda(p) + \lambda(q)]^2},$$

(3.7.27)

and $w_2(i)$ is given by

$$w_2(i) \triangleq \Psi^2(i, 1) = \frac{2}{N+1} \sin^2 \frac{i\pi}{N+1}.$$

(3.7.28)

Again we must make this specific for the interpolation which we shall use in our experiments by setting $\alpha = 0.25$ and then $\lambda(i) = \frac{1}{2}(1 - \cos \frac{i\pi}{N+1})$, and $w_1(p,q)$ becomes

$$w_1(p,q) = \frac{1}{2[2 - \cos \frac{p\pi}{N+1} - \cos \frac{q\pi}{N+1}]^2}.$$

(3.7.29)

Having measured the corner variable variance σ_{cnr}^2 and the unperturbed residual transform coefficient variances $\sigma_{row}^2(k)$, $\sigma_{col}^2(k)$, and $\sigma_{core}^2(p,q)$, we are ready to start the allocation. At each stage we must calculate the returns that we would get if we allocated this bit to the corner, or the coefficient with the maximum return in the row, column or core residuals.

If we allocate the bit to the corner variable, then the return will consist of three parts: the reduced distortion in the corner, and hence in each boundary, and hence in each core residual, viz.,

$$\Delta_{cnr} = \epsilon_{cnr} + \sum_{k=1}^{N} [\epsilon_{row,k}^{cnr} + \epsilon_{col,k}^{cnr}] + \sum_{p=1}^{N} \sum_{q=1}^{N} \epsilon_{core,p,q}^{cnr}.$$

(3.7.30)

Here ϵ_{cnr} is the reduction in the corner distortion and can be written as

$$\epsilon_{cnr} \triangleq [d_{cnr}(n_{cnr}) - d_{cnr}(n_{cnr}+1)]; \quad d_{cnr}(n_{cnr}) = \sigma_{cnr}^2 f(n_{cnr}),$$

(3.7.31)

and $\epsilon_{row,k}^{cnr}$ is the reduction in the kth row residual coefficient distortion due to the reduction ϵ_{cnr}, viz.,

$$\epsilon_{row,k}^{cnr} \triangleq \epsilon_{cnr} w(k) f(n_{row,k}),$$

(3.7.32)

and similarly for the column boundary

$$\epsilon_{col,k}^{cnr} \triangleq \epsilon_{cnr} w(k) f(n_{col,k}),$$

(3.7.33)

and finally the reduction in each core residual coefficient distortion is

$$\epsilon_{core,p,q}^{cnr} \triangleq$$

(3.7.34)

$$\epsilon_{cnr} w_1(p,q) \left[w_2(q) w(p) f(n_{col,p}) + w_2(p) w(q) f(n_{row,q}) \right].$$

If, instead, we allocate the next bit to the kth column residual coefficient, then the return will be the sum of the reduced distortion in the boundary coefficient and the resultant reduction in the kth row of the core residuals, viz.,

$$\Delta_{col,k} = \epsilon_{col,k} + \sum_{q=1}^{N} \epsilon_{core,k,q}^{col} \qquad (3.7.35)$$

where $\epsilon_{col,k}$ is the reduction in the kth column residual distortion and is defined as

$$\epsilon_{col,k} \triangleq d_{col,k}(n_{col,k}) - d_{col,k}(n_{col,k}+1), \qquad (3.7.36)$$

and the reduction in the kth row of the core residual distortion is

$$\epsilon_{core,k,q}^{col} \triangleq \epsilon_{col,k} w_1(k,q) w_2(q) f(n_{core,k,q}); \qquad q=1,...,N . \quad (3.7.37)$$

Similarly if the bit is allocated to the kth row residual coefficient, then the return is

$$\Delta_{row,k} = \epsilon_{row,k} + \sum_{p=1}^{N} \epsilon_{core,p,k}^{row} \qquad (3.7.38)$$

where $\epsilon_{row,k}$ is the reduction in the kth row residual distortion and is defined as

$$\epsilon_{row,k} \triangleq d_{row,k}(n_{row,k}) - d_{row,k}(n_{row,k}+1), \qquad (3.7.39)$$

and the reduction in the kth column of the core residual distortion is

$$\epsilon_{core,p,k}^{row} \triangleq \epsilon_{row,k} w_1(p,k) w_2(p) f(n_{core,p,k}); \qquad p=1,...,N . \quad (3.7.40)$$

If, instead, we allocate the next bit to core residual coefficient (p,q), then the return is simply the reduction in that coefficient, that is

$$\Delta_{core,p,q} = \epsilon_{core,p,q} \triangleq d_{core,p,q}(n_{core,p,q}) - d_{core,p,q}(n_{core,p,q}+1) \qquad (3.7.41)$$

where

$$d_{core,p,q}(n_{core,p,q}) = \qquad (3.7.42)$$

$$\left[\sigma_{core}^2(p,q) + w_1(p,q)[w_2(q)d_{col,p} + w_2(p)d_{row,q}] \right] f(n_{core,p,q}).$$

The resulting algorithm is given on page 81.

Alternative Minimization Strategy

One of the major advantages of RBC is that it suppresses the *tile effect* commonly observed in block by block transform coding. There is however a possibility of RBC producing its own form of block distortion if the distortion is perceived as being different between the corners, boundaries and core. The overall, or average, distortion D is

ALGORITHM 3.7.2. 2d RBC Bit Allocation

Algorithm 3.7.2

(1) initialize:

$n_{cnr} = 0, \quad d_{cnr} = \sigma_{cnr}^2;$

$n_{col,k} = 0, \quad d_{col,k} = \sigma_{col}^2(k) + w(k)d_{cnr}; \quad k = 1,...,N$

$n_{row,k} = 0, \quad d_{row,k} = \sigma_{row}^2(k) + w(k)d_{cnr}; \quad k = 1,...,N$

$n_{core,p,q} = 0,$

$d_{core,p,q} = \sigma_{core}^2(p,q) + w_1(p,q) [w_2(q)d_{col,p} + w_2(p)d_{row,q}];$
$\quad p,q = 1,...,N$

$total\_bits = 0, \quad R = 0.0$

$$D = \frac{1}{(N+1)^2} \left[d_{cnr} + \sum_{k=1}^{N} [d_{col,k} + d_{row,k}] + \sum_{p=1}^{N}\sum_{q=1}^{N} d_{core,p,q} \right]$$

(2) while there are bits to allocate ($total\_bits < (N+1)^2 p$)

begin

    (3) compute the returns $\Delta_{cnr}, \Delta_{col,k}, \Delta_{row,k}$ and $\Delta_{core,p,q}$

    (4) find the indices, $k_{col}^*, k_{row}^*, (p^*,q^*)$, for maximum
    return

$$\Delta_{col,k_{col}^*} = \max_k[\Delta_{col,k}], \quad \Delta_{row,k_{row}^*} = \max_k[\Delta_{row,k}]$$

$$\Delta_{core,p^*,q^*} = \max_{p,q}[\Delta_{core,p,q}]$$

    (5) allocate the next bit to obtain the maximum return

    if Δ_{cnr} is the largest

        (5a) $\Delta^* = \Delta_{cnr}$

        (5b) $n_{cnr} \leftarrow (n_{cnr} + 1)$

        (5c) $d_{cnr} \leftarrow d_{cnr} - \epsilon_{cnr}$

        (5d) $d_{col,k} \leftarrow d_{col,k} - \epsilon_{col,k}^{cnr}; \quad k = 1,...,N$

        (5e) $d_{row,k} \leftarrow d_{row,k} - \epsilon_{row,k}^{cnr}; \quad k = 1,...,N$

        (5f) $d_{core,p,q} \leftarrow d_{core,p,q} - \epsilon_{core,p,q}^{cnr}; \quad p,q = 1,...,N$

continued on next page ...

$$D = \frac{1}{(N+1)^2} \left[d_{cnr} + \sum_{k=1}^{N} [d_{col,k} + d_{row,k}] + \sum_{p=1}^{N}\sum_{q=1}^{N} d_{core,p,q} \right]$$

$$= \frac{1}{(N+1)^2} \left[d_{cnr} + N(\bar{d}_{col} + \bar{d}_{row}) + N^2\bar{d}_{core} \right] \tag{3.7.43}$$

where $\bar{d}_{row}, \bar{d}_{col},$ and $\bar{d}_{core}$ are the average distortions for the row,

Algorithm 3.7.2 continued.

else if $\Delta_{col,k^*_{col}}$ is the largest

    (5a) $k^* = k^*_{col}$, $\Delta^* = \Delta_{col,k^*}$

    (5b) $n_{col,k^*} \leftarrow (n_{col,k^*}+1)$

    (5c) $d_{col,k^*} \leftarrow (d_{col,k^*} - \Delta^*)$

    (5d) $d_{core,k^*,q} \leftarrow (d_{core,k^*,q} - \epsilon^{col}_{core,k^*,q})$; $q = 1,...,N$

else if $\Delta_{row,k^*_{row}}$ is the largest

    (5a) $k^* = k^*_{row}$, $\Delta^* = \Delta_{row,k^*}$

    (5b) $n_{row,k^*} \leftarrow (n_{row,k^*}+1)$

    (5c) $d_{row,k^*} \leftarrow (d_{row,k^*} - \Delta^*)$

    (5d) $d_{core,p,k^*} \leftarrow (d_{core,p,k^*} - \epsilon^{row}_{core,p,k^*})$; $p = 1,...,N$

else allocate to the core residual with maximum return

    (5a) $\Delta^* = \Delta_{core,p^*,q^*}$

    (5b) $n_{core,p^*,q^*} \leftarrow (n_{core,p^*,q^*}+1)$

    (5c) $d_{core,p^*,q^*} \leftarrow (d_{core,p^*,q^*} - \Delta^*)$

(6) $total\_bits \leftarrow (total\_bits + 1)$

$$R \leftarrow R + \frac{1}{(N+1)^2}$$

$$D \leftarrow D - \frac{\Delta^*}{(N+1)^2}$$

end

column and core components respectively and we refer to $\{d_{cnr}, \bar{d}_{row}, \bar{d}_{col}, \bar{d}_{core}\}$ as the component distortions. Since the above bit allocation only minimizes the average distortion D, it could produce allocations where, for example, the boundary distortion $\bar{d}_{row}$ or $\bar{d}_{col}$ is considerably larger than the average, D. This is because there are only $2N$ boundaries compared to N^2 core samples and so this design, which is concerned with the overall distortion, will tend to reduce the core distortion more than the boundary or corner distortion. However, this is balanced to a certain extent since reducing the boundary distortion has the side-effect of also reducing the core distortion which therefore makes the boundaries more important than they would otherwise be. The same problem arises in the 1d allocation where there are N residuals but only one boundary sample and so the boundary distortion may be above average and perceptibly different.

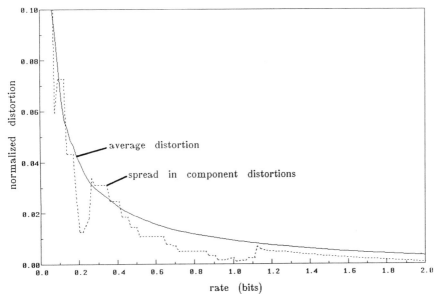

FIGURE 3.7.2. Average distortion and spread in component distortions for the traditional minimization strategy.

The normalized rate-distortion curve for a typical image which has been allocated bits using the above algorithm is shown in Fig. 3.7.2 where $N = 7$ and the normalized distortion is D/σ_x^2. The spread in the component distortions, that is the difference between the smallest and the largest of $\{d_{cnr}, \bar{d}_{row}, \bar{d}_{col}, \bar{d}_{core}\}$ is also shown superimposed on the same plot and notice that there is a large spread in the component distortions which is often of the same order as the average value. An alternative approach is to compute the returns and identify the best candidate in each component: k_{col}^*, k_{row}^*, and (p^*, q^*) as before but to allocate the next bit not to the component which minimizes the average distortion, but to the one which minimizes the spread in the component distortions. The result of this approach is shown in Fig. 3.7.3 where the reduced distortion spread is shown together with the original spread for the same set of variances. Note that the spread in component distortions is now often much narrower and, as seen in Fig. 3.7.4 where the overall rd curve for each of the two different minimization criteria are superimposed, the loss in average MSE is minimal. Consequently we favor this alternative minimization criterion which will produce better visual results by reducing the possibility of *boundary breakthrough* where the individual boundaries become visible and objectionable.

Finally, the rate-distortion and spread in component distortions using the alternative minimization are shown in Fig. 3.7.5 which should be compared with Fig. 3.7.2.

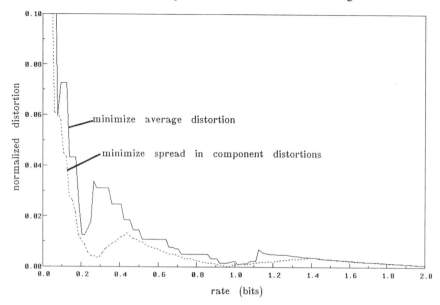

FIGURE 3.7.3. Spread in component distortions for the two minimization strategies.

3.8   Ensemble Design for DCT and RBC

From a computational point of view it is rather undesirable to have to measure the transform domain variances of an image and then make a bit allocation before encoding the image. Furthermore this would reduce the available data compression since the variances would have to be stored or transmitted for the decoder, as overhead, to allow the image to be reconstructed. (The bit allocation could either be transmitted or computed by the decoder using the same variances and algorithm as the encoder.) To avoid these drawbacks, we will now provide a method for designing a standard quantization scheme *off-line*.

An ensemble of images, with characteristics similar to the images to be encoded, are used to design a standard set of normalized variances from which a bit allocation can be derived for the whole ensemble at each desired rate. The variances and bit allocation are then stored or transmitted for the decoder.

As we have seen, the bit allocation depends on the variance distribution in the transform domain. Now for a unitary transform, like the DCT or DST, Parseval's relation states that the energy is the same in both domains. In particular, if

$$\hat{\mathbf{x}} = \mathbf{A}\mathbf{x} \tag{3.8.1}$$

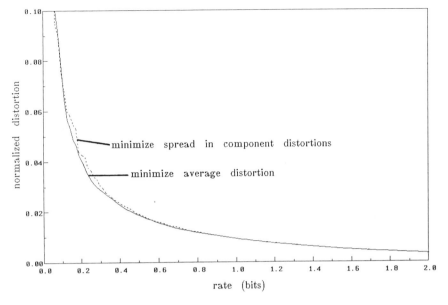

FIGURE 3.7.4. Rate-distortion plots for the two minimization strategies.

where **A** is a unitary transform, then applying Parseval's relation and taking expectations we get

$$\sum_{k=1}^{N} E[\hat{x}^2(k)] = \sum_{n=1}^{N} E[x^2(n)] = N(\sigma_x^2 + \mu_x^2) \qquad (3.8.2)$$

where we have assumed stationarity and (μ_x, σ_x^2) are the mean and variance in the spatial domain. Now we can rewrite the expected energy in the kth coefficient as the sum of the variance and squared mean for that channel, viz.,

$$E[\hat{x}^2(k)] = \sigma_{\hat{x}}^2(k) + \mu_{\hat{x}}^2(k) \qquad (3.8.3)$$

and the mean vector in the transform domain is

$$\boldsymbol{\mu_{\hat{x}}} \triangleq E[\hat{\mathbf{x}}] = \mathbf{A}E[\mathbf{x}] = \mathbf{A}[\mu_x \cdots \mu_x]^T. \qquad (3.8.4)$$

Using Parseval's relation we have

$$\sum_{k=1}^{N} \mu_{\hat{x}}^2(k) = N\mu_x^2 \qquad (3.8.5)$$

and then summing (3.8.3) leads to

$$\sum_{k=1}^{N} E[\hat{x}^2(k)] = N\mu_x^2 + \sum_{k=1}^{N} \sigma_{\hat{x}}^2(k) \qquad (3.8.6)$$

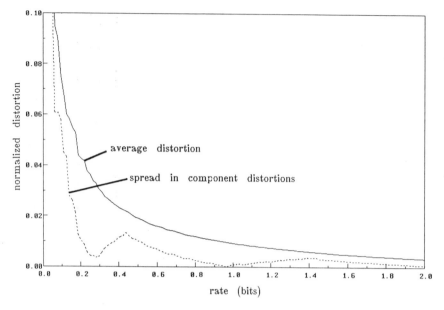

FIGURE 3.7.5. Average distortion and spread in component distortions for the alternative minimization strategy.

after substituting (3.8.5). Comparison with (3.8.2) shows that, not only the energy, but also the sum of the variances is preserved, viz.,

$$\sum_{k=1}^{N} \sigma_{\tilde{x}}^2(k) = N\sigma_x^2. \qquad (3.8.7)$$

Consequently if we scale the transform domain variances by the image variance σ_x^2, then these *normalized variances* will always sum to N for 1d coding and N^2 for 2d coding regardless of the input image, although the distribution may vary considerably. This observation is the key to the ensemble design which is illustrated in Fig. 3.8.1.

For each image in the ensemble we compute the transform coefficient variances and then scale these by their average value, which is also σ_x^2 to form the normalized variances as shown in Fig. 3.8.1(b). These variance distributions are then averaged over the ensemble to give the standard normalized variances. Since bit allocation is insensitive to absolute values and only depends on the relative magnitudes of the coefficient variances, we can use the standard normalized variances to generate the bit allocations for the ensemble. The standard normalized variances can now be made available to the encoder and decoder and used to encode any number of images.

To encode an image we use the standard bit allocation to select the specific Lloyd-Max quantizer for each coefficient but this unity variance quantizer must then be scaled to match the coefficient variance. Rather than measuring each coefficient variance we approximate it by measuring the spatial domain image variance and scaling the standard normalized variances by this value to give a set of estimated variances as shown in Fig. 3.8.2.

We then multiply the Lloyd-Max quantizers by the estimated standard deviation to give customized quantizers for this image; or equivalently we could divide the transform coefficient by its estimated standard deviation and quantize using the standard unity variance quantizers. There is a trade-off to be made since the latter suggestion requires an extra division for each coefficient while extra storage is needed in the former case.

Assuming that the bit map has been relayed to the decoder, we only need to measure and encode a single parameter, the image variance, as overhead for this specific image.

As an example of normalized variance distributions we computed, and plotted on a log scale in Fig. 3.8.3, the normalized 1d DCT domain variances for the ten 512 x 512 monochrome images from the USC image database shown in Fig. 4.2.1. Note that since $N = 8$ the sum of the normalized variances is 8 for each image but the distribution, although similar in form, is spread over a range whose upper limit is approximately 10 times the lower limit for all except the dc and first ac coefficient. The distributions are plotted on a log scale since the bit allocation depends on the relative magnitudes of, rather than differences between, the coefficient variances. This plot shows that this set of images is too diverse to be

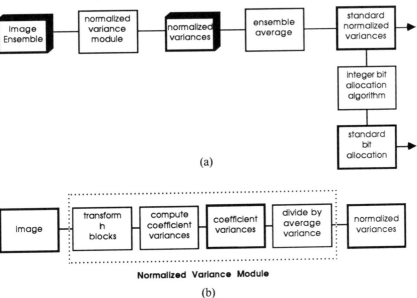

(a)

(b)

Normalized Variance Module

FIGURE 3.8.1. DCT ensemble design: (a) computing the standard normalized variances and the standard bit allocation; (b) detail of the normalized variance module shown in (a).

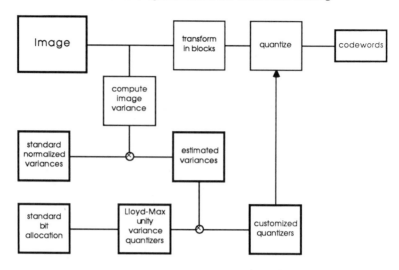

FIGURE 3.8.2. DCT coding an image using the ensemble design parameters.

considered as an ensemble of similar images suitable for a single bit allocation design and, as we shall see in chapter 4, it is appropriate to segment this set into two ensembles.

RBC Variance Reduction

Unlike traditional transform coding, RBC is not a unitary transformation when viewed as a whole because of its predictive nature, even though the DST is unitary. This means that we cannot simply scale the residual variances by the image variance and then average over the ensemble as we did before. The variance of the residual will depend on how *predictable* the original image is.

We will consider 1d coding first and if we denote the boundary variance as σ_b^2 ($\approx \sigma_x^2$) and the average residual variance as

$$\bar{\sigma}_y^2 \triangleq \frac{1}{N} \sum_{k=1}^{N} \sigma_y^2(k), \tag{3.8.8}$$

then we define the *prediction variance reduction ratio* η, as

$$\eta \triangleq \frac{\sigma_b^2}{\bar{\sigma}_y^2}. \tag{3.8.9}$$

The smoother, more predictable images, have a lower residual variance and consequently a higher value for η. The ratio η is shown in Table 3.8.1 for 1d RBC with $N = 7$ using the same ten images and varies in

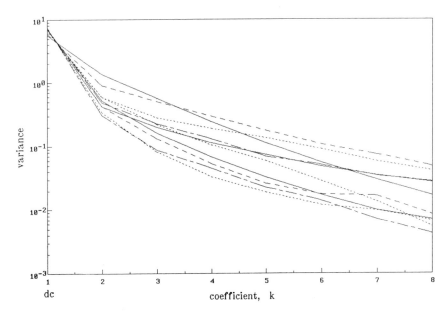

FIGURE 3.8.3. Normalized transform domain variances for 1d DCT ($N = 8$) of the ten USC monochrome images.

value from 2.36 for the most detailed aerial image to 13.75 for peppers which is the image with least detail.

We normalize the boundary variance and residual variances separately by dividing the boundary variance by σ_b^2 while dividing the residual variances by $\bar{\sigma}_{\hat{y}}^2 = \sigma_b^2/\eta$. The average normalized variance is then unity for all images and we can meaningfully average these distributions over the ensemble.

The design process is illustrated in Fig. 3.8.4 and although there is a lot of similarity to Fig. 3.8.1 the process is complicated by the prediction variance reduction ratio, η. During normalization, shown in Fig. 3.8.4(b) we compute the boundary variance σ_b^2, and the average residual variance $\bar{\sigma}_{\hat{y}}^2$, from which we calculate η using (3.8.9). In Fig. 3.8.4(a) the normalized variances are averaged over the ensemble as before to form

TABLE 3.8.1. Prediction variance reduction ratios for 1d RBC, $N = 7$.

image	η	image	η
aerial	2.36	airplane	5.85
baboon	2.38	couple	5.22
lenna	7.88	peppers	13.75
sailboat	9.34	splash	11.85
stream	5.57	tiffany	4.86

the standard normalized variances but we must first form a representative set of variances before making the bit allocation. This is done by using a typical value for η and dividing, that is reducing, the residual variances relative to the boundary variance value which remains at 1. Equivalently we could multiply the boundary variance by η while leaving the residuals unchanged, but this would not extend to the 2d case discussed below.

To select an appropriate η for an ensemble we could average the individual values over the ensemble. However it may be wiser to take the median to avoid obtaining a value which is biased towards those very smooth images. For example the lynda image, which is not part of the USC database but an image that we have used in the past, has a huge value of 60.24 for η. Assuming a 1st-order Markov model, the theoretical value for η is derived in Appendix C, equation (C.2.12), as

$$\eta = N \frac{(1 + \rho^2)}{(1 - \rho^2)} \frac{1}{\sum_{k=1}^{N} \lambda(k)} \tag{3.8.10}$$

which tends to infinity as $\rho \to 1$. In Table C.2.1 η is tabulated for various ranges of N and ρ and in particular, for $N = 7$, typical (ρ, η) pairs are: (0.9, 3.3), (0.95, 6.6), and (0.99, 33.2).

To code an image, we need to scale the standard normalized variances to generate estimated values, as with DCT coding, and this is shown in Fig. 3.8.5. For RBC we measure two parameters: the boundary variance σ_b^2, and the residual energy, and this constitutes the only overhead necessary to generate the correct quantizers at the encoder and decoder. Since the DST is unitary, the average DST domain residual variance $\bar{\sigma}_{\hat{y}}^2$, is also the spatial domain residual variance, or energy since the mean of the residual is zero. So we do not have to transform the residual to compute $\bar{\sigma}_{\hat{y}}^2$, just as with DCT coding when we measured the spatial domain variance σ_x^2. However, we do have to form the prediction so that we can compute the residual energy.

Note that we must make two passes through the image for either DCT or RBC compression. The first pass is required to calculate one (DCT) or two (RBC) parameters and the second pass is when the coding is actually done. This is not a requirement specific to the ensemble design since a single image design would also require a frame buffer and even more computation prior to coding. If a single pass coding scheme is required then this can easily be achieved by suitably estimating the image variance, or boundary and residual variances in the case of RBC, without actually computing them. In a full duplex system these parameters could be varied in a local loop back configuration and the decoded image viewed to subjectively select values which could be fixed for a number of subsequent images. This would be similar to adjusting the brightness and contrast settings on a TV monitor.

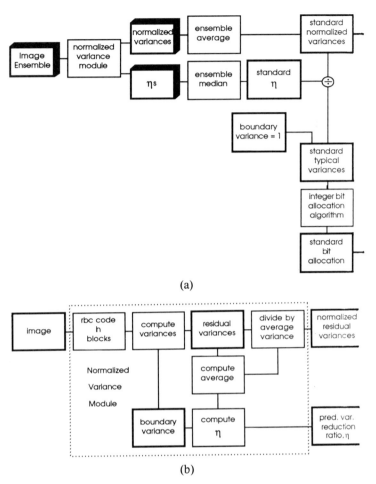

(a)

(b)

FIGURE 3.8.4. RBC ensemble design: (a) computing the standard normalized variances and the standard bit allocation; (b) detail of the normalized variance module shown in (a).

The normalized variances are plotted on a log scale in Fig. 3.8.6 and it can be seen that after normalization the distributions for the ensemble are much more similar than for DCT coding. This is to be expected since the distribution is fairly insensitive to ρ for a 1st-order Markov process as shown in Appendix C.

Variance Reduction With 2D RBC

The normalization procedure must now be generalized to allow for three prediction variance reduction ratios: η_{row}, η_{col}, and η_{core}, which are defined as

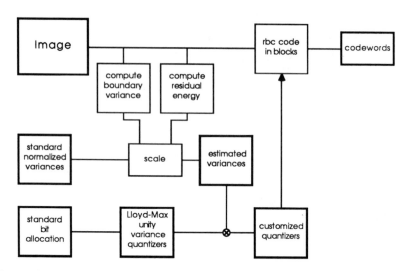

FIGURE 3.8.5. RBC coding an image using the ensemble design parameters.

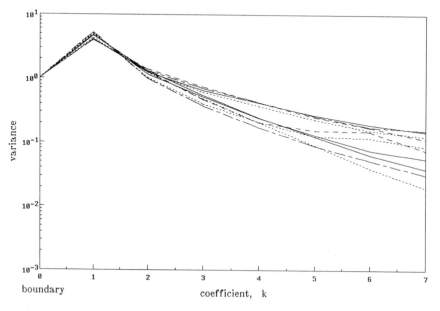

FIGURE 3.8.6. Normalized transform domain variances for 1d RBC ($N=7$) of the ten USC monochrome images.

$$\eta_{row} \overset{\Delta}{=} \frac{\sigma_{cnr}^2}{\bar{\sigma}_{row}^2}; \quad \bar{\sigma}_{row}^2 \overset{\Delta}{=} \frac{1}{N} \sum_{k=1}^{N} \sigma_{row}^2(k), \tag{3.8.11}$$

$$\eta_{col} \overset{\Delta}{=} \frac{\sigma_{cnr}^2}{\bar{\sigma}_{col}^2}; \quad \bar{\sigma}_{col}^2 \overset{\Delta}{=} \frac{1}{N} \sum_{k=1}^{N} \sigma_{col}^2(k), \tag{3.8.12}$$

and

$$\eta_{core} \overset{\Delta}{=} \frac{\sigma_{cnr}^2}{\bar{\sigma}_{core}^2}; \quad \bar{\sigma}_{core}^2 \overset{\Delta}{=} \frac{1}{N^2} \sum_{p=1}^{N} \sum_{q=1}^{N} \sigma_{core}^2(p,q). \tag{3.8.13}$$

Each set of variances is scaled by (σ_{cnr}^2, $\bar{\sigma}_{row}^2$, $\bar{\sigma}_{col}^2$, $\bar{\sigma}_{core}^2$) to form a normalized distribution and median values of (η_{row}, η_{col}, η_{core}) are used to produce the typical variances for bit allocation. When coding we must now send four parameters: the corner variance, and the row, column, and core residual energies. The prediction variance reductions for the ten USC images are tabulated in Table 3.8.2.

3.9   Color Coding

A color image is represented by the three primary components R(ed), G(reen) and B(lue) and the original images are typically encoded at 8 bits per component or 24 bits/pixel. We could encode color images by applying the same coding algorithm to each of these components, but if we first transform the (R,G,B) image to the (Y,I,Q) or (Y,U,V) space [62] then we can get increased performance since the spatial bandwidth of the (I,Q) or (U,V) chrominance signals can be limited to about 1/5th of that of the luminance signal Y, with no noticeable degradation on coding performance [63]. This possible bandwidth reduction, together with other *tricks*, is currently used in the NTSC, PAL and SECAM systems to enable color broadcast TV to be transmitted within the bandwidth previously used for monochrome TV distribution.

TABLE 3.8.2. Prediction variance reduction ratios for 2d RBC, $N = 7$.

image	η_{row}	η_{col}	η_{core}	image	η_{row}	η_{col}	η_{core}
aerial	2.37	1.85	3.11	airplane	5.89	8.31	10.07
baboon	2.34	2.01	3.09	couple	6.05	4.56	6.32
lenna	7.82	13.10	15.41	peppers	14.28	14.74	21.41
sailboat	9.54	7.96	13.00	splash	11.82	26.68	25.17
stream	5.27	4.27	6.94	tiffany	4.71	11.31	9.70

We would use the (Y,U,V) space for color coding and encode the Y luminance component just as we would a monochrome image. This is to be expected since the luminance of a color scene is indeed the monochrome information, that is the Y signal is a weighted sum of the R,G,B signals where the weights are chosen to achieve a reference white, viz.,

$$Y = 0.299R + 0.587G + 0.114B. \qquad (3.9.1)$$

The chrominance signals are normalized color difference signals and the (U,V) pair used in PAL and SECAM systems are defined as

$$U \triangleq (B - Y)/2.03 = -0.147R - 0.289G + 0.436B$$

$$V \triangleq (R - Y)/1.14 = 0.615R - 0.515G - 0.1B. \qquad (3.9.2)$$

We would take advantage of the reduced spatial bandwidth of these channels and subsample each by two in both the horizontal and vertical directions. We would then apply the same coding algorithm to the subsampled signal and then, after decoding, expand to the original resolution by linear interpolation. After decoding, the inverse transformation

$$R = Y + 1.14V$$

$$G = Y - (0.581V + 0.394U) \qquad (3.9.3)$$

$$B = Y + 2.03U$$

would give the reconstructed image in (R,G,B) space.

The remaining bit allocation problem with color coding is how to distribute the bits between the three channels: Y, U and V.

4

Zonal Coding

4.1 Introduction

Zonal coding is the simplest transform coding scheme where each block is coded in the same way without any reference to local image content. That is, we measure statistics for the complete image and then use these to design a bit allocation and set of quantizers to code every block of the image. The bit allocation process, as discussed in chapter three, naturally leads to a *zone* of active coefficients and this leads to the term *zonal coding*. However, some researchers choose the zone first and then, using only the coefficient variances within this zone, make the bit allocation. This is a sub-optimal approach and instead we will let the bit allocation determine the zone directly.

With this technique the same coefficients are transmitted for each block whether the block is smooth or contains a high contrast edge. Naturally with such a fixed scheme there will be a compromise and the number of coefficients will be more than enough for the smooth block and, unless the rate is very high, too few to accurately reconstruct the edge. However, it does not follow that this scheme will perform well in smooth regions and poorly in active blocks. This is because the number of active coefficients in itself does not control the quality since the amplitude of each coefficient is quantized. In fact in the smooth blocks it would be a better use of resources to reallocate the bits from the high frequency coefficients to the lower coefficients to provide smaller steps in the amplitude scale. This of course would require side information to inform the decoder of the local block characteristics and this would lead to some adaptive scheme such as threshold coding or transform coding based on activity classification. We will discuss adaptive coding techniques later in chapter five.

In the next three sections of this chapter we will describe the framework for all of the subsequent chapters which describe our experimental results for different coding strategies. In section 4.2 we will present the images which will be used to evaluate the performance of the coding algorithms. In section 4.3 we will then describe the simulation facilities and software implementation and in the final general section, 4.4, we will discuss the very important topic of image quality measurement. Of course the best methodology would be to conduct extensive subjective tests and have the reconstructed images rated on a suitable descriptive scale. However this is not practical within our research environment and so we will discuss an objective measure which correlates with subjective evaluation.

In the remaining sections we will present material which is specific to the zonal coding approach to data compression. In section 4.5 we will discuss the segmentation of the input images into suitable ensembles and then present results of 1d coding these ensembles using both DCT and RBC. The results of 2d coding will be given in section 4.6. In section 4.7 we will discuss hybrid transform predictive coding methods, apply them to RBC, and present the experimental results. Conclusions will then be drawn in section 4.8.

4.2   Original Images

It is very important to verify the robustness of any proposed coding technique by coding not one, but a number of images. Furthermore, it is undesirable from a computational standpoint that an algorithm is so sensitive that it requires that each image be coded using a specifically designed quantization stage. Consequently we will design our quantizers using statistics gathered from an image ensemble, as discussed in chapter three, so that such algorithms will perform poorly and therefore not be recommended.

The images are taken primarily from the USC image database [64] because they are readily available and have become a *de facto* standard, at least within the U.S.A. (We would add, however, that the image quality is far from perfect: the color balance is often poor and the film sprockets are visible in some of the digitized slides). In addition we include some images generated here at U.C. Davis which we have coded in earlier work [24]. In all cases the images contain 512×512 pixels with each pixel represented by 8 bits per band: Y or (R,G,B).

The USC database consists of the following volumes: textures, aerials, miscellaneous, motion picture sequences and military equipment. We shall use the miscellaneous images, some of which are available in color (R,G,B) while others are only available in monochrome. USC distributes the color images as one volume, and the green component, G, of the color images together with true monochrome images as a second volume. As we have already seen in section 3.9, the monochrome information of

TABLE 4.2.1. Monochrome test images.

image	G:Y	source	μ	σ^2	min	max	entropy	ρ
aerial	Y	USC	180.6	1556	12	255	7.0	.90
airplane	G	USC	177.9	2687	0	234	6.8	.95
baboon	G	USC	128.9	2282	0	236	7.5	.86
buildings	Y	UCD	101.0	2640	0	255	7.4	.96
couple	Y	USC	123.2	1605	0	255	7.2	.94
lenna	G	USC	99.1	2796	3	248	7.6	.97
lynda	Y	UCD	98.6	4625	0	255	7.2	.995
peppers	G	USC	115.6	5632	0	237	7.5	.98
sailboat	G	USC	124.3	6027	0	249	7.6	.97
splash	G	USC	70.5	3640	0	247	6.9	.98
stream	Y	USC	113.8	2996	0	255	5.7	.94
tiffany	G	USC	208.6	1126	0	255	6.7	.87

a color image is the luminance, Y, and not G. However, since the green component has been used in the past as if it were a true monochrome image we will do the same. We took the ten 512×512 green components or monochrome images from the miscellaneous images volumes and added two monochrome images from UCD to form the input set for monochrome coding. The original images are shown in Fig. 4.2.1 and their statistics and origin are given in Table 4.2.1.

Color Images

The statistics for the seven 512×512 color images from the USC database are presented in Table 4.2.2.

Comparing the statistics for the Y, U, and V components we see that the entropy and variance of the chrominance channels is less than the corresponding values for the luminance channel and in some cases the reduction is dramatic. For example, with the airplane, the entropy drops by $(2.3, 2.5)$ bits for the (U, V) channels respectively and the variance is reduced by a factor of $(22.5, 15.5)$. At the other extreme, the baboon entropy drops by $(1.1, 0.6)$ bits and the variance is only reduced by $(4.4, 1.3)$.

Comparing the U and V channels notice that in all but one case (airplane) the entropy of the V channel is greater and in every case the V component has a higher variance.

4.3   Simulation Facilities

All of the algorithms presented in this and the following chapters were simulated in software written in the C language [65] running on a Sun-3/160M computer under the Sun 3.0 Unix operating system which is their

(a) aerial   (b) airplane

(c) baboon   (d) buildings

(e) couple   (f) lenna

Fig. 4.2.1   Original monochrome test images

(a) lynda

(b) peppers

(c) sailboat

(d) splash

(e) stream

(f) tiffany

Fig. 4.2.1 contd.   Original monochrome test images.

TABLE 4.2.2. Color test images.

image	source	μ	σ^2	min	max	entropy	ρ
airplane	USC	179.7	2154	17	232	6.7	.96
baboon	USC	130.1	1790	0	231	7.4	.87
lenna	USC	124.6	2290	25	246	7.4	.97
peppers	USC	120.7	2903	0	228	7.6	.97
sailboat	USC	125.7	4301	2	240	7.5	.97
splash	USC	103.7	2657	9	243	7.3	.98
tiffany	USC	211.6	858.1	0	255	6.6	.92

(a) Luminance, Y

image	source	μ	σ^2	min	max	entropy	ρ
airplane	USC	5.9	95.6	-40	63	4.4	.90
baboon	USC	-7.6	407.1	-78	49	6.3	.91
lenna	USC	-8.7	141.5	-88	29	5.5	.95
peppers	USC	-25.9	163.4	-64	80	5.6	.93
sailboat	USC	-4.6	129.3	-61	60	5.4	.87
splash	USC	-10.9	145.1	-75	82	5.4	.97
tiffany	USC	-22.9	108.2	-57	82	5.2	.73

(b) Chrominance, U

image	source	μ	σ^2	min	max	entropy	ρ
airplane	USC	-0.9	139.0	-83	118	4.2	.80
baboon	USC	7.3	1403	-83	126	6.8	.95
lenna	USC	49.8	249.5	-8	96	5.9	.95
peppers	USC	26.5	1884	-85	135	7.0	.98
sailboat	USC	5.6	737.2	-119	135	6.6	.93
splash	USC	64.6	1354	-91	127	6.6	.99
tiffany	USC	20.7	176.9	-35	136	5.6	.81

(c) Chrominance, V

implementation of Berkeley version 4.2. Since images are not yet a generic data type like bytes and integers, we have defined a fixed file structure for images and written a set of special purpose routines to access images of arbitrary size and data type. The format is the same as that used by the Image Processing Facility (IPF) at Davis who in addition have written an image processing executive called DAISY which stands for DAvis Interactive SYstem, which runs on top of the VMS 4.4 operating system on their VAX 11/750. We chose not to use a special purpose image processing operating system since the C Shell [66] under Unix is a very powerful and flexible general purpose environment which is also well suited to algorithm evaluation.

The software was written to be very modular by only incorporating one coding block, e.g. transformation or quantization, in each program so that a large percentage of the coding blocks are reused for many algorithms. The overall connection of these coding blocks to form an algorithm is achieved in a C Shell script. This provides a flexible testbed since different algorithms can be quickly tested by simply writing scripts, which are interpreted rather than compiled. Interpreted code executes slower than compiled code, but in this case only the overall control is in the script while the time consuming computation is done by compiled programs so that this overhead is minimal. Another advantage of using the C Shell is that it provides features to easily manipulate strings such as file names and lists of them which is very useful since we need to process image ensembles which are simply lists of file names.

```
#
# -----------------------------------
# SuperBatch
# -----------------------------------
set list = (lenna.grn lynda.bw peppers.grn sailboat.grn splash.grn)

# --------------------------------------------------------
# code each image with ensemble stats
# --------------------------------------------------------
setenv DESIGNLIST "${list}"   # use all images in design stage
setenv CODELIST "${list}"     # code all images using this design

# --------------------------------------------------------
# 1d coding at rates in RATELIST
# --------------------------------------------------------
setenv RATELIST "3.0 2.5 2.0"
Batch -b 8 1                   # 1d coding block size = 8

# --------------------------------------------------------
# 2d coding at rates in RATELIST
# --------------------------------------------------------
setenv RATELIST "2.0 1.5 1.0"
Batch -b 8 2                   # 2d coding block size = 8

exit(0)
# -----------------------------------
```

For example, consider the short script above which provides the highest level control for zonal DCT coding. All text following the " # " symbol are comments and so there are only eight lines of code here. Of these, five are defining the coding parameters: DESIGNLIST, the list of images to use in the design phase; CODELIST, the images to be coded; and RATELIST, the rates at which they are to be coded.

We simply choose which images will form the design and coding ensembles: DESIGNLIST and CODELIST. In this case the five images: lenna,...,splash are used to design the coding scheme and then each image is coded. This script *SuperBatch* calls the *Batch* script twice to actually do the work. *Batch* is initiated via "*Batch [options] n*" where *n* is the dimensionality of the coding algorithm, 1 or 2 for example. The first time: *Batch -b 8 1*, the block size option -b is used to set the block size to 8 and then each image is coded using the 1d DCT zonal algorithm at rates of 2, 2.5, and 3 bits/pixel, as indicated by the RATELIST variable. The second time: *Batch -b 8 2*, the 2d algorithm is used at 1, 1.5, and 2 bits/pixel, again with a block size of 8. Underlying this script are a number of other scripts which take care of the design and coding stages by calling C programs as necessary for each image in the ensemble and combining the results to form standard normalized variance files and bit allocations before actually coding, generating statistics, etc. To run another simulation with different images, at other rates and with a different block size requires only simple editing of this script to change the block size option, and the design, code, and rate lists.

The Sun has a bit-mapped display which is useful for graphics but since each display pixel is only one bit deep it is unable to display gray level images. Initially, the images were viewed for subjective evaluation on a Conrac monitor driven by a Gould IP8500 image processing system attached to the IPF's VAX 11/750, but toward the end of this research a diskless Sun-3/110G workstation became available. This has a 1152×900 8-bit display and was used to directly view the images within windows on the workstation. In fact two images could be viewed side by side which was very useful when comparing results. The images were photographed using a Matrix PCR digital film recorder hosted by an IBM PC/AT. These different machines run different operating systems but by using a standard DAISY image file structure, programs on each machine can process the same images. The Sun, VAX and AT are all connected via an ethernet local network under the TCP/IP protocol so images can be transferred from host to host albeit rather slowly and somewhat awkwardly.

4.4   Image Quality Measures

The traditional objective quality measure is the MSE between the original image and the reconstructed image after coding, viz.,

$$\text{MSE} \triangleq \frac{1}{total\_pixels} \sum_n [x(n) - x^{\bullet}(n)]^2, \qquad (4.4.1)$$

where $x(n)$ is an original pixel and $x^*(n)$ is the corresponding pixel in the reconstructed image. The MSE is sometimes normalized by the image variance to give the NMSE, or percentage distortion

$$\text{NMSE} \triangleq \frac{\text{MSE}}{\sigma_x^2}; \quad \% \text{ distortion} = \text{NMSE} \times 100\%. \tag{4.4.2}$$

This is done since one might expect that we will be more forgiving of a fixed MSE in a very active image as opposed to a smooth image and the NMSE would then be better correlated to the subjective image quality. Unfortunately the variance of an image is not necessarily related to the smoothness or activity of the image as can be seen in Table 4.2.1 where lynda has a relatively large variance and yet is the smoothest image in the set with a horizontal correlation coefficient of 0.995. As another counterexample, consider tiffany with a very low correlation of 0.87, but also a low variance which is more than four times smaller than the variance of the smooth lynda image.

Directly related to the NMSE figure is the logarithmic signal to noise ratio (SNR) used by communications engineers, viz.,

$$\text{SNR} \triangleq 10 \log_{10} \frac{\sigma_x^2}{\text{MSE}} = -10 \log_{10} \text{NMSE} \quad \text{dB}. \tag{4.4.3}$$

A second logarithmic measure which does not normalize by the image variance but rather by the squared peak to peak value, a constant independent of the image, is SNR', viz.,

$$\text{SNR}' \triangleq 10 \log_{10} \frac{255^2}{\text{MSE}} \quad \text{dB} \tag{4.4.4}$$

where we have assumed an 8-bit image (replace 255 by 1023 for a 10-bit image for example).

Although widely used, it is also widely accepted that this measure, in its various forms (4.4.1)-(4.4.4), which consists of a single number for the whole image is at best of limited use. It is certainly true that in the limit as the MSE tends to zero, then we will have a perfect pixel by pixel reconstruction and presumably when the MSE is small enough this corresponds to a high quality reconstruction. Furthermore for a given algorithm and a given image the MSE increases as the rate decreases, but it does not follow in general that if the MSE increases in an arbitrary manner, then the image quality is always reduced. As a simple example take an image and add a constant to each pixel. Assuming that the dynamic range is not exceeded, such a dc shift will result in an image with the same quality as the original and yet the MSE will equal the square of the intensity offset. Another problem is that the same MSE does not guarantee that two images are of the same subjective quality which is rather unsettling. In particular, Miyahara and Kotani [19] have conducted subjective studies and shown that *tile effect distortion is ten times more objectionable than equal energy white noise.* In other words we are sensitive to the structure of the noise and not just the noise energy.

Recent work by Hosaka [30] shows great promise for an objective measure that can be interpreted in terms of subjective qualities.

Hosaka Plots (h-plots)

Hosaka proposes that we measure a number of features of the reconstructed image and compare these with the corresponding features in the original image with the difference between the two feature vectors generating a vector error measure. The input and output features are compared, but corresponding individual pixels are not which seems reasonable since when we subjectively evaluate an image, even in a side by side A-B comparison, we compare features of the images rather than the quarter of a million error values for a 512×512 image. We make comments like: this image is noisy, or blurred, or blocky, and so we seek features which correspond to these attributes.

The evaluation process consists of first segmenting the original image into blocks whose variance is less than some threshold and these are then grouped together to form a number of classes depending on the size of the blocks as outlined in Algorithm 4.4.1. We then compute two features for each class: the first is related to the mean intensity values, and the second is the mean standard deviation which represents the magnitude of the intensity variations due to edges and textures, for example.

The two parameters: the initial block size N and the threshold T were chosen as 16 and 10 respectively as in Hosaka's paper [30].

Each class k, is then treated separately and the mean of the nth block in class k, $\mu_k(n)$:

$$\mu_k(n) = \frac{1}{k^2} \sum_{i=1}^{k} \sum_{j=1}^{k} u(i,j), \qquad n = 1, 2, \ldots, n_k \qquad (4.4.5)$$

and the standard deviation, $\sigma_k(n)$:

$$\sigma_k(n) = \sqrt{\frac{1}{k^2} \sum_{i=1}^{k} \sum_{j=1}^{k} [u(i,j) - \mu_k(n)]^2}; \qquad n = 1, 2, \ldots, n_k. \quad (4.4.6)$$

are evaluated. The average mean is then computed for each class as

$$\bar{\mu}_k \triangleq \frac{1}{n_k} \sum_{n=1}^{n_k} \mu_k(n) \qquad (4.4.7)$$

where n_k is the number of blocks in the kth class. The $\{\bar{\mu}_k\}$ are then averaged to form m, viz.,

ALGORITHM 4.4.1. Segmentation Prior to Feature Measurement.

Algorithm 4.4.1

(1) segment the original image into NxN blocks, where N is a power of 2

(2) for each block

begin

        (3) measure the block variance, σ^2
if $\sigma^2 > T$ and block size, $k > 1$

                (3a) subdivide the block into 4 sub-blocks by splitting at the midpoint both horizontally and vertically

                (3b) repeat step 3 for each of the new blocks

end

(4) group all of the blocks of size k to form class k where $k = 1, 2, 4, ..., N$

$$m = \frac{1}{[\log_2 N + 1]} \left[\bar{\mu}_1 + \bar{\mu}_2 + \bar{\mu}_4 + \cdots + \bar{\mu}_N \right]. \qquad (4.4.8)$$

Note that this is not the same as the image mean unless $(n_k k^2)$ is a constant so that each class contains the same number of pixels. We subtract m from the $\{\bar{\mu}_k\}$ to form the first feature, dm_k, viz.,

$$dm_k \triangleq \bar{\mu}_k - m. \qquad (4.4.9)$$

The reason for subtracting m is to remove the effects of any dc drift which has no adverse effect on the perceived image quality.

The second feature is just the average standard deviation, $\bar{\sigma}_k$,

$$\bar{\sigma}_k \triangleq \frac{1}{n_k} \sum_{n=1}^{n_k} \sigma_k(n) \qquad (4.4.10)$$

and we measure these features for each class in both the original $(dm_k, \bar{\sigma}_k)$ and reconstructed images $(dm_k^*, \bar{\sigma}_k^*)$. We do not segment the reconstructed image separately, instead we apply the segmentation that was used for the original image, that is for each block in the original we construct a block of the same size at the same spatial location in the reconstructed image.

The error diagram, or *h-plot*, is constructed by plotting the errors in the corresponding features

$$dS_k \stackrel{\Delta}{=} |\bar{\sigma}_k - \bar{\sigma}_k^*| \qquad (4.4.11)$$

and

$$dM_k \stackrel{\Delta}{=} |dm_k - dm_k^*| \qquad (4.4.12)$$

in polar coordinates where the radius is the feature error value, the left half plane contains dS vectors with dM vectors in the right half plane each equally spaced for the different classes so as to fill the plane, as shown in Fig. 4.4.1. Note that there is no dS_1 since, by definition, the variance is zero in a block of size 1 and the error in this class shows up in the dM_1 error feature.

To illustrate the use of the diagram we will consider three controlled examples and study the corresponding h-plots. The first consists of adding a dc shift to the image, the second is the addition of noise and the third is blurring of the image.

In the first case, if we let s be the amount of the shift, then we have

$$\bar{\mu}_k^* = \bar{\mu}_k + s, \quad \text{and} \quad m^* = m + s,$$

so

$$dm_k^* = dm_k \qquad (4.4.13)$$

and we also have

$$\bar{\sigma}_k^* = \bar{\sigma}_k \qquad (4.4.14)$$

so the feature vectors are the same for both the input and output images and the diagram is simply the origin, indicating that the image quality is unchanged.

If we add noise to the image, we would expect that the dS_k would all be non-zero with equal magnitudes proportional to the noise power. If the noise has zero mean, then the means of class k should be the same in both images which in turn implies that m is unchanged and so we would expect the dM_k to be zero. In practice, the dM_k will only be close to zero since the fluctuations within a single class may not completely cancel. Another source of error leading to non-zero dM_k is clipping which arises when noise is added to pixels which are close to black or white and the resulting pixel is beyond the range of allowable values. Two h-plots for the buildings image when uniformly distributed zero mean noise at two different powers is added are shown superimposed in Fig. 4.4.2. The structure of the diagram is as expected with equal dS_k and small dM_k and when the noise power is increased the shape of the diagram remains the same but at a larger scale. This shows that the area of the h-plot is

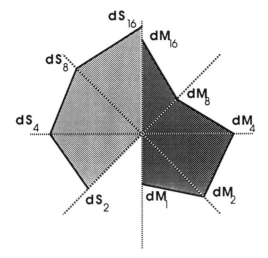

FIGURE 4.4.1. Hosaka plot (h-plot).

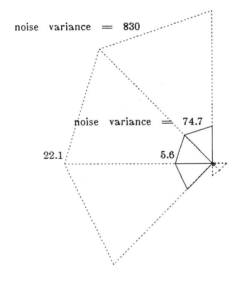

FIGURE 4.4.2. H-plot for images with added zero mean uniformly distributed noise: in the outer plot the noise variance = 830; and in the inner plot the noise variance = 74.7.

proportional to the image quality while the structure of the diagram depends on the type of distortion. The lower noise variance is 74.7 which corresponds visually to a typical noisy coded image in zonal coding while the higher variance is 830 which is visually totally unacceptable. The values for dS_4 are 5.63 and 22.1 for the two cases and as noted already these values are approximately the same for all the dS_k.

If we blur a stationary image then we would expect to see little change in the means of each class, while the change in the standard deviation will be different for each class. This is because the lower activity classes may be characterized by a lower bandwidth which will be unaffected by a small amount of blurring while the most active classes with a bandwidth equal to the system bandwidth will immediately be affected. As the amount of blurring increases then the effect will be felt in the lower activity classes as the filter bandwidth drops below the class bandwidth. In practice however, the images are not stationary and the major effect is at the boundaries between smooth and active regions where the intensities will change away from their local block means as the image is blurred. These non-zero values for the dM_k will then increase with the amount of blurring. It is more difficult to predict what will happen to the standard deviations since there are two conflicting mechanisms: the standard deviation will increase in a low activity block if it is at a class boundary and decrease if the surrounding blocks are similar, that is the image is locally stationary. The overall effect will depend on both the image and the filter structure. To illustrate this we again took the buildings image and digitally smoothed it by replacing each pixel with the average of itself and its North, South, East and West neighbors. The corresponding h-plot is shown in Fig. 4.4.3 for three cases. The second image was obtained by applying the same blurring operator to the blurred original. This was continued by blurring the second image to produce the third. As can be seen the pattern on the right side of the diagram remains fixed and increases in magnitude as the blurring increases while the left side is less predictable.

So, with some appreciation of the new graphical error measure we can now present the coding results. However there is a caveat: if we wish to detect the tile effect distortion with this method we need to shift the Hosaka block structure relative to the transform block structure. Consequently, we discard the first four lines and left columns of the image and compute the h-plot over a 496×496 region.

4.5   1d Coding Results

The first task is to decide on suitable image ensembles for coding. As shown in Appendix C (Figs. C.2.1 and C.3.1) when $\rho \approx 1$, as is the case with the monochrome test images here where $.86 \le \rho \le .995$, the normalized variance distribution for 1d RBC varies only slowly with ρ while the 1d DCT distribution varies a good deal. With RBC, it is the variance prediction ratio η which varies greatly with ρ and so we could use either ρ, η or the DCT variance distribution to group our images into suitable ensembles of similar images. We considered all of these parameters and decided to split the twelve test images into two ensembles: A and B. We

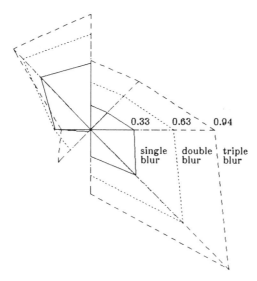

FIGURE 4.4.3. H-plot for blurred images.

show the images below ranked in order of unpredictability, or lack of smoothness, with their values for ρ and η. The first image, aerial, is the most unpredictable and as we move down the table to the smoother images, the trend is for both ρ and η to increase.

The seven images above the line in Table 4.5.1 are the more difficult images and form ensemble A while the remaining five images are the low activity B ensemble. When choosing the ensembles, most weight was placed on η_{row}, η_{col} and η_{core} since they measure predictability in both directions while ρ only measures correlation in the horizontal direction—we did not calculate the vertical correlation. At first sight

TABLE 4.5.1. Test images in order of coding difficulty.

ensemble	image	ρ	η	η_{row}	η_{col}	η_{core}
	aerial	.90	2.36	2.37	1.85	3.11
	baboon	.86	2.38	2.34	2.01	3.09
	buildings	.96	4.18	4.08	3.31	5.95
A	couple	.94	5.22	6.05	4.56	6.32
	stream	.94	5.57	5.27	4.27	6.94
	tiffany	.87	4.86	4.71	11.31	9.70
	airplane	.95	5.85	5.89	8.31	10.07
	sailboat	.97	9.34	9.54	7.96	13.00
	lenna	.97	7.88	7.82	13.10	15.41
B	peppers	.98	13.75	14.29	14.74	21.41
	splash	.98	11.85	11.82	26.68	25.17
	lynda	.995	60.24	60.22	98.16	121.99

tiffany seems to be placed too low in the list based on low values for both ρ and η_{row} but these measure horizontal smoothness and as we can see from η_{col} and η_{core} this image is non-isotropic and is much more predictable in the vertical direction—in fact the vertical correlation for this image is .92. Comparing this segmentation with the normalized DCT variances shown in Fig. 3.8.3 for the 10 USC images we see that the A ensemble images all belong to the upper group of curves at $k = 3$ while the B ensemble images form the lower grouping so the various indicators are in agreement.

Having fixed the ensembles, we proceeded to encode all twelve images with a block size of 8 at four different rates using a bit allocation designed for the ensemble to which each image belonged.

1d DCT Design

The normalized variances for each ensemble are given in Table 4.5.2 and plotted in Fig. 4.5.1. The resulting standard bit allocations for each rate are given in Table 4.5.3.

1d RBC Design

For RBC, the normalized variances are listed in Table 4.5.4 and plotted in Fig. 4.5.2. Note that the differences in the normalized distributions are minimal when compared with the spread for DCT in Fig. 4.5.1 which is close to a factor of 5.

The bit allocation is determined using a representative distribution which is obtained by scaling each residual coefficient variance by $\frac{1}{\bar{\eta}}$, where $\bar{\eta}$ is the median value for η within the ensemble, and these are shown in Table 4.5.5 and Fig. 4.5.3 with the resulting bit allocations given in Table 4.5.6.

Initially, when the A ensemble was coded at 1.5 bits/pixel using the allocation (3,4,3,1,1,0,0,0) from Table 4.5.6, there was a very objectionable *boundary breakthrough* problem when the boundaries appeared to be very distorted. In fact the boundary MSE distortion was typically 80 which was close to the residual distortion but visually perceived as being much higher. We have determined that at least 4 bits are necessary for the boundary points to prevent this breakthrough problem, so the

TABLE 4.5.2. Normalized variances for 1d DCT coding.

ensemble	coefficient							
	1 (dc)	2	3	4	5	6	7	8
A	6.535	0.748	0.333	0.167	0.093	0.055	0.036	0.024
B	7.437	0.358	0.096	0.040	0.020	0.012	0.009	0.005

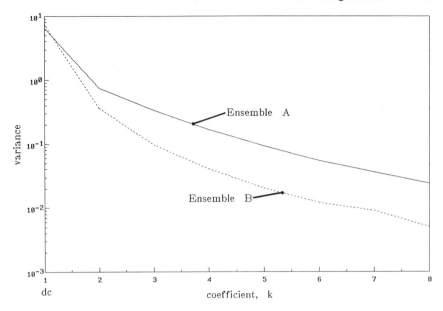

FIGURE 4.5.1. Ensemble normalized DCT variances for 1d DCT ($N = 8$).

TABLE 4.5.3. Bit allocations for 1d DCT coding.

ensemble	rate	coefficient							
		1 (dc)	2	3	4	5	6	7	8
A	3.0	6	4	4	3	3	2	1	1
	2.5	5	4	3	3	2	2	1	.
	2.0	5	4	3	2	1	1	.	.
	1.5	4	3	3	1	1	.	.	.
B	3.0	7	5	4	3	2	2	1	.
	2.5	6	4	3	3	2	1	1	.
	2.0	6	4	3	2	1	.	.	.
	1.5	6	3	2	1	.	.	.	.

allocation was changed to ensure that the boundary was allotted 4 bits and the results to be presented here were all coded with the modified allocation of (4,4,3,1,0,0,0,0) which is also shown in Table 4.5.6.

Discussion of Results

In this experiment each of the twelve images was coded at four rates using both the RBC and DCT algorithms. To save space we will not include all 96 reconstructed images here but rather use the h-plots, a few typical images, and a verbal description to convey the characteristic performance of each algorithm. The h-plots are given in Fig. 4.5.4 and are

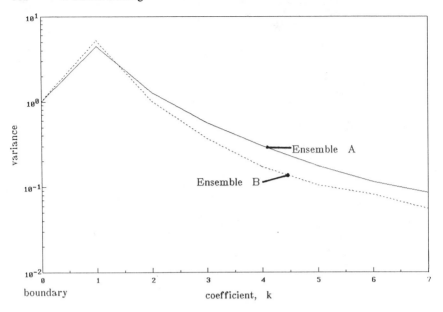

FIGURE 4.5.2. Ensemble normalized RBC variances for 1d RBC ($N = 7$).

TABLE 4.5.4. Normalized variances for 1d RBC coding.

ensemble	$\bar{\eta}$	coefficient							
		boundary	1	2	3	4	5	6	7
A	4.86	1.0	4.459	1.281	0.570	0.303	0.176	0.115	0.086
B	11.85	1.0	5.205	1.003	0.369	0.172	0.105	0.081	0.055

all drawn to the same scale. There are six diagrams per page with four plots, one for each rate, in each diagram. For a given image, the RBC results are placed directly to the left of the DCT results for easy comparison, so the row fixes the image and the column determines the algorithm. The left side of each plot contains the dS_k and the right the dM_k, as in Fig. 4.4.1, but to avoid cluttering the diagram we exclude the labels. The top left represents 1.5 bits/pixel, the top right 2 bits/pixel, the bottom left 2.5 bits/pixel and finally the bottom right is for 3 bits/pixel. The scale of each diagram was fixed so that a horizontal or vertical radius extending from the center to the edge of the window is 2 units. To avoid clipping and make the structure of the dS_k more visible they are first scaled by a factor of 0.5 before being drawn, so the dynamic range for the left side of the plot is actually 4 units. The diagrams are arranged alphabetically within each ensemble with the seven images from ensemble A coming before those of ensemble B.

The plots do provide insight into the subjective quality, for example the noise in the reconstructed image as measured by the dS_k is generally

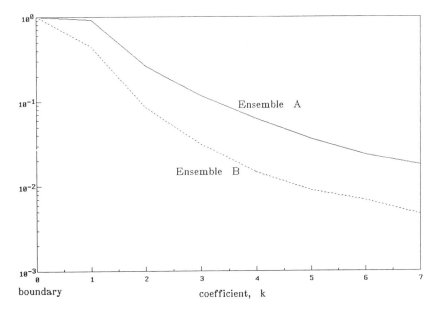

FIGURE 4.5.3. Typical or ensemble representative RBC variances for 1d RBC ($N = 7$).

TABLE 4.5.5. Typical variances for 1d RBC coding.

ensemble	coefficient							
	boundary	1	2	3	4	5	6	7
A	1.0	0.917	0.263	0.117	0.062	0.036	0.024	0.018
B	1.0	0.439	0.085	0.031	0.015	0.009	0.007	0.005

less with RBC and this is verified by subjective evaluation of the images. We describe the image quality below in Table 4.5.7(a) for ensemble A and 4.5.7(b) for ensemble B.

For reference we give the MSE and corresponding SNR' results for the 1d coding experiments in Table 4.5.8 although they should not be used to judge the image quality without reference to the subjective descriptions. In nearly all cases RBC leads to an increased SNR' figure with the exception of the baboon when coded at 1.5 bits, and the couple at rates of 3, 2.5, and 2 bits/pixel.

Ensemble A

As a good example of when the MSE figures can be very misleading, consider the baboon which, with the exception of tiffany discussed below, has the highest MSE value for both RBC and DCT coding at all rates.

TABLE 4.5.6. Bit allocations for 1d RBC coding.

ensemble	rate	coefficient							
		boundary	1	2	3	4	5	6	7
A	3.0	5	5	4	3	3	2	1	1
	2.5	4	5	4	3	2	1	1	.
	2.0	4	4	3	3	1	1	.	.
	1.5	3	4	3	1	1	.	.	.
	1.5†	4	4	3	1	.	.	.	.
B	3.0	5	5	4	3	3	2	1	1
	2.5	5	5	3	3	2	1	1	.
	2.0	5	4	3	2	1	1	.	.
	1.5	4	4	3	1	.	.	.	.

† Modified allocation to prevent *boundary breakthrough*

However the subjective quality is very good and perhaps better than all of the other images, at least in ensemble A. Interestingly, the h-plot for the baboon is not the largest deviating from the trend in MSE values. In particular with DCT coding, it has the smallest area within the ensemble indicating the superior quality observed, while with RBC it is similar to all of the other plots for the A ensemble, again indicating the good quality.

For ensemble A, although the performance of RBC is better than DCT, the subjective improvement is not dramatic at rates of 2 bits/pixel or more. This is also indicated by the h-plots where the size of the plot for RBC is of the same order as the DCT plot at the higher rates except for the couple, and tiffany of course which is discussed below.

However as the rate drops from 2 to 1.5 bits/pixel, there is a significant increase in the area of the h-plot for DCT coding of all of the images while with RBC the change is marginal and the airplane and buildings images are significantly better when coded with RBC at these rates, instead of using the DCT, although the quality is now only acceptable. When coded using the DCT, these images exhibit lots of noise, contours, and visible blocks—the *tile effect*. The RBC images are much better with only a low frequency texture visible. This texture has a period equal to the block size and is visible in the smooth regions of all of the images.

This texture arises because the pixels within the interior of the block although flat in the original image now have some characteristic shape determined by the bit allocation. As we discussed earlier in section 3.5, traditionally in zonal coding whole bits are allocated to each coefficient which results in quantizers with an even number of output levels and consequently no reconstruction level at zero. This means that even these smooth blocks which have zero, or very small, residuals contain all of the active residual coefficients in the output image and the amplitude of

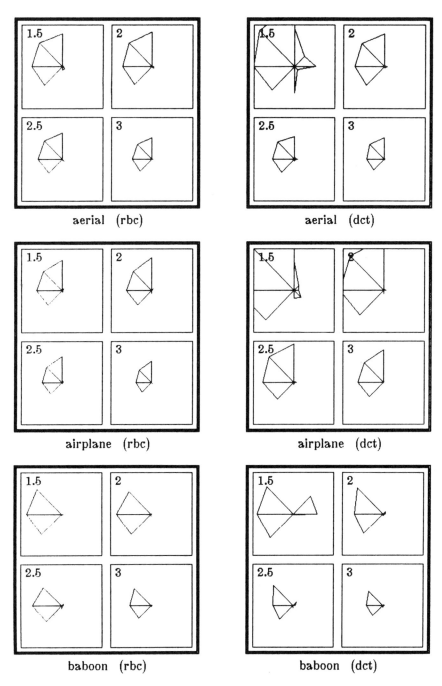

FIGURE 4.5.4. H-plots for 1d zonal coding at rates of 1.5, 2, 2.5, and 3 bits/pixel. RBC plots on the left; DCT plots on the right.

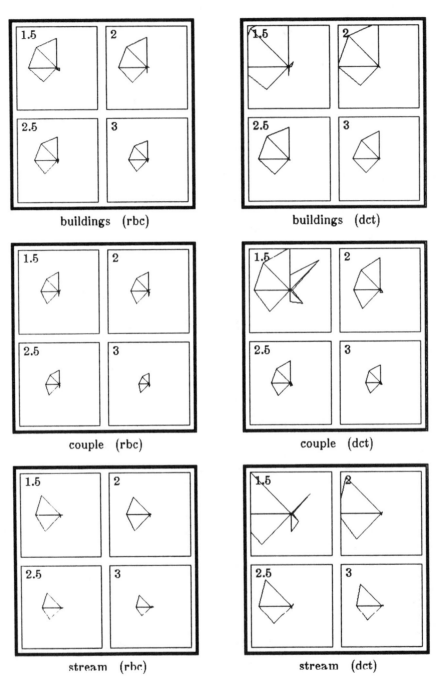

FIGURE 4.5.4. Continued.

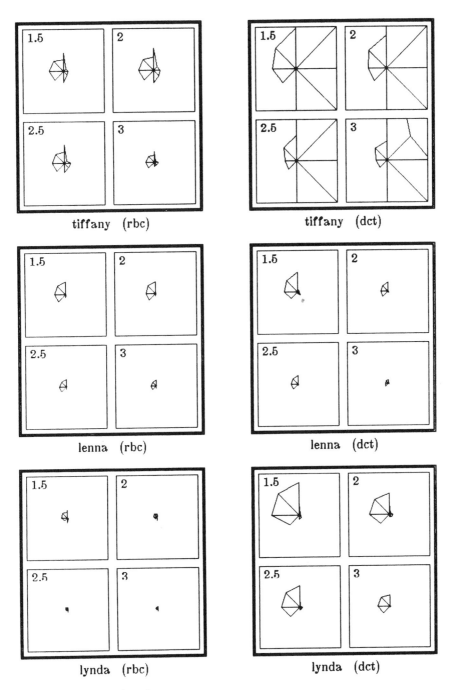

FIGURE 4.5.4. Continued.

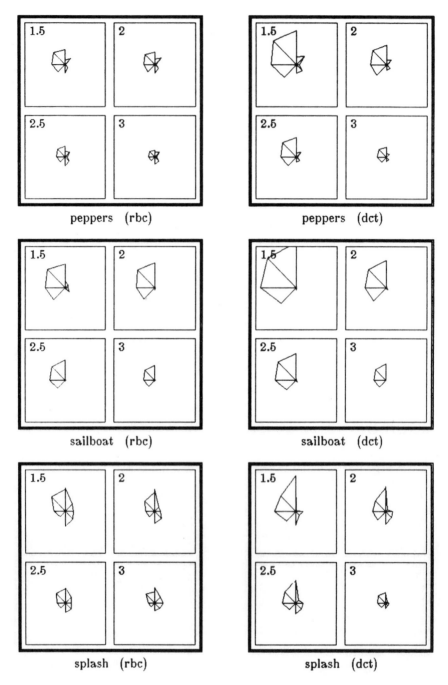

FIGURE 4.5.4. Continued.

TABLE 4.5.7(a). 1d coding results for ensemble A.

image	DCT	RBC
aerial	1.5 bits − very blocky, 　　　　many dc problems 2 bits − ok, a few dc problems 2.5 bits − good, a few dc problems 3 bits − excellent	1.5 bits − texture 2 bits − good, slight texture 2.5 bits − very good, 　　　　very slight texture 3 bits − excellent
airplane	1.5 bits − heavy contouring, 　　　　very blocky 2 bits − contours, texture 2.5 bits − good, slight contours (sky) 3 bits − excellent	1.5 bits − texture 2 bits − good, slight texture 2.5, 3 bits − excellent
baboon	1.5 bits − ok, blocks & dc problems (cheeks) 2, 2.5 bits − very good, 　　　　very slight dc problems 3 bits − excellent	1.5 bits − very good, slight texture (cheeks) 2, 2.5, 3 bits − excellent
buildings	1.5 bits − extremely noisy, contours 2 bits − ok, grainy 2.5 bits − good 3 bits − very good, slight grain	1.5 bits − strong texture (preferable to DCT) 2 bits − ok, grainy 2.5, 3 bits − very good, slight grain
couple	1.5 bits − extremely grainy, blocky 2, 2.5 bits − very good, slight grain 3 bits − excellent	1.5 bits − ok, texture 2 bits − very good, slight grain 2.5, 3 bits − excellent
stream	1.5 bits − grainy, dc problems (handrail) 2 bits − good, texture (handrail) 2.5 bits − very good, slight texture 3 bits − excellent	1.5 bits − ok, texture (handrail) 2, 2.5 bits − very good, 　　　　slight texture (handrail) 3 bits − excellent
tiffany	1.5, 2, 2.5 bits − very blocky, contours, 　　　　too dark: dc problems 3 bits − better but still very blocky	1.5 bits − boundaries visible at peak 　　　　white (hand, teeth) 2, 2.5 bits − very good, 　　　　boundaries barely visible 3 bits − excellent

each coefficient is the inner level of the corresponding quantizer. This *aliased* residual is the texture observed in the reconstructed images.

Before discussing the results for ensemble B, we will first explain the terrible performance obtained when DCT coding tiffany.

Tiffany

Tiffany is difficult to code because, as the statistics in Table 4.2.1 indicate, it spans the whole dynamic range of intensities (0,255) and yet the image variance is particularly small at 1126. When coding the dc coefficient we use a Lloyd-Max quantizer for a Gaussian pdf. Since tiffany is in ensemble A, the allocation for the dc coefficient is 6 bits when the average rate is 3 bits/pixel as shown in Table 4.5.3. In this case the Lloyd-Max quantizer has a range of $\pm 3.75\, \sigma$ [29] where σ is the estimated dc variance or $6.535\sqrt{1126}$ using Table 4.5.2. Since the dc coefficient for a constant block is $\sqrt{8}$ times the constant intensity when

TABLE 4.5.8(a). MSE and SNR′ figures for 1d coding of ensemble A.

image	algorithm	MSE				SNR′ (dB)			
		rate				rate			
		3.0	2.5	2.0	1.5	3.0	2.5	2.0	1.5
aerial	dct	21.3	36.0	58.6	116.7	34.9	32.6	30.5	27.5
	rbc	16.4	26.2	45.3	81.0	36.0	34.0	31.6	29.1
airplane	dct	24.8	37.4	63.4	117.5	34.2	32.4	30.1	27.4
	rbc	16.3	24.2	42.2	66.9	36.0	34.3	31.9	29.9
baboon	dct	40.8	62.5	111.1	172.2	32.0	30.2	27.7	25.8
	rbc	35.8	61.1	98.8	178.3	32.6	30.3	28.2	25.6
buildings	dct	18.3	27.5	38.4	71.0	35.5	33.7	32.3	29.6
	rbc	13.3	17.9	27.6	40.2	36.9	35.6	33.7	32.1
couple	dct	30.6	40.6	56.2	93.6	33.3	32.1	30.6	28.4
	rbc	33.7	41.7	56.9	77.2	32.9	32.0	30.5	29.2
stream	dct	26.4	41.7	69.8	116.5	33.9	31.9	29.7	27.5
	rbc	23.8	40.2	61.5	103.3	34.4	32.1	30.3	28.0
tiffany	dct	39.4	131.0	150.8	426.9	32.2	27.0	26.4	21.8
	rbc	16.9	27.4	43.4	67.7	35.9	33.8	31.8	29.8

the block size is 8 this corresponds to a dynamic range of $\frac{(2)(3.75)(6.535)\sqrt{1126}}{\sqrt{8}} = 225$ intensity values in the spatial domain. If the quantizer is centered at an intensity value of 127.5, then the quantization error for a constant black or white block leads to a constant error for each pixel within the block of 15 intensity levels. On the other hand, if we center the quantizer about the image mean which is 209 for this image then the range of reconstructed constant intensity blocks would be 209 ± 113 or (96, 322). This clearly makes the problem worse because although the peak white blocks will now be correctly represented, any blocks with a mean of 96 or less will be reconstructed as if their mean were actually 96. Consequently we choose to center the quantizer at mid-range rather than the actual image mean in all cases.

Since this image has many blocks with a large mean close to 255, they are all reconstructed with a mean of 240 and this leads to a large number of neighboring blocks in the output image with the same mean which causes the contours and blocks observed even at the high rate of 3 bits/pixel.

The boundary coefficient in RBC is PCM coded which avoids this problem. Since we are very sensitive to the dc coefficient it would be better to also use a uniform quantizer in this case and it should span the whole dynamic range of $255\sqrt{N}$ for the dc coefficient, unlike the Lloyd-Max quantizer whose dynamic range is determined by the image variance. This approach is adopted for adaptive coding in the following chapter and is detailed in section 5.2.

Ensemble B

The improvement with RBC is even greater with this ensemble than with the more active A ensemble. This is anticipated because of increased SNR′ improvements which now reach as much as 4.9 dB, and substantially smaller h-plots in many cases.

Since the residual variances are smaller for this ensemble, the low frequency texture which is due to the non-zero smallest quantizer reconstruction level is reduced so that the image quality at 1.5 bits/pixel is now good rather than acceptable in general.

Subjectively, RBC is better able to handle the edges in these less detailed images. This is seen most clearly in the splash and lenna images which have well defined edges separating large smooth regions. DCT coding blurs these edges and this becomes more extreme as the rate is lowered. As this happens, the edge is blurred throughout the block but not into neighboring blocks which are completely within the smooth regions on either side of the edge. This makes those blocks which contain a high contrast edge very noticeable and objectionable. The SNR′ improvement and h-plot indicate the improvement for the splash but neither indicator shows substantial gain for RBC coding lenna which is used as the 1d coding example in Fig. 4.5.5.

1d coding of lenna at 1.5 bits/pixel, using the ensemble B design, is shown in Fig. 4.5.5(a) for RBC, and the quality is very good, especially when compared with the DCT coded image in (b). The DCT coding produces extremely bad *stepping* along diagonal edges and is most noticeable along the edges of the hat and the shoulder. In (c) and (d) a portion of the same image is zoomed by a factor of two in both directions, using

TABLE 4.5.7(b). 1d coding results for ensemble B.

image	DCT	RBC
lenna	1.5 bits − very blocky (hat, shoulder) 2, 2.5 bits − still blocky at edges 3 bits − very good, slight blocks (shoulder)	1.5 bits − very good, slight texture 2, 2.5, 3 bits − excellent
lynda	1.5 bits − extremely textured 2, 2.5 bits − good, texture 3 bits − excellent	1.5 bits − good, boundaries slightly visible 2, 2.5, 3 bits − excellent
peppers	1.5 bits − grainy, blocks at edges 2, 2.5 bits − very good, slight grain 3 bits − excellent	1.5 bits − good, blurred edges 2 bits − very good, slight grain 2.5, 3 bits − excellent
sailboat	1.5 bits − texture 2 bits − ok, grainy 2.5 bits − very good, slight grain 3 bits − excellent	1.5 bits − texture 2 bits − ok, grainy 2.5, 3 bits − excellent
splash	1.5 bits − extensive block structured blurring 2, 2.5 bits − good, blocks still visible at high contrast edges 3 bits − excellent	1.5 bits − good, slight texture 2, 2.5, 3 bits − excellent

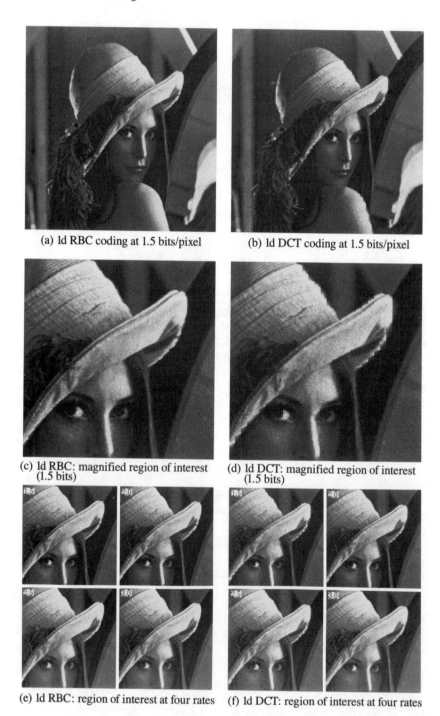

(a) 1d RBC coding at 1.5 bits/pixel   (b) 1d DCT coding at 1.5 bits/pixel

(c) 1d RBC: magnified region of interest (1.5 bits)   (d) 1d DCT: magnified region of interest (1.5 bits)

(e) 1d RBC: region of interest at four rates   (f) 1d DCT: region of interest at four rates

Fig. 4.5.5   1d coding results for lenna.

TABLE 4.5.8(b). MSE and SNR' figures for 1d coding of ensemble B.

image	algorithm	MSE				SNR' (dB)			
		rate				rate			
		3.0	2.5	2.0	1.5	3.0	2.5	2.0	1.5
lenna	dct	16.9	28.6	40.9	76.2	35.9	33.6	32.0	29.3
	rbc	11.9	20.4	32.5	49.8	37.4	35.1	33.0	31.2
lynda	dct	6.2	12.6	13.4	25.6	40.2	37.1	36.8	34.1
	rbc	3.3	4.1	6.6	9.9	43.0	42.0	39.9	38.2
peppers	dct	20.4	30.7	46.5	85.2	35.0	33.3	31.5	28.8
	rbc	13.8	24.3	38.5	55.5	36.7	34.3	32.3	30.7
sailboat	dct	27.4	41.4	67.4	120.7	33.8	32.0	29.9	27.3
	rbc	19.9	34.6	56.1	85.7	35.2	32.8	30.7	28.8
splash	dct	14.3	24.4	35.8	68.7	36.6	34.3	32.6	29.8
	rbc	7.5	13.7	21.5	32.4	39.4	36.8	34.8	33.1

pixel replication, to more clearly illustrate the coding artifacts. It is now possible to see general *tiling* problems with the DCT in addition to the stepping already mentioned. RBC, on the contrary, produces a much better picture with no obvious artifacts. In (e) and (f) the region of interest is shown at normal magnification at all four coding rates: 1.5, 2, 2.5, and 3 bits/pixel. From these images it can be seen that the blocky edges persist with the DCT until the rate doubles to 3 bits/pixel, while with RBC all of the images are very good and there is little to choose between those images coded at the lowest and highest rates.

4.6 2d Coding Results

The same set of experiments described in the previous section for the 1d zonal coding algorithms is now repeated for the 2d case using the same two image ensembles.

2d DCT Design

The normalized DCT variances for each ensemble are given in Table 4.6.1. It should be noted that the two dimensional array is laid out in such a way that the dc coefficient is at the top left corner and the horizontal frequency increases down the table while the vertical frequency increases across each row. This transposition is due to our implementation of a 2d transform as the cascade of: 1d transform; transpose; 1d transform which gives the *transposed* 2d transform. On inverse transformation, using the same method, the effect of transposition cancels so that in the spatial domain the image is oriented correctly despite the transposition in the frequency domain. This then saves the computational effort

TABLE 4.6.1. Normalized variances for 2d DCT coding.

	1	2	3	4	5	6	7	8
1	43.792	5.121	1.632	0.706	0.457	0.255	0.176	0.122
2	3.494	1.167	0.563	0.305	0.194	0.122	0.080	0.060
3	1.266	0.531	0.329	0.200	0.135	0.090	0.063	0.046
4	0.563	0.242	0.174	0.125	0.090	0.061	0.045	0.034
5	0.299	0.128	0.097	0.071	0.055	0.040	0.031	0.024
6	0.158	0.071	0.056	0.046	0.035	0.031	0.024	0.021
7	0.088	0.044	0.037	0.030	0.025	0.023	0.022	0.015
8	0.049	0.033	0.027	0.022	0.018	0.017	0.015	0.012

(a) Ensemble A

	1	2	3	4	5	6	7	8
1	57.385	1.504	0.330	0.132	0.071	0.039	0.020	0.009
2	2.244	0.388	0.138	0.047	0.022	0.012	0.007	0.006
3	0.469	0.148	0.077	0.034	0.016	0.009	0.006	0.004
4	0.179	0.059	0.036	0.020	0.012	0.008	0.005	0.004
5	0.084	0.025	0.018	0.012	0.008	0.005	0.004	0.004
6	0.046	0.013	0.010	0.007	0.006	0.005	0.006	0.005
7	0.022	0.008	0.006	0.006	0.005	0.007	0.010	0.006
8	0.011	0.005	0.004	0.004	0.004	0.004	0.005	0.004

(b) Ensemble B

of needlessly transposing the image twice. Consequently, for ensemble A, it is seen that there is more energy in the vertical transitions, that is more horizontal edges, while this trend is reversed with ensemble B.

The resulting standard bit allocations at the four rates: 2.0, 1.5, 1.0, and 0.75 bits/pixel, are given in Table 4.6.2. Each image is coded using the standard bit allocation and the normalized variances scaled by the actual image variance, given in Table 4.2.1, provide the estimated variances to fix the dynamic range for each of the quantizers.

2d RBC Design

For RBC, the normalized variances are listed in Table 4.6.3. The variances for the corner, row, column and core coefficients are shown together as a composite. The various components are shown separated by lines: the top left value is for the corner; the rest of the top row corresponds to the 7 row residual coefficients; the rest of the first column corresponds to the column residual coefficients; and the lower right 49 values are for the core residual coefficients. Again the 2d core residual variances are transposed just as with the 2d DCT variances described above.

TABLE 4.6.2. Bit allocations for 2d DCT coding.

```
7  6  5  4  4  3  3  3        6  5  4  4  3  3  2  2
5  4  4  3  3  3  2  1        5  4  3  3  3  2  1  1
4  4  3  3  3  2  1  1        4  3  3  3  2  1  1  1
4  3  3  3  2  1  1  1        3  3  2  2  1  1  .  .
3  3  2  2  1  1  1  .        3  2  1  1  1  .  .  .
3  2  1  1  1  1  .  .        2  1  1  1  .  .  .  .
2  1  1  1  .  .  .  .        1  .  .  .  .  .  .  .
1  1  .  .  .  .  .  .        1  .  .  .  .  .  .  .
        2.0 bits                      1.5 bits


6  5  4  3  3  2  1  1        6  4  3  3  2  1  1  .
4  3  3  2  1  1  .  .        4  3  3  1  1  .  .  .
3  3  2  2  1  1  .  .        3  3  2  1  .  .  .  .
3  2  1  1  1  .  .  .        3  1  1  .  .  .  .  .
2  1  1  .  .  .  .  .        1  .  .  .  .  .  .  .
1  .  .  .  .  .  .  .        1  .  .  .  .  .  .  .
.  .  .  .  .  .  .  .        .  .  .  .  .  .  .  .
.  .  .  .  .  .  .  .        .  .  .  .  .  .  .  .
        1.0 bit                      0.75 bits
```

(a) Ensemble A

```
8  6  5  4  3  3  3  1        8  6  4  4  3  3  2  1
6  5  4  3  3  2  1  1        6  4  4  3  2  1  .  .
5  4  4  3  2  1  1  .        5  4  3  2  1  1  .  .
4  3  3  2  2  1  1  .        4  3  3  2  1  .  .  .
4  3  2  2  1  1  .  .        3  2  1  1  .  .  .  .
3  2  1  1  1  .  1  .        3  1  1  .  .  .  .  .
3  1  1  1  .  1  1  1        2  .  .  .  .  .  1  .
1  1  .  .  .  .  1  .        1  .  .  .  .  .  .  .
        2.0 bits                      1.5 bits


7  5  4  3  3  1  1  .        7  4  3  3  1  1  .  .
5  4  3  2  1  .  .  .        5  3  3  1  .  .  .  .
4  3  3  1  .  .  .  .        3  3  2  1  .  .  .  .
3  2  1  1  .  .  .  .        3  1  1  .  .  .  .  .
3  1  .  .  .  .  .  .        2  .  .  .  .  .  .  .
2  .  .  .  .  .  .  .        1  .  .  .  .  .  .  .
1  .  .  .  .  .  .  .        .  .  .  .  .  .  .  .
.  .  .  .  .  .  .  .        .  .  .  .  .  .  .  .
        1.0 bit                      0.75 bits
```

(b) Ensemble B

TABLE 4.6.3. Normalized variances for 2d RBC coding.

	0	1	2	3	4	5	6	7
0	1.0	4.501	1.257	0.574	0.304	0.168	0.109	0.082
1	4.386	16.322	4.925	2.563	1.333	0.710	0.582	0.413
2	1.164	5.629	1.972	1.116	0.661	0.436	0.299	0.227
3	0.611	2.427	0.983	0.692	0.446	0.297	0.212	0.166
4	0.347	1.154	0.556	0.412	0.269	0.199	0.148	0.123
5	0.205	0.612	0.318	0.247	0.187	0.146	0.118	0.093
6	0.159	0.350	0.202	0.165	0.131	0.108	0.093	0.073
7	0.122	0.243	0.157	0.130	0.099	0.083	0.072	0.058

(a) Ensemble A

	0	1	2	3	4	5	6	7
0	1.0	5.200	1.005	0.370	0.171	0.103	0.082	0.055
1	5.124	23.557	4.608	1.516	0.626	0.306	0.174	0.112
2	1.029	6.078	1.809	0.733	0.327	0.186	0.111	0.088
3	0.387	2.165	0.790	0.446	0.241	0.147	0.097	0.076
4	0.188	0.903	0.367	0.251	0.158	0.104	0.084	0.068
5	0.109	0.471	0.195	0.156	0.107	0.091	0.092	0.082
6	0.080	0.231	0.120	0.116	0.095	0.108	0.149	0.100
7	0.068	0.135	0.088	0.084	0.070	0.076	0.090	0.113

(b) Ensemble B

As in the 1d case, the bit allocation is determined using a representative distribution which is obtained by scaling the boundary and core normalized variances relative to the normalized corner value of unity. The core residuals are scaled by a typical $\frac{1}{\bar{\eta}_{core}}$ where $\bar{\eta}_{core}$ is the ensemble median of the individual values given above in Table 4.5.1. We scale the row and column boundaries by a single factor, $\frac{1}{\bar{\eta}_1}$, where $\bar{\eta}_1$ is the ensemble median of the individual average values: $\frac{1}{2}(\eta_{row}+\eta_{col})$. For ensembles A and B the values for $(\bar{\eta}_1, \bar{\eta}_{core})$ are (4.77, 6.32) and (14.51, 21.41) respectively. The typical variances formed using these scale factors are found in Table 4.6.4 with the resulting bit allocations in Table 4.6.5.

When coding the images, the standard bit allocations dictate the quantizers and to determine the dynamic range of these quantizers, the normalized variances (Table 4.6.3) are multiplied by the measured variances of each component: $(\sigma^2_{cnr}, \sigma^2_{row}, \sigma^2_{col}, \sigma^2_{core})$, or equivalently we multiply the whole array by σ^2_{cnr} and then divide the residual components by $(\eta_{row}, \eta_{col}, \eta_{core})$ which are given in Table 4.5.1. When we implemented this quantizer design technique and coded the two ensembles, most of the images looked good but in some cases the individual boundaries were

TABLE 4.6.4. Typical variances for 2d RBC coding.

	0	1	2	3	4	5	6	7
0	1.0	0.944	0.264	0.120	0.064	0.035	0.023	0.017
1	0.920	2.584	0.780	0.406	0.211	0.112	0.092	0.065
2	0.244	0.891	0.312	0.177	0.105	0.069	0.047	0.036
3	0.128	0.384	0.156	0.109	0.071	0.047	0.034	0.026
4	0.073	0.183	0.088	0.065	0.043	0.032	0.023	0.019
5	0.043	0.097	0.050	0.039	0.030	0.023	0.019	0.015
6	0.033	0.055	0.032	0.026	0.021	0.017	0.015	0.012
7	0.026	0.038	0.025	0.021	0.016	0.013	0.011	0.009

(a) Ensemble A

	0	1	2	3	4	5	6	7
0	1.0	0.358	0.069	0.026	0.012	0.007	0.006	0.004
1	0.353	1.100	0.215	0.071	0.029	0.014	0.008	0.005
2	0.071	0.284	0.085	0.034	0.015	0.009	0.005	0.004
3	0.027	0.101	0.037	0.021	0.011	0.007	0.005	0.004
4	0.013	0.042	0.017	0.012	0.007	0.005	0.004	0.003
5	0.008	0.022	0.009	0.007	0.005	0.004	0.004	0.004
6	0.006	0.011	0.006	0.005	0.004	0.005	0.007	0.005
7	0.005	0.006	0.004	0.004	0.003	0.004	0.004	0.005

(b) Ensemble B

clearly visible. For some images this was only a problem at low rates: 0.75 bits/pixel, and sometimes also 1 bit/pixel, but as the rate increased this *boundary breakthrough* artifact disappeared. However, in the case of airplane, lynda, and splash, the boundary breakthrough remained even at the highest rate of 2 bits/pixel. We observed boundary breakthrough in the 1d case, but it was a global problem and the solution was to ensure that enough bits were used to code the boundary points. However in 2d coding these *problem boundaries* are located at high contrast edges and are only visible in a few places in a few images. The situation is worst when the two corner points used to predict the boundary are both white while the boundary values are black, or vice versa, since then the prediction is of no use and the residual will have maximum amplitude. When this occurs, the quantizers clip the inputs and the visual outcome is boundary breakthrough. The quantizer dynamic ranges are determined by the estimated variances which are a function of the measured residual energy and the normalized variances. Since both of these are average values it is not surprising that a MSE design is unable to accurately reproduce these infrequent problem boundaries. From a MSE point of view, the large error in reconstructing these high energy residuals is insignificant because they seldom occur. However, they are visually annoying and the design must be compensated to allow a larger dynamic range for the boundary quantizers.

TABLE 4.6.5. Bit allocations for 2d RBC coding.

4	5	4	3	2	1	1	.
4	5	4	4	3	3	3	2
3	4	4	3	3	3	2	1
3	4	3	3	3	2	1	1
3	3	3	2	2	1	1	1
2	3	2	1	1	1	1	.
1	2	1	1	1	.	.	.
1	1	1	1	.	.	.	.

2.0 bits

4	4	3	3	1	1	.	.
4	5	4	3	3	3	2	1
3	4	3	3	2	2	1	1
3	3	3	2	2	1	1	.
2	3	2	2	1	1	.	.
1	2	1	1	1	.	.	.
1	1	1	.	.	.	.	.
.	1	.	.	.	.	.	.

1.5 bits

3	4	3	1	1	.	.	.
4	4	4	3	3	1	1	1
3	4	3	2	1	1	.	.
2	3	2	2	1	.	.	.
1	2	1	1	.	.	.	.
.	1	.	.	.	.	.	.
.	1	.	.	.	.	.	.
.	.	.	.	.	.	.	.

1.0 bit

3	4	3	1	.	.	.	.
3	4	3	3	2	1	1	.
3	3	2	1	1	.	.	.
1	3	1	1	.	.	.	.
1	1	1	.	.	.	.	.
.	1	.	.	.	.	.	.
.	.	.	.	.	.	.	.
.	.	.	.	.	.	.	.

0.75 bits

(a) Ensemble A

5	5	4	3	2	1	1	.
5	6	5	4	3	3	1	1
4	5	4	3	3	2	1	1
3	4	3	3	2	1	1	.
2	3	3	2	1	1	1	.
1	3	2	1	1	1	1	1
1	2	1	1	1	1	1	1
1	1	1	1	.	.	1	1

2.0 bits

5	5	3	3	1	1	1	.
5	6	4	3	3	2	1	.
3	5	4	3	2	1	.	.
3	4	3	2	1	1	.	.
2	3	2	1	1	.	.	.
1	3	1	1	.	.	.	1
1	1	1	1	.	.	1	.
.	1	.	.	.	.	.	.

1.5 bits

5	4	3	2	1	.	.	.
4	5	4	3	2	1	.	.
3	4	3	2	1	.	.	.
2	3	2	1	1	.	.	.
1	3	1	1	.	.	.	.
.	1	.	.	.	.	.	.
.	1	.	.	.	.	.	.
.	.	.	.	.	.	.	.

1.0 bit

4	4	3	1	.	.	.	.
4	5	3	3	1	.	.	.
3	4	3	1	.	.	.	.
1	3	1	1	.	.	.	.
.	2	.	.	.	.	.	.
.	1	.	.	.	.	.	.
.	.	.	.	.	.	.	.
.	.	.	.	.	.	.	.

0.75 bits

(b) Ensemble B

The simplest approach to rectify the situation is to stretch the quantizer characteristic by assuming a higher residual energy, or equivalently a lower value for η_{row} and η_{col}. Alternatively we could move only some of the levels to provide an increased dynamic range but a largely unchanged characteristic so as not to introduce too much graininess to the smaller inputs. We chose the former solution here although in practice it would probably be worth the extra time to subjectively optimize the quantizers. In the spirit of the ensemble design we chose to make a global modification and re-estimate the boundary residual variances as $\dfrac{\sigma^2_{cnr}}{\eta}$ times the normalized variances in Table 4.6.3 with $\eta^* = 2$ for ensemble A, and 4 for ensemble B. These values were determined empirically by coding the ensembles with values of 1, 2, 4, 6, and 8 and trading off the reduced boundary breakthrough with increased boundary graininess.

Note that the modification only applies to the coding stage with the design stage remaining the same, that is the bit allocation and normalized variances are unchanged.

By using fixed values for η_{row} and η_{col} there is the added advantage that there is no longer a need to compute the residual energies: σ^2_{row} and σ^2_{col}, before coding since they are now both estimated as $\dfrac{\sigma^2_{cnr}}{\eta^*}$. However, we must still compute σ^2_{core} which does involve forming the 2d prediction but by fixing η_{core} we could also remove this computational overhead. We leave this possibility for future work.

Discussion of Results

In this experiment each of the twelve images was coded at four rates: 0.75, 1, 1.5, and 2 bits/pixel using both the 2d RBC and DCT algorithms. This again leads to a great amount of data, so as before we will not present all of the images but rather use a number of techniques to describe the results. The h-plots are presented in Fig. 4.6.1 and are drawn to the same scale as the plots for the 1d coding in Fig. 4.5.4 to allow comparison. The subjective evaluation is summarized in Tables 4.6.6(a) and (b) for ensembles A and B respectively and the MSE results are given in Tables 4.6.7(a) and (b).

As the rate is reduced, zonal coding with the DCT produces images which are progressively more grainy or noisy, and after some point the *tile-effect* artifact, where the individual blocks become discernible, limits the attainable compression. In these experiments, RBC produces images which are often better than DCT coding. In particular the noise and tile-effect are both reduced.

By manually setting η_{row} and η_{col} to small values the boundary breakthrough problem was eliminated with no noticeable degradation in the

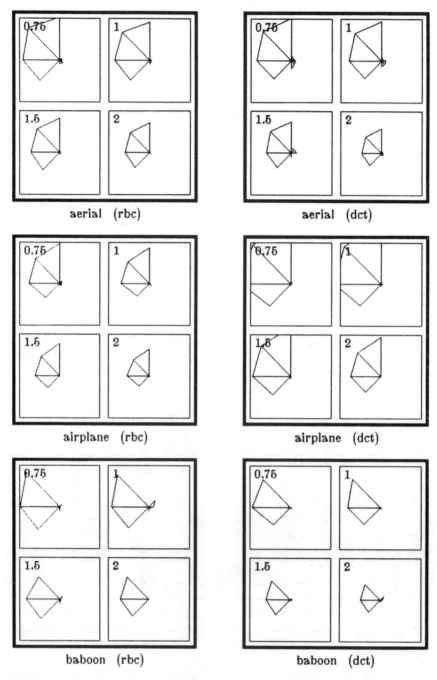

FIGURE 4.6.1. H-plots for 2d zonal coding at rates of 0.75, 1, 1.5, and 2 bits/pixel. RBC plots on the left; DCT plots on the right.

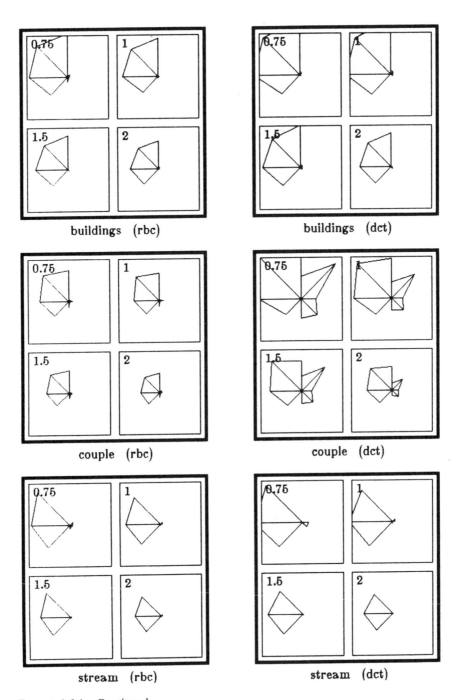

FIGURE 4.6.1. Continued.

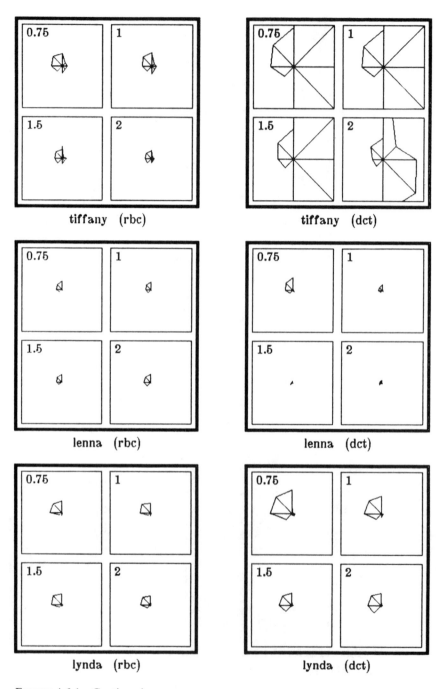

FIGURE 4.6.1. Continued.

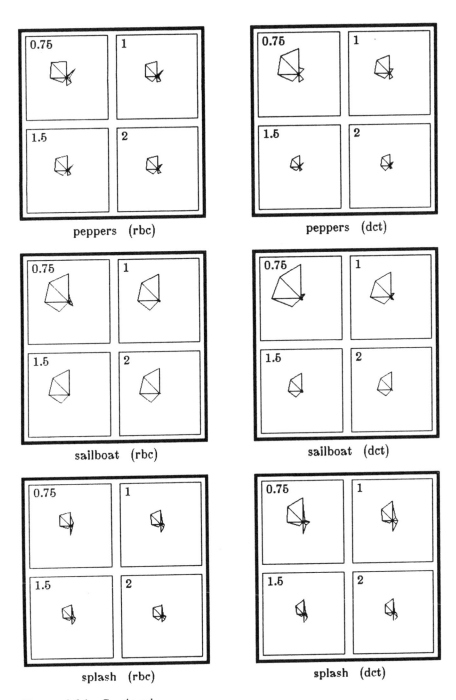

FIGURE 4.6.1. Continued.

TABLE 4.6.6(a). 2d coding results for ensemble A.

image	DCT	RBC
aerial	0.75 bits – very grainy, blocky 1 bit – ok, grainy 1.5, 2 bits – very good, slight grain	0.75 bits – very grainy, some boundaries 1 bit – ok, grainy 1.5, 2 bits – very good, slight grain
airplane	0.75, 1 bits – extremely grainy 1.5 bits – ok, grainy 2 bits – very good, slight grain	0.75 bits – few columns in fuselage, slight background structure 1 bit – ok, grainy, background barely visible 1.5, 2 bits – very good, slight grain
baboon	0.75, 1 bits – good, upper fur slightly blocky 1.5, 2 bits – excellent	0.75, 1 bits – good, slight boundary structure in upper fur 1.5, 2 bits – excellent
buildings	0.75, 1 bits – extremely grainy 1.5 bits – ok, grainy 2 bits – very good, slight grain	0.75 bits – very grainy, some boundaries 1 bit – ok, grainy 1.5, 2 bits – very good, slight grain
couple	0.75, 1 bits – extremely grainy 1.5, 2 bits – very good, slight grain	0.75 bits – very grainy 1 bit – ok, grainy 1.5 bits – very good, slight grain 2 bits – excellent
stream	0.75 bits – blocky texture 1 bit – ok, grainy 1.5, 2 bits – very good	0.75 bits – some boundaries (handrail) 1 bit – ok, grainy 1.5, 2 bits – very good
tiffany	0.75, 1, 1.5 bits – very blocky and grainy too dark, lost highlights dc problems 2 bits – intensity ok, still blocky	0.75 bits – ok, grainy 1 bit – very good, slight grain 1.5, 2 bits – excellent

other boundaries and the three images: airplane, lynda, and splash are now free of artifacts. For most of the images the visual quality is unchanged using the fixed value of η^* instead of the actual η_{row} and η_{col}, while the MSE is usually a little larger, or the same, but occasionally smaller although the change is never more than 0.5 dB. The exception is lynda which shows a large MSE increase of between 2.3 and 4.1 dB over the range of data rates. This is because the value of $\eta^* = 4$ is much smaller than lynda's own $(\eta_{row}, \eta_{col}) = (60.2, 98.2)$ and although the individual boundary breakthrough has been eliminated, the quantizer step sizes have increased by a factor of 4 or 5 and a grainy boundary structure is visible in the smooth regions. The boundary structure remains at all rates for lynda but is not visible in the other images except for airplane and peppers at the lowest rate of 0.75 bits. So after the modification we conclude that RBC is clearly superior to DCT with the exception of the lynda image where a larger value for η^* would be more appropriate.

For the example of 2d coding we show the splash coded at 0.75 bits/pixel using RBC with $\eta^* = 4$ in Fig. 4.6.2(a) and the result of using the DCT at the same rate is given in (b). Both images are grainy with

TABLE 4.6.7(a). MSE and SNR′ figures for 2d coding of ensemble A.

image	algorithm	MSE				SNR′ (dB)			
		rate				rate			
		2.0	1.5	1.0	0.75	2.0	1.5	1.0	0.75
aerial	dct	41.5	67.2	115.3	154.4	32.0	29.9	27.5	26.2
	rbc	31.9	51.4	89.0	127.2	33.1	31.1	28.6	27.1
airplane	dct	32.2	50.1	80.1	100.7	33.1	31.1	29.1	28.1
	rbc	25.1	36.5	55.6	77.6	34.2	32.5	30.7	29.2
baboon	dct	123.1	177.1	270.1	343.2	27.2	25.7	23.8	22.8
	rbc	104.2	161.7	259.3	327.2	27.9	26.1	24.0	23.0
buildings	dct	24.2	34.3	55.1	68.3	34.3	32.8	30.7	29.8
	rbc	21.4	27.9	38.5	52.6	34.8	33.7	32.3	30.9
couple	dct	53.5	82.9	111.6	152.5	30.9	29.0	27.7	26.3
	rbc	53.4	68.8	91.8	111.3	30.9	29.8	28.6	27.7
stream	dct	45.8	71.8	113.7	149.6	31.5	29.6	27.6	26.4
	rbc	43.4	66.8	107.9	140.0	31.7	29.9	27.8	26.7
tiffany	dct	45.7	104.5	127.5	142.9	31.5	27.9	27.1	26.6
	rbc	28.4	39.2	56.3	70.5	33.6	32.2	30.7	29.7

TABLE 4.6.6(b). 2d coding results for ensemble B.

image	DCT	RBC
lenna	0.75, 1 bits − blocky (hat brim, shoulder) 1.5, 2 bits − good, still artifacts on brim	0.75, 1 bits − ok, boundaries slightly visible on hat brim 1.5, 2 bits − excellent
lynda	0.75 bits − ok, blocky texture 1 bit − very good, slight texture 1.5, 2 bits − excellent	0.75, 1, 1.5, 2 bits − boundary structure slightly visible; otherwise excellent
peppers	0.75 bits − blocky texture 1 bit − very good, slight grain 1.5, 2 bits − excellent	0.75 bits − slight background breakthrough 1 bit − very good, slight grain 1.5, 2 bits − excellent
sailboat	0.75 bits − very grainy 1 bit − good, grainy 1.5, 2 bits − excellent	0.75 bits − very grainy 1 bit − very good, slight grain 1.5, 2 bits − excellent
splash	0.75 bits − grainy and blocky at edges 1, 1.5, 2 bits − still blocky but not so bad	0.75 bits − good, grainy 1 bit − very good, slight grain 1.5, 2 bits − excellent

DCT being worse and the underlying block structure is seen in the DCT image especially along the contours separating the splash from the dark background. A 128×128 portion is zoomed by four in each direction, using pixel replication, to provide (c) and (d) where the tiling and distorted edges associated with DCT coding are clearly visible. In (e) and (f) the same region, now magnified only by two, is shown when coded at each of the rates: 0.75, 1, 1.5, and 2 bits/pixel. With DCT coding, the

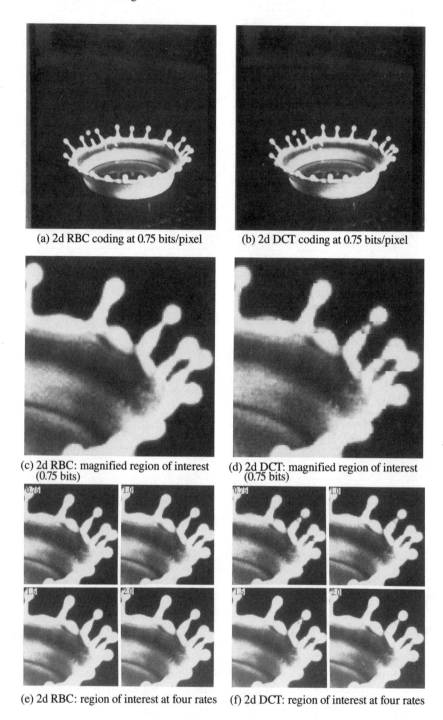

(a) 2d RBC coding at 0.75 bits/pixel   (b) 2d DCT coding at 0.75 bits/pixel

(c) 2d RBC: magnified region of interest   (d) 2d DCT: magnified region of interest
    (0.75 bits)   (0.75 bits)

(e) 2d RBC: region of interest at four rates   (f) 2d DCT: region of interest at four rates

Fig. 4.6.2   2d coding results for the splash.

TABLE 4.6.7(b). MSE and SNR′ figures for 2d coding of ensemble B.

image	algorithm	MSE				SNR′ (dB)			
		rate				rate			
		2.0	1.5	1.0	0.75	2.0	1.5	1.0	0.75
lenna	dct	21.0	29.8	46.2	62.5	34.9	33.4	31.5	30.2
	rbc	15.9	23.1	35.7	47.3	36.1	34.5	32.6	31.4
lynda	dct	7.0	7.5	11.7	17.3	39.7	39.4	37.5	35.7
	rbc	6.1	7.8	9.1	11.0	40.3	39.2	38.6	37.7
peppers	dct	32.2	44.3	66.1	91.6	33.1	31.7	29.9	28.5
	rbc	24.9	37.7	54.1	70.4	34.2	32.4	30.8	29.7
sailboat	dct	48.4	70.2	106.1	145.9	31.3	29.7	27.9	26.5
	rbc	36.7	57.9	88.0	117.7	32.5	30.5	28.7	27.4
splash	dct	17.1	23.5	37.9	58.0	35.8	34.4	32.4	30.5
	rbc	9.8	14.1	22.3	30.5	38.2	36.6	34.7	33.3

general tile effect is still evident at 1 bit/pixel while the most distorted blocks are still clearly visible even at the highest rate of 2 bits/pixel. The RBC images are much better at all rates. They are judged to be excellent at 1.5 bits/pixel and above, and at 0.75 and 1 bit/pixel are very good with only a very faint boundary structure barely visible.

4.7 Hybrid Coding

Hybrid coding is so-called because it is a combination of predictive and transform coding techniques. The image is transformed in one of its dimensions, as in 1d transform coding, and then each transform coefficient sequence is coded independently by a 1d predictive technique such as DPCM in the orthogonal direction. For example, if each row is divided into blocks and transformed, then the 1d transform coding algorithm takes advantage of the horizontal correlation within the image and then a set of DPCM coders, one for each transform coefficient, achieves extra compression by exploiting correlation in the vertical direction.

The DPCM coder works down the columns and codes the current coefficient using an indirect method. A prediction is made using previous values for this coefficient from earlier blocks located directly above the current block and the prediction error is encoded. Given an initial value and a sequence of prediction errors the decoder is able to reconstruct the coefficient values.

The simplest 1d predictor uses only the previous pixel, so if the current coefficient is $\hat{x}(k)$ and we use a subscript to denote the current line, i, as $\hat{x}_i(k)$ then instead of coding $\hat{x}_i(k)$ directly, we code the prediction error, $e_i(k)$, where

$$e_i(k) = \hat{x}_i(k) - a_k \hat{x}_{i-1}(k) \qquad (4.7.1)$$

and the weight a_k is chosen to minimize the variance of the prediction error signal. It is easy to show that the optimum MSE performance is obtained by setting the weight equal to the sequence correlation coefficient, viz.,

$$a_k = \frac{E[\hat{x}_i(k)\hat{x}_{i-1}(k)]}{E[\hat{x}_i^2(k)]} \qquad (4.7.2)$$

when the sequence $\{\hat{x}_i(k); i=0,1,...\}$ is stationary. To derive the correlation coefficient for each of the transform coefficients let us first consider the correlation between blocks on different lines in the spatial domain. If the two blocks are separated by m lines, then

$$\mathbf{R}_x^m \triangleq E[\mathbf{x}_i \mathbf{x}_{i+m}^T]$$

$$= \rho_v^{|m|} \mathbf{R}_x \qquad (4.7.3)$$

where $\mathbf{R}_x$ is the autocorrelation matrix of the vector $\mathbf{x}$, viz.,

$$\mathbf{R}_x \triangleq E[\mathbf{x}_i \mathbf{x}_i^T] \qquad (4.7.4)$$

and we have assumed stationarity so that $\mathbf{R}_x$ is independent of the subscript i. The result in (4.7.3) also assumes a separable covariance function for the image so that the autocorrelation sequence, $r_x(m,n)$, is

$$r_x(m,n) \triangleq E[x(i,j)x(i+m,j+n)] = \sigma_x^2 \rho_h^{|m|} \rho_v^{|n|} \qquad (4.7.5)$$

where ρ_h is the one-step horizontal correlation coefficient and ρ_v is the vertical counterpart. Moving to the transform domain via $\mathbf{A}$, we have

$$\mathbf{R}_{\hat{x}} \triangleq E[\hat{\mathbf{x}}_i \hat{\mathbf{x}}_i^T] = \mathbf{A}\mathbf{R}_x\mathbf{A}^T \qquad (4.7.6)$$

and

$$\mathbf{R}_{\hat{x}}^m \triangleq E[\hat{\mathbf{x}}_i \hat{\mathbf{x}}_{i+m}^T] = \rho_v^{|m|} \mathbf{R}_{\hat{x}} \qquad (4.7.7)$$

and therefore the correlation between the kth transform coefficient on neighboring lines is

$$\rho_k \triangleq \frac{\mathbf{R}_{\hat{x}}^1(k,k)}{\mathbf{R}_{\hat{x}}(k,k)} = \rho_v. \qquad (4.7.8)$$

Note that, under the assumed separable covariance model, the transform domain correlation, ρ_k, is the same for all coefficients. To verify the validity of this assumption, the correlation coefficient was measured for each coefficient using two different images: buildings and lynda. The results are shown in Table 4.7.1 where it is seen that the constant correlation assumption is appropriate for at least half of the coefficients.

For simplicity, we have assumed the separable covariance model so that the correlation coefficient for each coefficient sequence is ρ_v and

TABLE 4.7.1. Correlation of 1d DCT coefficients.

image	ρ_v	coefficient							
		1 (dc)	2	3	4	5	6	7	8
buildings	0.94	0.94	0.95	0.95	0.93	0.86	0.87	0.88	0.34
lynda	0.996	0.997	0.98	0.94	0.89	0.76	0.60	0.37	-0.40

further set the weight a_k equal to 1 since ρ_v is indeed close to unity. This is a suboptimal design and is particularly susceptible to channel errors which will not decay with a prediction weight of 1 however it does give a particularly simple algorithm to compare RBC and DCT coding.

DPCM Equations

Predictor: $\hat{x}^{\bullet}{}_{i-1}(k)$

Quantizer Input: $q_i(k) = \hat{x}_i(k) - \hat{x}^{\bullet}{}_{i-1}(k)$ (4.7.9)

Reconstructor: $\hat{x}^{\bullet}{}_i(k) = \hat{x}^{\bullet}{}_{i-1}(k) + q_i^{\bullet}(k)$

Bit Allocation

As shown in Fig. 4.7.1, the predictor uses reconstructed values for the previous coefficients when predicting the current coefficient rather than the true values so that the prediction will be the same both at the encoder and decoder. If this were not done, then the system would be open-loop and the decoder would drift as quantization errors accumulated. This

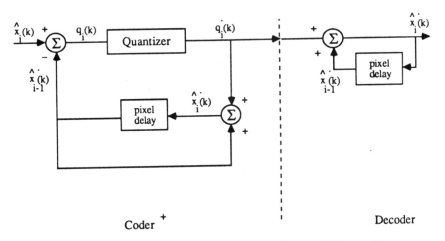

FIGURE 4.7.1. DPCM loop used to code each coefficient in hybrid coding.

makes the analysis of the prediction error variance more difficult since we must now account for the quantization error in the previous samples which will increase the variance of the current prediction error above the inherent uncertainty we would obtain with a prediction based on the true values.

Jain and Wang [67] have shown that to calculate the distortion in each channel we should use the coefficient prediction error variances assuming perfect data but use an increased quantizer distortion function. In particular, for the simple nearest neighbor predictor with weight a_k, then the distortion in coding the kth channel is

$$d_k = \sigma_k^2 \frac{f(n)}{1 - a_k^2 f(n)} = \sigma_k^2 g(n) \qquad (4.7.10)$$

where σ_k^2 is the prediction error variance in the kth channel assuming a predictor based on original rather than reconstructed data, viz.,

$$\sigma_k^2 = E\left[[\hat{x}_i(k) - a_k \hat{x}_{i-1}(k)]^2 \right], \qquad (4.7.11)$$

$f(n)$ is the actual quantizer distortion function, and $g(n)$ is the increased effective quantizer distortion function.

To cast this in the framework of 1d coding we see that σ_k^2 can be calculated in a slightly different form if the prediction weight a_k, is ρ_v, the same for all channels, viz.,

$$\sigma_k^2 = E\left\{ [\mathbf{A}\mathbf{x}_i(k) - \rho_v \mathbf{A}\mathbf{x}_{i-1}(k)]^2 \right\}$$

$$= E\left\{ [\mathbf{A}[\mathbf{x}_i - \rho_v \mathbf{x}_{i-1}](k)]^2 \right\} \qquad (4.7.12)$$

$$= E[\hat{e}_i^2(k)]$$

where

$$\mathbf{e}_i = \mathbf{x}_i - \rho_v \mathbf{x}_{i-1}. \qquad (4.7.13)$$

This is in the form of a 1d coding design for the input $\{\mathbf{e}_i\}$. So after pre-processing by subtracting ρ_v times the previous row from the current row, the design is identical to the 1d case except we should replace $f(.)$ by $g(.)$. The difference between $f(.)$ and $g(.)$ is great at low rates but becomes smaller as the rate increases. For example if we consider the Shannon rd function, 2^{-2n}, then for the rates of $0,...,3$ bits we have $f(n) = \{1, 0.25, 0.0625, 0.0156\}$ and $g(n) = \{\infty, 0.3333, 0.0666, 0.0158\}$ and the difference is only really significant at 1 bit. So for this experiment which is simply intended to illustrate hybrid RBC we will neglect this correction and set $\rho_v = 1$ and $g(.) = f(.)$.

Hybrid Coding Results

The same set of experiments described in previous sections for the 1d and 2d zonal coding algorithms is now repeated for the hybrid case using the same two image ensembles.

As noted above, the design for hybrid coding is the same as 1d coding after pre-processing the image by subtracting ρ_v times the previous row from the current row to obtain the error image. Consequently the transform domain variances are normalized relative to the variance of this processed image rather than the original and we present the statistics of the line by line difference images ($\rho_v = 1$) in Table 4.7.2 where we append a subscript e to show that they refer to the prediction *error* source.

TABLE 4.7.2. Statistics for row by row differences.

image	DCT σ_e^2	RBC boundary σ_{be}^2	RBC residual σ_{ye}^2	$\eta_e = \dfrac{\sigma_{be}^2}{\sigma_{ye}^2}$
aerial	559.7	558.2	438.3	1.27
airplane	234.5	233.8	115.7	2.02
baboon	1104.8	1107.7	1256.6	0.88
buildings	237.8	272.4	75.5	3.61
couple	339.9	332.1	191.4	1.73
stream	484.5	489.6	439.1	1.12
tiffany	211.2	210.5	134.4	1.57

(a) Ensemble A

image	DCT σ_e^2	RBC boundary σ_{be}^2	RBC residual σ_{ye}^2	$\eta_e = \dfrac{\sigma_{be}^2}{\sigma_{ye}^2}$
lenna	122.1	121.0	129.8	0.93
lynda	43.2	43.3	10.5	4.11
peppers	204.6	202.8	152.2	1.33
sailboat	405.4	401.6	372.7	1.08
splash	96.8	97.0	59.9	1.62

(b) Ensemble B

Hybrid DCT Design

The normalized variances for each ensemble are given in Table 4.7.3 and plotted in Fig. 4.7.2. It should be noted that the difference between the two ensembles is now marginal, especially when compared with the 1d distributions in Fig. 4.5.1. The resulting standard bit allocations for each rate are given in Table 4.7.4.

Hybrid RBC Design

For RBC, the normalized variances are listed in Table 4.7.5 and plotted in Fig. 4.7.3. However the bit allocation is determined using the representative distributions, shown in Table 4.7.6 and plotted in Fig. 4.7.4, which are obtained by scaling each residual coefficient by $\dfrac{1}{\bar{\eta}_e}$, where $\bar{\eta}_e$ is the median value for the values of η_e within the ensembles given in Table 4.7.2. Again the distributions are more similar than for the 1d

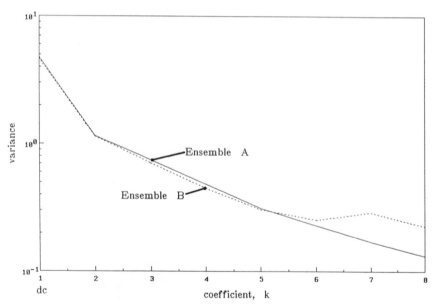

FIGURE 4.7.2. Ensemble normalized DCT variances for hybrid DCT ($N = 8$).

TABLE 4.7.3. Normalized variances for hybrid DCT coding.

ensemble	coefficient							
	1 (dc)	2	3	4	5	6	7	8
A	4.782	1.147	0.748	0.481	0.311	0.228	0.170	0.132
B	4.642	1.144	0.698	0.446	0.305	0.253	0.288	0.224

TABLE 4.7.4. Bit allocations for hybrid DCT coding.

ensemble	rate	coefficient							
		1	2	3	4	5	6	7	8
A	2.5	4	3	3	3	3	2	1	1
	2.0	4	3	3	2	2	1	1	.
	1.5	3	3	2	2	1	1	.	.
	1.0	3	2	2	1	.	.	.	.
B	2.5	4	3	3	3	2	2	2	1
	2.0	4	3	3	2	1	1	1	1
	1.5	3	3	2	1	1	1	1	.
	1.0	3	2	2	1	.	.	.	.

algorithm. The resulting bit allocations are given in Table 4.7.7.

The bit allocations provided insufficient bits for the boundaries in some cases. In 1d RBC coding we noted that the boundary allocation must be 4 bits or more to prevent subjectively unacceptable boundaries. In hybrid RBC, the boundary threshold is 3 bits, so as before some modifications were necessary and they are marked with a † in Table 4.7.7. Since the distributions are so similar, the bit allocations are actually the same for both ensembles at the rates of 1 and 2 bits/pixel.

Note that the variances fail to drop off for the higher coefficients in Ensemble B for both DCT and RBC. This is because the DPCM prediction weight $a_k = 1$, is much too large in these cases as seen in Table 4.7.1 where the correlation falls off for the higher coefficients, especially for lynda—a member of the B ensemble.

Discussion of Results

The major problem with initial attempts at hybrid RBC was *slope overload* coding errors in the boundaries at horizontal edges. Slope overload occurs in DPCM when a large transition is encountered such that the rate of change of the input is so great that the prediction error exceeds the dynamic range of the quantizer. Consider a step function which changes in one pixel from one constant level to a second constant level, and assume that the prediction error was zero before the transition, that is the predictor was tracking the input signal. After the transition, if it is very large, the predictor will change by the maximum quantizer output level. If the predictor is still lagging the input, then the predictor will continue to increase by the same amount at each pixel until the predictor finally reaches the new input level. The visual result is a blurred edge.

This problem can be eased by scaling the quantizer to increase the dynamic range, but the granularity in smooth regions will increase as a result of the larger steps in the quantizer characteristic, and so a balance must be reached. Using the MSE design to derive the hybrid normalized

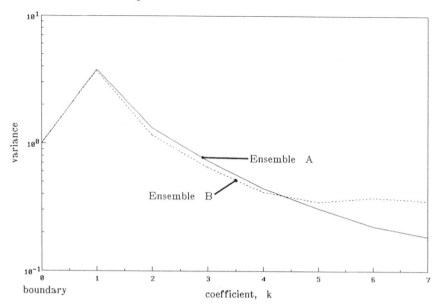

FIGURE 4.7.3. Ensemble normalized RBC variances for hybrid RBC ($N = 7$).

TABLE 4.7.5. Normalized variances for hybrid RBC coding.

ensemble	$\bar{\eta}_e$	coefficient							
		boundary	1	2	3	4	5	6	7
A	1.57	1.0	3.771	1.326	0.735	0.447	0.308	0.225	0.186
B	1.33	1.0	3.694	1.164	0.648	0.415	0.348	0.376	0.354

variances and bit allocation produces slope overload in the boundaries but not in the residual. This *boundary overshoot* is very objectionable and the design must be compensated. Rather than *fine tuning* the parameters for each image we made a single modification to the standard variances which still results in a unified design process. The problem is one of dynamic range rather than insufficient bits except for the modified allocations in Table 4.7.7 which we have already described above. So we modified the normalized variances to change the quantizer dynamic range after using the true normalized variances to generate the bit allocation.

In this case we doubled the boundary prediction error variance, that is changed 1.0 to 2.0 in Table 4.7.5, which increases the boundary quantizer dynamic range by $\sqrt{2}$. This limited the boundary overshoot in those images with problems but without introducing any noticeable granularity. Some images had no boundary problems even with the original dynamic range, and after increasing the range for the boundary elements there was no noticeable visual change or significant change in MSE for

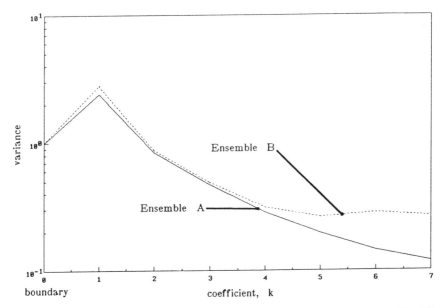

FIGURE 4.7.4. Typical or ensemble representative RBC variances for hybrid RBC
($N = 7$).

TABLE 4.7.6. Typical variances for hybrid RBC coding.

ensemble		coefficient						
	boundary	1	2	3	4	5	6	7
A	1.0	2.407	0.847	0.469	0.285	0.197	0.144	0.118
B	1.0	2.773	0.874	0.486	0.312	0.261	0.282	0.265

these images. Hence the modified design was not a compromise and lead
to improvements in all cases.

The two images which benefited most from this new design were the
airplane and splash but they still show slight problems and could be
improved even more by further increasing the dynamic range of the
boundary quantizers. Judging by the lack of detrimental effects in the
other images we conjecture that this would be a satisfactory solution.

The results are described in Tables 4.7.8 and 4.7.9 with h-plots in Fig.
4.7.5. As with 1d and 2d coding, hybrid RBC performs very favorably
when compared to DCT coding and to illustrate the hybrid coding results
we show lenna coded at 1 bit/pixel in Fig. 4.7.6. At this rate, both DCT
and RBC have problems with the diagonal edges. The DCT image in (b)
is extremely blocky in these regions and is clearly worse than the RBC
image in (a) where these edges are also broken but masked by blurring.
A region of the image is magnified by a factor of two to provide (c) and
(d) where the DCT tiling is now more clearly visible and can now also be

TABLE 4.7.7. Bit allocations for hybrid RBC coding.

ensemble	rate	coefficient							
		boundary	1	2	3	4	5	6	7
A	2.5	3	4	3	3	3	2	1	1
	2.0	3	4	3	2	2	1	1	.
	1.5	2	3	3	2	1	1	.	.
	1.5†	3	3	3	2	1	.	.	.
	1.0	2	3	2	1	.	.	.	.
	1.0†	3	3	2	.	.	.	.	.
B	2.5	3	4	3	3	2	1	2	2
	2.0	2	4	3	2	2	1	1	1
	2.0†	3	4	3	2	2	1	1	.
	1.5	2	3	2	1	1	1	1	1
	1.5†	3	3	2	1	1	1	1	.
	1.0	1	3	2	1	1	.	.	.
	1.0†	3	3	2	.	.	.	.	.

† Modified allocation to prevent *boundary breakthrough*

seen in the eyes. In (e) and (f) the same region is shown, but no longer magnified, at rates of 1, 1.5, 2, and 2.5 bits/pixel. At 2 bits/pixel and above the RBC images are judged to be excellent while blocking is still visible even at the highest rate using DCT. At 1.5 bits the RBC image is acceptable with some distortion still slightly visible along the diagonal edges.

4.8   Conclusions

The two major artifacts associated with zonal coding are:

(i)   noise (DCT); texture (RBC); and

(ii)   the tile effect as the rate is lowered.

As indicated in section 3.5 the first artifact can be reduced by using zero-level or mid-tread quantizers. Unfortunately this tends to make the second artifact more noticeable since the noise actually disguises the block structure. Consequently the major artifact is the tile effect and as we have shown RBC reduces this, leading to improved image quality.

Apart from noting the artifacts, we should also like to discuss the advantages and disadvantages of zonal coding. Zonal coding is very simple but performs poorly in non-stationary images. The baboon is well suited to zonal coding while the buildings image is not. It is not true that adaptive coding will always produce better pictures since when some of the data rate is used for the adaptivity, the available coding rate is

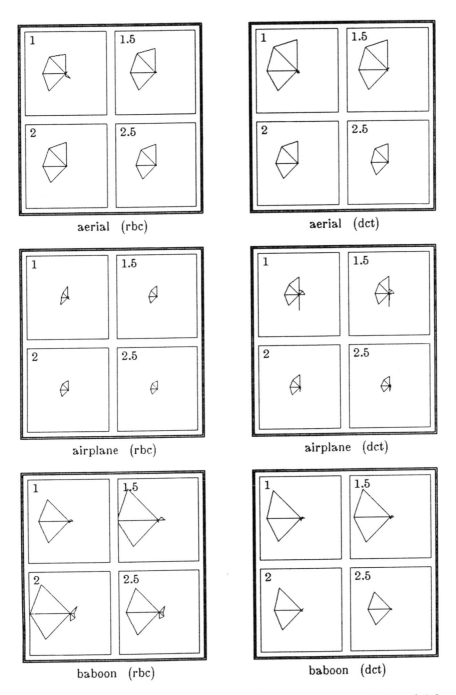

FIGURE 4.7.5. H-plots for hybrid zonal coding at rates of 1, 1.5, 2, and 1.5 bits/pixel. RBC plots on the left; DCT plots on the right.

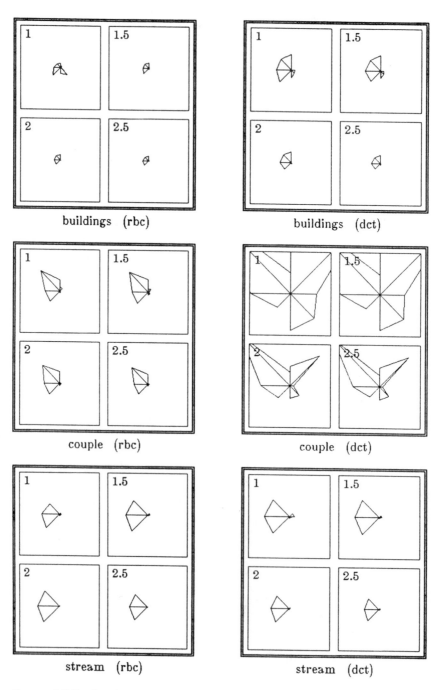

FIGURE 4.7.5. Continued.

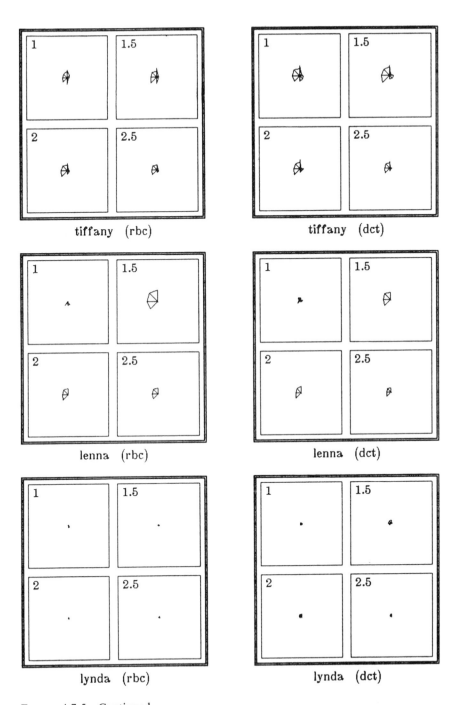

FIGURE 4.7.5. Continued.

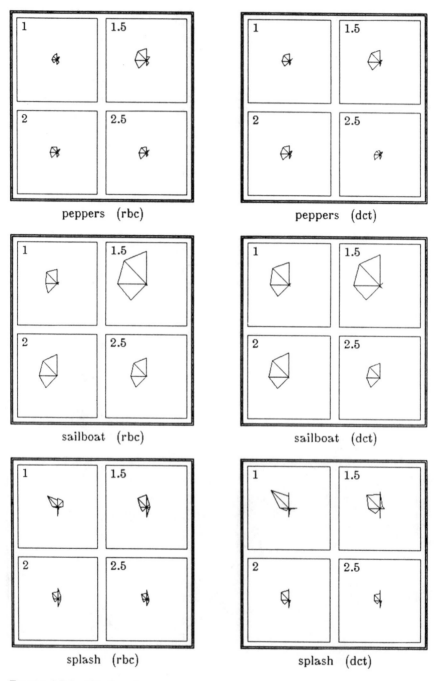

peppers (rbc)

peppers (dct)

sailboat (rbc)

sailboat (dct)

splash (rbc)

splash (dct)

FIGURE 4.7.5. Continued.

TABLE 4.7.8(a). Hybrid coding results for ensemble A.

image	DCT	RBC
aerial	1 bit − very blocky at edges 1.5 bits − good, blocky at edges 2, 2.5 bits − excellent	1 bit − blurred, edges stepped 1.5 bits − very good, slightly blurred 2, 2.5 bits − excellent
airplane	1 bit − very blocky (edges, mountains) 1.5 bits − very blocky (edges) 2, 2.5 bits − good, edges stepped (nose)	1 bit − blurred, few boundaries (mountains) 1.5 bits − good except plane insignia blurred 2, 2.5 bits − very good
baboon	1 bit − blocky, loss of contrast (eyes) 1.5, 2, 2.5 bits − excellent	1 bit − some boundaries visible, loss of contrast (eyes) 1.5, 2, 2.5 bits − excellent
buildings	1 bit − blurred, slight grain 1.5, 2, 2.5 bits − excellent	1 bit − blurred 1.5, 2, 2.5 bits − excellent
couple	1 bit − ok, slightly blocky and grainy 1.5, 2, 2.5 bits − excellent	1 bit − blurred 1.5, 2, 2.5 bits − excellent
stream	1 bit − blurred, blocky 1.5 bits − very good, slight blurring 2, 2.5 bits − excellent	1 bit − blurred, boundaries (background) 1.5, 2, 2.5 bits − excellent
tiffany	1 bit − blocky (chin, eyes) 1.5, 2, 2.5 bits − excellent	1 bit − boundaries (hair) 1.5 bits − very good, few boundaries 2, 2.5 bits − excellent

reduced. The baboon is an example where a simple adaptive coding is not useful since the image is uniformly active with heavy textures. Thus imposing a four class adaptive coding scheme, as we shall see in the next chapter, can actually produce worse results. The buildings image is a contrasting example with smooth low activity blocks in the background and yet very high activity blocks in the office buildings in the foreground. This image responds very well to adaptive coding as we shall see.

Finally we would like to stress that RBC is a more robust algorithm in the sense that the parameters needed to make an ensemble design—the normalized variance distributions—fluctuate much more slowly as a function of image activity than with DCT coding. This is similar to the observation that the DPCM prediction error statistics are much more stable than original image statistics as typified by their histograms.

(a) Hybrid RBC coding at 1 bits/pixel

(b) Hybrid DCT coding at 1 bits/pixel

(c) Hybrid RBC: magnified region of interest (1 bit)

(d) Hybrid DCT: magnified region of interest (1 bit)

(e) Hybrid RBC: region of interest at four rates

(f) Hybrid DCT: region of interest at four rates

Fig. 4.7.6   Hybrid coding results for lenna.

TABLE 4.7.9(a). MSE and SNR′ figures for hybrid coding of ensemble A.

image	algorithm	MSE				SNR′ (dB)			
		rate				rate			
		2.5	2.0	1.5	1.0	2.5	2.0	1.5	1.0
aerial	dct	37.1	51.9	90.7	146.5	32.4	31.0	28.6	26.5
	rbc	28.6	42.9	68.9	128.0	33.5	31.8	29.8	27.1
airplane	dct	22.2	28.8	67.2	110.5	34.7	33.5	29.9	27.7
	rbc	13.5	19.9	35.5	79.6	36.9	35.1	32.7	29.1
baboon	dct	79.4	119.1	189.8	281.0	29.1	27.4	25.4	23.6
	rbc	73.9	114.0	172.5	285.1	29.4	27.6	25.8	23.5
buildings	dct	20.4	22.5	49.0	69.4	35.0	34.6	31.2	29.7
	rbc	11.6	13.4	23.7	55.8	37.4	36.9	34.4	30.6
couple	dct	137.0	145.0	228.3	252.7	26.8	26.5	24.6	24.1
	rbc	78.1	86.9	109.3	142.5	29.2	28.7	27.8	26.6
stream	dct	37.3	56.6	96.1	141.9	32.4	30.6	28.3	26.6
	rbc	34.0	53.7	83.7	142.8	32.8	30.8	28.9	26.6
tiffany	dct	40.3	49.1	68.5	97.9	32.1	31.2	29.8	28.2
	rbc	29.2	38.6	55.2	90.9	33.5	32.3	30.7	28.5

TABLE 4.7.8(b). Hybrid coding results for ensemble B.

image	DCT	RBC
lenna	1 bit − extremely blocky (hat, shoulder) 1.5 bits − very bad blocking 2, 2.5 bits − staircase (hat brim, shoulder)	1 bit − blurred stepped edges (hat brim, shoulder) 1.5 bits − ok, busy edges (not staircase) 2, 2.5 bits − excellent
lynda	1, 1.5 bits − very blocky (collar, eyebrows, nose, mouth) 2, 2.5 bits − slightly blocky (collar)	1, 1.5 bits − blurred stepped edges (collar, jaw) 2, 2.5 bits − excellent
peppers	1 bit − very blocky edges 1.5 bits − blocky edges 2, 2.5 bits − very good, slightly blocky edge (bottom left)	1 bit − blurred stepped edges 1.5 bits − slightly blurred stepped edges 2, 2.5 bits − very good, slight boundary pull (bottom left pepper)
sailboat	1 bit − blocky 1.5 bits − good, slight texture 2, 2.5 bits − excellent	1 bit − blurred 1.5 bits − good, slight texture 2, 2.5 bits − excellent
splash	1 bit − extensive block structured blurring 1.5 bits − more localized 2, 2.5 bits − still very blocky	1 bit − very blurred 1.5 bits − blurred 2.5, 2 bits − very good, slight boundary pull at transitions

TABLE 4.7.9(b). MSE and SNR' figures for hybrid coding of ensemble B.

image	algorithm	MSE				SNR' (dB)			
		rate				rate			
		2.5	2.0	1.5	1.0	2.5	2.0	1.5	1.0
lenna	dct	23.8	35.4	55.9	78.8	34.4	32.6	30.7	29.2
	rbc	16.5	23.6	48.8	65.3	36.0	34.4	31.3	30.0
lynda	dct	6.9	7.5	17.5	21.5	39.8	39.4	35.7	34.8
	rbc	3.9	4.3	7.9	9.0	42.3	41.8	39.2	38.6
peppers	dct	47.5	56.6	91.7	120.3	31.4	30.6	28.5	27.3
	rbc	26.7	34.3	54.4	78.0	33.9	32.8	30.8	29.2
sailboat	dct	42.9	61.5	102.5	145.5	31.8	30.2	28.0	26.5
	rbc	31.8	45.1	81.8	119.8	33.1	31.6	29.0	27.4
splash	dct	48.0	51.7	89.3	119.9	31.3	31.0	28.6	27.3
	rbc	20.1	22.8	36.1	54.5	35.1	34.6	32.5	30.7

5

Adaptive Coding
Based on Activity Classes

5.1 Introduction

Since images are not stationary a number of techniques have been used to adapt the coding scheme to the local image content. As the image changes, the most complex schemes adapt the transform [68], while simpler schemes modify the bit allocation [69], or leave the allocation unchanged but scale the quantizers [70] from block to block. Some adaptive schemes lead to a variable rate code, where the rate increases for more complex images, while others go to some length to ensure that the rate remains the same for all images. Since most communication systems require that the data be transmitted at a constant rate, the transmission time for a still image coded using a variable rate scheme will vary according to the image content which may be quite acceptable. However this is not possible with broadcast TV and videoconferencing where the data is generated and must be reconstructed by the receiver at a constant rate and an elaborate buffering scheme must be employed to smooth out the non-uniform data generation rate for subsequent fixed rate transmission. In such cases it may be more attractive to use a fixed rate scheme which can be made quite complex before it becomes as involved as a variable rate coder and accompanying buffer and controller which together can meet the fixed rate constraint.

A popular example of a variable rate scheme is *threshold* coding [71] where the transform domain coefficients in each block are compared to some threshold, determined *a priori* or adaptively, and only transmitted when they exceed this value. In this way only frequencies which are significant are transmitted and none of the rate is wasted on those frequencies which have a small amplitude or are not even present in this particular block. Even the highest frequencies which are rare and therefore not transmitted in zonal coding are reconstructed in this scheme if they exceed the threshold. Of course there is a price to pay for this flexibility since we must now continually inform the decoder which coefficient is being transmitted. This overhead or side information consists of a bit map for each block indicating those super-threshold coefficients and there have been a number of suggestions to efficiently code this bit map so that the overhead is minimized [72]. A second disadvantage is that, to maintain a fixed rate over a whole frame, we must do some additional processing to determine the threshold value for each particular image.

In this chapter we will be using another very popular adaptive technique based on a paper by Chen and Smith [51] in which they segment the image blocks into a number of classes according to the local image activity within each block [73]. Each class is then coded using a zonal scheme but the bit allocation is different for each class. This allows more bits to be used to code the active blocks by using less for the smoother regions which do not require such a high rate. As with threshold coding, if we require a fixed rate, then there is some on-line pre-processing for each image to determine the activity thresholds used in classification so that each class contains the desired number of blocks.

We observe that the classification is usually done so as to ensure equal occupation of each class which then leads to the same average rate for each image. However, to guarantee a constant average rate it is only required that each class contains a fixed number of blocks which can be different for each class, and it should be possible to improve performance by carefully selecting appropriate (non-equal) class occupation levels. Jain and Wang [67] have shown that in order to determine the activity thresholds and minimize the overall distortion we must solve a set of simultaneous nonlinear equations.

In section 5.2 we will discuss adaptive transform coding based on image classification and derive an ensemble design methodology which we will then extend to RBC in section 5.3. In section 5.4 we will present the results of DCT and RBC coding within this adaptive framework and in the final section, 5.5, we will draw conclusions.

Since the tables containing the normalized variances and bit allocations are quite extensive in a four class coding scheme, we refer the reader to Appendix D for the details.

5.2   Adaptive DCT

Let us first consider traditional transform coding, leaving RBC until the next section. In this case we wish to distinguish between blocks that are smooth and those that are active. Chen and Smith [51] used four classes: 1, 2, 3, and 4 where class 1 is the most active and class 4 is the smoothest. Cox and Tescher [74] used eight classes and since we are unaware of any conclusive study indicating how many classes should be used for optimum performance, we choose to use four classes here.

To decide which class a particular block belongs to we first measure the variance of each block within the image relative to its local mean. In particular, if the intensity of the pixels in this, the nth, block are denoted as $u(i,j)$ and the block size is N, then we compute the local mean, m_n, as

$$m_n \triangleq \frac{1}{N^2} \sum_{i=1}^{N} \sum_{j=1}^{N} u(i,j) \tag{5.2.1}$$

and the local block variance, v_n, is

$$v_n \triangleq \frac{1}{N^2} \sum_{i=1}^{N} \sum_{j=1}^{N} [u(i,j) - m_n]^2. \tag{5.2.2}$$

The $\{v_n\}$ are then arranged in increasing order and thresholds determined so that they can be separated into four groups each containing 25% of the variances and the corresponding blocks are then labeled as belonging to one of the four classes. This results in an overhead of 2 bits per block to identify the class which corresponds to an overhead rate of $2/N^2$ or 0.03125 bits/pixel for a block size of 8 and only 0.00781 bits/pixel if a block of size 16 is used.

Since each block is transformed during coding it is advantageous to make the variance measurements in the DCT domain directly. The variance, v_n, is equivalently evaluated by summing the energy of the ac coefficients, viz.,

$$v_n = \frac{1}{N^2} \sum_{(p,q) \neq (1,1)} \hat{u}^2(p,q) \tag{5.2.3}$$

which avoids the necessity to compute the mean and of course, since we only need the relative magnitudes to determine the thresholds, there is no need to scale by $\frac{1}{N^2}$ in either (5.2.2) or (5.2.3).

The thresholds for the various images when divided into blocks of sizes 8 and 16 are shown below in Table 5.2.1. For each image there are three thresholds, $\tau_{k\,k-1}$ for the transition from class k to class $k-1$ where $k = 4$, 3, and 2.

If we compare these threshold values with Fig. 4 in [51] there is a discrepancy which may be due to a non-unitary implementation of the DCT in Chen's simulation. Chen uses an image which is similar to our aerial image and if we take our thresholds for this image when coded with a block size of 16 and divide by 256 then we obtain (1.1, 2.5, 5.6) which are close to Chen's values. As can be seen from the table the thresholds vary for different images and block sizes and must be computed for each image before coding if the rate is to be maintained constant. However if the rate is allowed to vary, for example in a storage application, then the

TABLE 5.2.1. Class transition thresholds.

image	block size = 8			block size = 16		
	τ_{43}	τ_{32}	τ_{21}	τ_{43}	τ_{32}	τ_{21}
aerial	101.9	360.0	1008.2	278.3	654.5	1425.5
airplane	6.7	24.8	485.0	12.5	135.0	1357.7
baboon	202.7	700.4	1365.7	357.9	950.5	1581.5
buildings	17.3	422.4	1547.4	76.5	812.7	3197.4
couple	27.9	120.3	390.2	70.5	270.5	575.3
stream	167.1	399.4	769.4	337.0	668.1	1180.8
tiffany	19.4	63.8	220.1	47.3	172.0	482.4

(a) Ensemble A

image	block size = 8			block size = 16		
	τ_{43}	τ_{32}	τ_{21}	τ_{43}	τ_{32}	τ_{21}
lenna	17.8	56.5	318.4	40.0	181.5	778.6
lynda	11.7	37.1	140.6	45.9	143.7	640.1
peppers	20.9	52.2	339.2	40.5	198.7	1576.2
sailboat	43.0	194.5	1035.3	79.0	680.9	2154.5
splash	16.8	30.1	89.7	28.7	62.5	405.0

(b) Ensemble B

thresholds could be fixed ahead of time and the pre-processing eliminated. In this case the more complex images would contain a higher percentage of class 1 blocks leading to a higher overall rate but would be reconstructed with less distortion than using the fixed rate.

Fig. 5.2.1 graphically illustrates the classification map for the buildings image with block sizes of 8 and 16. All of the blocks in class 1, the most active class, are white while class 4 is mapped to black and classes 2 and 3 are represented by two shades of gray so that the intensity increases with the class activity.

Having discussed the classification procedure, there are now two basic considerations: first, how do we design the quantizers for each class and then, how do we adaptively code each block.

Design Methodology

Chen and Smith make different bit allocations for each image and transmit these bit maps as overhead. However, rather than transmitting the coefficient variances which are needed to scale the quantizers at the decoder, they model them using only a single parameter to minimize the extra information which must be sent. Despite this, we will continue to design our coder for an image ensemble rather than repeating the design for each image although it could be argued that since we are already

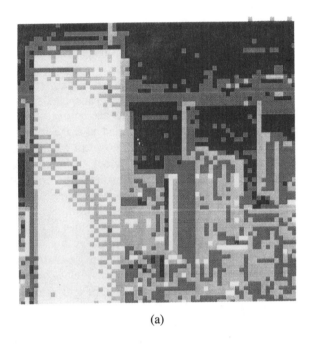

(a)

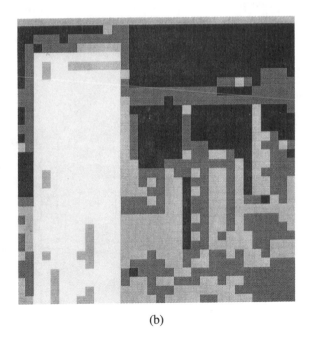

(b)

Fig. 5.2.1   Classification map for buildings using the DCT: (a) N=8; (b) N=16.

allowing considerable on-line computation then perhaps we could complete the whole design on-line rather than just the threshold determination. We will discuss the possible performance improvement when we allow this additional adaptivity in our conclusions in section 5.5.

The ensemble design begins with the computation of the variance thresholds for each image within the ensemble as shown in Fig. 5.2.2(a). These thresholds are then used to classify this image into four sub-images each containing the blocks from only one class. The sub-images corresponding to each class are then grouped to form a class ensemble. We then make four zonal coding designs, one for each class, as shown in Fig. 5.2.2(b). However, the individual designs are coupled together since we must first determine how to allocate a fixed average number of bits per block between the four classes so that the overall MSE is minimized. This is represented by the central processing block in Fig. 5.2.2(b) which takes in the four performance curves and determines the optimal rate for each class. This is then used with the normalized variances to drive the integer bit allocation algorithm and generate the bit allocation as before. Before discussing how the rate allocation is achieved, we will first describe the other new processing block which was not needed in the nonadaptive zonal design. This processing element generates the normalized variances and performance curve for each class and is shown expanded in Fig. 5.2.2(c). The determination of the normalized variances is slightly different from the method used in the zonal design because we wish to ensure that, after reconstruction, there are no dc shifts at boundaries between adjacent blocks from different classes. In zonal coding we used a Lloyd-Max quantizer where the exact structure depended on the number of bits, assumed pdf, and estimated variance for the dc coefficient. If we were to use this method here, then fluctuations in these parameters between classes would indeed lead to dc

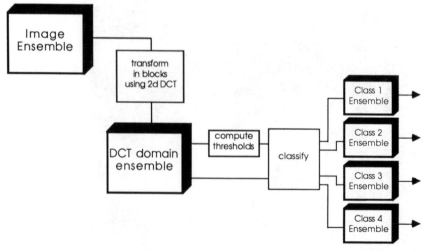

FIGURE 5.2.2. Adaptive DCT ensemble design: (a) Classification.

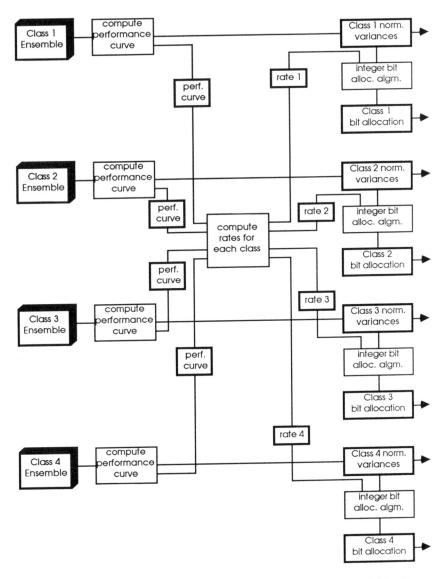

FIGURE 5.2.2(b). Computing the standard normalized variances and bit allocations for each class.

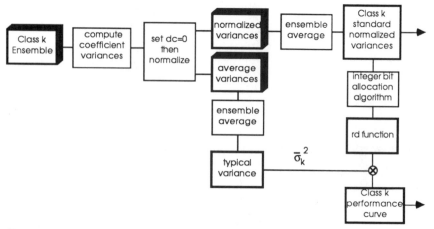

FIGURE 5.2.2(c). Detail of the class k performance curve module shown in (b).

shifts and an accentuated tile effect. Consequently we use the same dc quantizer for each class, or in other words, the dc coefficient is treated separately and not subject to classification.

DC Quantizer

For the reasons just mentioned, we replace the Lloyd-Max dc quantizer by a uniform quantizer whose step size is simply determined by the dynamic range of the dc coefficient and the number of bits available. The dynamic range of the dc coefficient is $\sqrt{N}$ times that of the input for 1d coding and N times greater for 2d coding. Consequently, for 2d coding, if the input image is represented by b bits and the dc coefficient is allotted $rate_{dc}$ bits, then the dc step size, q_{dc}, is given by

$$q_{dc} = \frac{N \, 2^b}{2^{rate_{dc}}}. \qquad (5.2.4)$$

For example, when coding an 8-bit image with a block size of 16 and using 7 bits for the dc coefficient, the step size is $\dfrac{(16)(256)}{128} = 32$. Using a pre-determined dc quantizer has the added advantage of avoiding the clipping problems which we encountered in chapter four when coding tiffany using a statistically designed Lloyd-Max quantizer.

Standard Normalized Variances

Since the dc coefficient is to be treated separately, we compute the transform coefficient variances for each image as before but set the dc entry to zero before normalizing. In this way the allocation algorithm will not assign any bits to the dc coefficient and we can manually select an appropriate dc rate. The ac variances are normalized by their average value and these normalized variances are then averaged over the class ensemble to give the standard normalized variances which are shown in Tables D.2.1 and D.2.2 in Appendix D for image ensembles A and B respectively.

Performance Curve

The second, and new, output in Fig. 5.2.2(c) is the performance curve which is proportional to the block rate-distortion function, $f(n)$. As shown in the figure, we first input the normalized variances into the integer bit allocation algorithm and by saving the $(n, f(n))$ pairs as the rate increases by $\frac{1}{N^2}$ bits/pixel at each iteration, as shown in Fig. 3.4.1 for the 1d case, we form the rd function up to the desired final rate.

The rd function is based on the normalized variances while the performance curve, which is the actual block coding distortion, is based on the actual variances and is $\sigma^2 f(n)$ where σ^2 is the normalizing factor used to generate the normalized variances from the actual values. In this case it is the average ac coefficient variance and since the DCT is a unitary transform, σ^2 is also the average pixel domain block variance, or ac energy. The average variances for each image and class are given in Table 5.2.2.

Since each image i, has a different average ac energy $\sigma_k^2(i)$, for each class k, we must use some typical values to scale each class rd function and we use the average over the ensemble $\bar{\sigma}_k^2$, which is also given in the table. So for ensemble A we scale the four rd functions by (1878.8, 512.0, 168.0, 35.2) and for ensemble B by (1603.4, 186.4, 40.6, 11.5) to get the performance curve for each class. Note that we could have scaled the standard normalized variances by $\bar{\sigma}_k^2$ prior to the bit allocation and obtained the performance curve directly without introducing the rd function.

Class Rate Allocation

To optimize the overall performance, the bits are allocated between the different classes so that each class is reconstructed with the same level of distortion. Using this criterion we can combine the individual performance curves into an overall performance curve which will then give the distortion, the same for each class, at any specified overall average rate. This distortion is then used to determine the four class rates via the individual performance curves and the bit allocation can then proceed.

To combine the performance curves we select a distortion level d, and examine the individual curves to determine the rates $\{r_1, r_2, r_3, r_4\}$

TABLE 5.2.2. Average ac energy for each class, $N = 8$.

image	σ_4^2	σ_3^2	σ_2^2	σ_1^2
aerial	34.9	212.5	626.1	2126.3
airplane	3.0	12.4	165.2	2040.3
baboon	88.4	420.2	1016.5	1928.3
buildings	6.4	160.9	848.2	2853.1
couple	14.3	61.6	236.8	1750.3
stream	86.9	271.2	564.8	1513.0
tiffany	12.5	37.1	126.8	939.9
average	35.2	168.0	512.0	1878.8

(a) Ensemble A

image	σ_4^2	σ_3^2	σ_2^2	σ_1^2
lenna	11.7	32.0	142.5	1236.2
lynda	5.2	22.5	74.4	724.9
peppers	12.5	31.9	138.8	2049.1
sailboat	18.7	93.7	526.6	2719.8
splash	9.4	22.6	49.5	1286.8
average	11.5	40.6	186.4	1603.4

(b) Ensemble B

needed to achieve this distortion level in each class. In general this will involve interpolation of the discrete characteristics whose rates are multiples of $\frac{1}{N^2}$. We then have one point located at $(\frac{r_1+r_2+r_3+r_4}{4}, d)$ and by varying d and repeating we can evaluate the overall performance curve. We are able to generate an overall curve for distortion values down to the smallest common distortion level. To increase the range, the bit allocation will have to be repeated with a higher final rate for one or more of the classes to bring their performance curves down to the required distortion level.

An example of the performance curves when $N = 8$ is shown for ensemble A in Fig. 5.2.3 where the four individual curves are drawn and the overall characteristic is superimposed.

If the block size is N, the desired rate is p bits/pixel, there are c classes, and $rate_{dc}$ is the rate used for the dc coefficient, then the ac data rate is

$$rate_{ac} = \frac{N^2 p - rate_{dc} - \log_2 c}{N^2 - 1} \qquad (5.2.5)$$

which is then distributed between the c classes.

For example, if we desire an average rate of 1 bit/pixel then, with a block size of 8, a dc rate of 8 bits, and four classes, we have

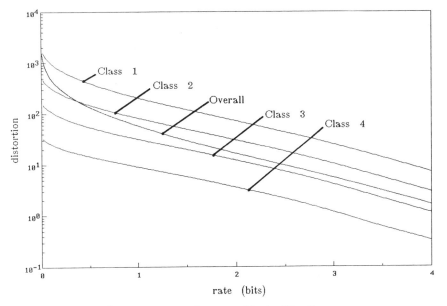

FIGURE 5.2.3. Performance curves for ensemble A, ($N = 8$).

$$rate_{ac} = \frac{64 - 8 - 2}{63} = 0.857 \text{ bits/pixel}$$

and for ensemble A the ac rate for each of the four classes is (2.00, 1.13, 0.30, 0.00) bits/pixel with the rate decreasing for the less active classes. To get the overall *coding rate* for each class we add in the rate for the dc coefficient: 8/64 = 0.125 bits to give (2.13, 1.25, 0.42, 0.13) and the *overhead rate* is 2/64 = 0.031 bits/pixel leading to a combined average rate of 1.01 bits/pixel, which slightly exceeds the desired rate due to rounding errors in the design process.

The bit allocations for adaptive coding at rates of 1.5, 1.0, 0.5, and 0.25 bits/pixel with a block size of 8 are given in Appendix D in Table D.2.3 for ensemble A and D.2.4 for ensemble B. These allocations are summarized here in Table 5.2.3 where the total number of bits allocated to each class is tabulated for each rate and ensemble.

In the case of DCT coding we can calculate the bit allocations rather more directly. After forming the standard normalized variances for each class, we scale each by $\bar{\sigma}_k^2$ to form typical variances which are then pasted together to form a composite block of size $2N$. When input to the integer bit allocation algorithm, the algorithm guarantees equal distortion for the four classes and will provide the correct allocations for each class if we specify a final rate which is four times the required value. However, this is not possible for the RBC design because of the interaction between the corner, boundary, and core distortions. So we introduce the performance curves at this stage to provide a uniform discussion.

TABLE 5.2.3. Distribution of bits between different classes for adaptive DCT.

average rate	dc bits	ac bit allocations							
		Ensemble A				Ensemble B			
		Class 1	Class 2	Class 3	Class 4	Class 1	Class 2	Class 3	Class 4
1.5	8	172	119	57	0	169	126	59	0
1.0	8	128	72	19	0	127	80	12	0
0.5	7	70	23	0	0	72	21	0	0
0.25	6	30	2	0	0	31	0	0	0

Coding Methodology

When coding an image, the only difference from zonal coding is that we must first compute the class variance thresholds: τ_{43}, τ_{32}, and τ_{21}, which are needed at the encoder, and the average ac energy $\bar{\sigma}_k^2$ for each class which must also be transmitted to the decoder. This is illustrated in Fig. 5.2.4 where the image is first transformed and these calculations are made in the transform domain, although we could equally well work in the spatial domain as noted earlier. The ac energy for each class is then used to form the estimated variances which then scale the generic Lloyd-Max unity variance quantizers to provide a set of customized quantizers for each class. Coding is shown in Fig. 5.2.5 where the transformed image block is first classified based on its ac energy and the 2-bit class identification code is stored or transmitted for the decoder. The block is then quantized using the appropriate set of class quantizers.

5.3   Adaptive RBC

As with adaptive DCT, we classify the input to the transform coder which is now a residual rather than a normal image. During the design phase, we must use an ideal residual image since we do not know in advance how much distortion there will be in each component. We therefore use perfect corner points to predict the row and column boundary interiors and subtract to form the residuals, and similarly the perfect boundaries are used to form the core residual. We now have a set of ideal row, column, and core residuals to classify.

The residual signals have zero mean on the average and are classified according to their total block energy rather than variance or ac energy. In the DST domain this is the squared sum of all of the coefficients including the (1,1) coefficient which is not a dc coefficient. We must now decide how many classes to use for each residual signal. To save overhead, we could group the right column and bottom row with the core

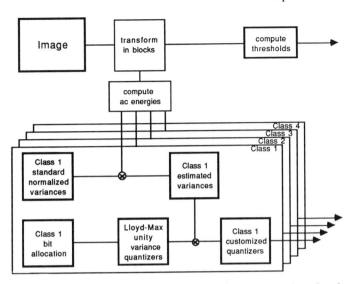

FIGURE 5.2.4. Setting up for adaptive DCT coding—computing the thresholds and customized quantizers for each class.

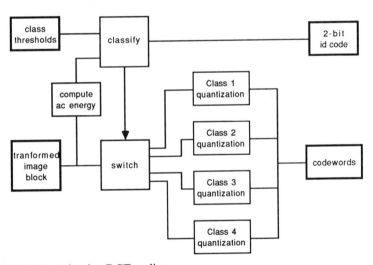

FIGURE 5.2.5. Adaptive DCT coding.

residual when classifying the current block so that, with the exception of the first column and top line of the image which we would treat as a special case, the overhead would still be $\log_2 c$ bits/block just as with adaptive DCT. However, to allow greater flexibility in this initial study, we have chosen to classify each of the three residual sources independently. This approach permits a class 4 core to be surrounded by boundaries belonging to classes 2 and 3 for example. This results in a higher overhead of $3 \log_2 c$ bits/block if each residual is classified as belonging to one of c classes. An intermediate approach would be to use fewer classes for the boundaries, for example when $c = 4$ for the core classification we could allow just 2 classes for each boundary so that the overhead would then be $[2 + (2)(1)] = 4$ bits per block instead of 6. The thresholds for each residual source: row, column, and core, are presented in Table 5.3.1.

Since we are allowing four classes there are three thresholds for each residual source. In many cases the residual energy is considerably less than the ac energy and so the threshold values here tend to be smaller than with adaptive DCT. It can also be seen from the table that the individual thresholds for the three residual sources are usually of the same order although there are still large variations between the images.

To illustrate the RBC classification, the buildings image was segmented with block sizes of 8 and 16 with all residuals classified into one of four classes and the resulting classification map is shown in Fig. 5.3.1 with white corresponding to class 1 and black to class 4 as before. If we compare the core classifications with the DCT classifications in Fig. 5.2.1 then we see that they are very similar. However note that the boundary and core classifications for a given block are not always the same. This is clearly seen in the background where the black class 4 cores are often surrounded by dark gray class 3 boundaries.

Design Methodology

The adaptive RBC design is similar to the method described for DCT with some additional considerations. In Fig. 5.3.2(a) we classify the transform domain residuals into four class ensembles for each residual component. After classification, we form the normalized variances for each (row, column, core) residual component and class as shown in Fig. 5.3.2(b). The normalization factor is the average coefficient variance which is also the average residual energy e_k since the DST is unitary. These energy values are given in Table 5.3.2 for each image, class, and residual component. The standard normalized variances are obtained as the ensemble average for each class and component and are listed in Appendix D in Tables D.3.1 and D.3.2 for ensembles A and B respectively.

In the non-adaptive case we measured the residual energy indirectly via the prediction variance reduction ratio η, and then took the median of these values as a typical value with which to scale the residuals relative to the corner variance. Since, as we shall soon see, the corner variance will be set to zero, we can no longer use this approach and so we measure the residual energies directly. The residual energies are averaged over the sub-image ensemble for each component and these typical values $\bar{e}_k$,

TABLE 5.3.1. Class transition thresholds.

image	residual	τ_{43}	τ_{32}	τ_{21}
aerial	row	21.4	152.2	708.0
	column	33.9	239.0	917.4
	core	63.1	227.2	670.3
airplane	row	4.4	15.2	161.3
	column	4.1	17.7	183.1
	core	4.6	16.0	249.0
baboon	row	141.5	482.1	1304.4
	column	137.5	580.8	1614.3
	core	154.0	560.9	1174.1
buildings	row	6.8	62.9	631.5
	column	8.2	84.2	888.1
	core	10.2	191.5	664.0
couple	row	10.9	38.9	205.5
	column	10.0	39.0	194.0
	core	20.3	65.8	226.1
stream	row	66.7	245.0	665.0
	column	102.9	307.3	786.7
	core	117.1	286.6	579.5
tiffany	row	16.6	42.2	174.9
	column	13.9	32.7	114.4
	core	15.0	34.7	133.9

(a) Ensemble A

image	residual	τ_{43}	τ_{32}	τ_{21}
lenna	row	16.5	42.5	213.7
	column	12.1	26.7	96.9
	core	13.9	28.8	143.9
lynda	row	3.0	8.3	32.0
	column	2.5	6.3	21.0
	core	2.8	6.3	22.3
peppers	row	15.8	39.0	138.6
	column	15.8	35.9	114.1
	core	17.9	36.2	140.5
sailboat	row	35.1	131.0	624.5
	column	37.4	123.2	599.1
	core	40.0	145.7	592.6
splash	row	10.7	23.3	56.2
	column	9.9	24.3	57.4
	core	14.0	23.1	48.8

(b) Ensemble B

TABLE 5.3.2. Average residual energy for each class.

image	residual	e_4	e_3	e_2	e_1
aerial	row	7.5	70.2	367.1	2144.5
	column	11.3	113.9	501.9	2694.0
	core	22.2	136.6	409.5	1406.8
airplane	row	2.1	8.6	53.3	2049.0
	column	1.8	9.3	65.1	1411.2
	core	2.4	8.8	86.7	1132.1
baboon	row	64.2	284.9	829.6	2764.1
	column	59.7	319.4	1038.7	3190.8
	core	67.5	328.5	849.3	1743.8
buildings	row	3.1	23.5	248.8	2383.4
	column	3.7	31.8	366.9	2871.3
	core	4.3	74.2	402.9	1341.0
couple	row	5.4	21.8	99.3	989.1
	column	4.9	21.6	95.8	1363.5
	core	10.8	36.9	134.0	889.2
stream	row	25.5	143.4	415.7	1655.0
	column	46.5	192.8	511.8	2012.6
	core	57.9	194.1	415.3	1030.8
tiffany	row	9.1	27.0	88.9	1287.7
	column	7.1	22.0	60.9	494.8
	core	10.4	22.3	74.5	577.1
AVERAGE	row	16.7	82.8	300.4	1896.1
	column	19.3	101.5	377.3	2005.4
	core	25.1	114.5	338.9	1160.1

(a) Ensemble A

image	residual	e_4	e_3	e_2	e_1
lenna	row	9.5	26.9	99.0	1267.6
	column	7.1	18.5	49.2	762.3
	core	9.6	19.7	66.5	615.8
lynda	row	1.6	5.1	16.8	281.1
	column	1.4	4.1	11.6	169.7
	core	1.8	4.2	12.0	132.3
peppers	row	7.9	25.7	73.8	1528.7
	column	7.7	24.8	63.3	1494.0
	core	10.8	25.1	71.9	986.3
sailboat	row	13.2	77.5	300.8	2224.5
	column	15.7	72.3	281.6	2772.7
	core	16.4	81.7	323.0	1500.2
splash	row	4.6	16.2	36.3	1167.8
	column	3.4	16.5	37.0	485.4
	core	7.5	18.2	32.6	516.6
AVERAGE	row	7.4	30.3	105.3	1294.0
	column	7.1	27.2	88.5	1136.8
	core	9.2	29.8	101.2	750.2

(b) Ensemble B

(a)

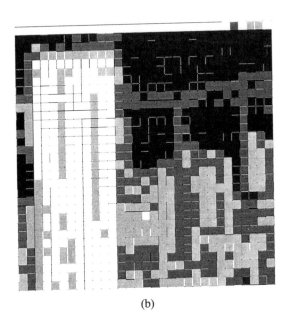

(b)

Fig. 5.3.1   Classification map for buildings using RBC: (a) N=7; (b) N=15.

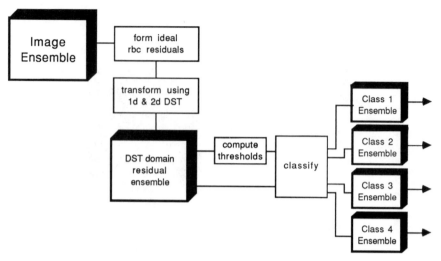

FIGURE 5.3.2. Adaptive RBC ensemble design: (a) Classification.

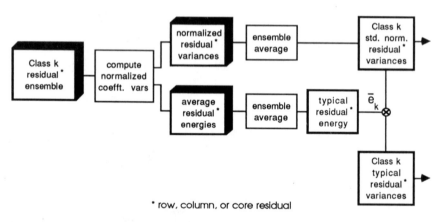

* row, column, or core residual

FIGURE 5.3.2(b). Computing the class k row, column, and core residual variances.

which are also given in Table 5.3.2, scale the standard normalized variances to form the typical variances for each residual component.

These typical values are now combined to form a typical composite set of variances in Fig. 5.3.2(c). However, it should be noted that when the boundaries are classified independently of the core, then the boundaries and core from a particular class are not necessarily adjacent to each other in the image in general but this is implicitly assumed by forming a class composite using the row, column, and core variances from a common class. We are forced to make this assumption, or simplification,

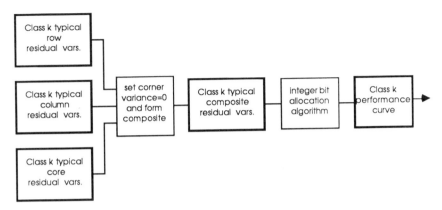

FIGURE 5.3.2(c). Computing the class k performance curve.

because we would otherwise be unable to compute the performance curves and bit allocations.

We code the corner point in a fixed way as we did with the dc coefficient in adaptive DCT, and therefore set the corner variance to zero to allow this rate to be selected manually. Using typical class k composite residual variances we use the RBC integer bit allocation algorithm (Algorithm 3.7.2) to compute the class k performance curve directly. The performance curves for each class are shown in Fig. 5.3.3 for ensemble A with a block size of 8.

To form the overall performance curve, the individual curves are combined in exactly the same way as shown in Fig. 5.2.2(b) for adaptive DCT. This is then used with the individual curves to fix the individual class rates and hence the bit maps which are shown in Appendix D in Tables D.3.3 and D.3.4. These bit allocations are summarized in Table 5.3.3.

Coding Methodology

The set up for adaptive RBC coding is illustrated in Fig. 5.3.4 and as can be seen the major deviation from zonal RBC coding is that we must first compute the three transition thresholds and the four class average residual energies for each of the residual sources. The average residual energies are also sent to the decoder and used to customize the quantizers at both the encoder and decoder. To avoid an overly complex diagram, the customization is shown in detail for only one set of quantizers (row residual, class 1) although it must actually be done for all twelve sets.

As we noted during the design stage, the thresholds must be based on ideal residuals assuming perfect boundaries because until we know the thresholds we cannot code the boundaries and hence have no access to the actual core residuals at this point. Consequently the classification

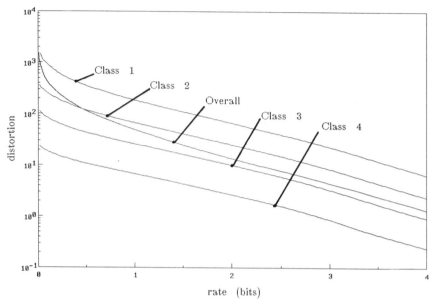

FIGURE 5.3.3. Performance curves for ensemble A, $(N = 7)$.

TABLE 5.3.3. Distribution of bits between different classes for adaptive RBC.

average rate	corner bits	residual bit allocations							
		Ensemble A				Ensemble B			
		Class 1	Class 2	Class 3	Class 4	Class 1	Class 2	Class 3	Class 4
1.5	7	173	113	51	0	164	116	56	0
1.0	6	130	67	14	0	125	74	12	0
0.5	5	68	16	0	0	69	15	0	0
0.25	4	24	0	0	0	24	0	0	0

must also be made using these ideal residuals rather than the residuals generated during actual coding. This is done by storing the ideal residual energies for each block during the threshold determination and later retrieving these values to classify and then code the block.

The coding process is shown for a single residual component in Fig. 5.3.5 and again it should be understood that the same process is repeated for the row, column, and core residuals. First we code the boundaries using the previously computed ideal residual energies to switch in the appropriate set of quantizers and two 2-bit class identification codes are sent to the receiver which reconstructs the boundaries. Using the reconstructed boundaries the core is predicted and the residual coded with the appropriate quantizers again determined by the stored ideal energy value. A third 2-bit code informs the receiver which quantizers to use. This procedure is repeated for each block to adaptively code the image.

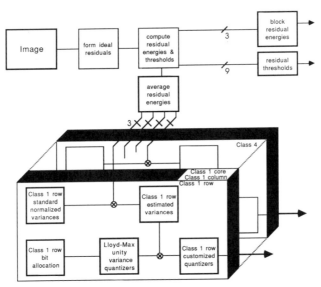

FIGURE 5.3.4. Setting up for adaptive RBC coding—computing the thresholds and customized quantizers for each component in each class.

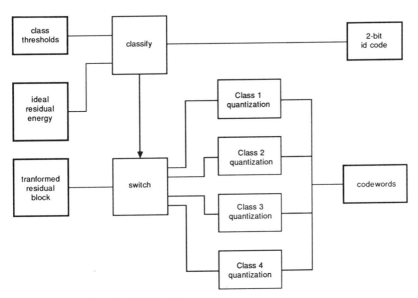

FIGURE 5.3.5. Adaptive RBC coding.

5.4   Coding Results

We would like to point out that there are not four distinct classes when coding at the low rates. In particular, as can be seen from Tables 5.2.3

and 5.3.3, classes 3 and 4 merge at 0.5 bits/pixel and, with the exception of DCT coding ensemble A, classes 2, 3, and 4 all become the same at 0.25 bits/pixel. This results in an effective misuse of bits, and at 0.25 bits/pixel since there are only two classes, class 1 and the rest, we are wasting one bit per block for DCT but 3 bits per block for RBC. This is a significant proportion of the available rate for RBC and at 0.25 bits/pixel we have (24, 0, 0, 0) bits for classes 1 through 4 with 4 bits for the corner and 6 bits for classification. If the 3 wasted bits were recouped then we could increase the allocation to (24, 4, 4, 4) for example.

We will now present results based on ensemble and individual design techniques.

Ensemble Design

The subjective evaluations for adaptive coding at rates of 0.25, 0.5, 1.0, and 1.5 bits/pixel are summarized in Tables 5.4.1(a) and (b) for ensembles A and B respectively and the MSE results are then given in Table 5.4.2. H-plots, drawn to the same scale as those in chapter four, are shown in Fig. 5.4.1 and examples of images from both ensembles, coded using adaptive RBC at 0.5 bits/pixel, are presented in Fig. 5.4.2.

Adaptive DCT provides good quality images at 1.5 and 1 bits/pixel in most cases. Exceptions to this rule in ensemble A are the baboon and stream images, where class 4 blocks are reconstructed as blocks of constant intensity which is highly objectionable. The buildings image has problems in the smooth background region where the blocks from different classes are clearly differentiable leading to visible contours along block boundaries. All of the images in ensemble B, except for the sailboat, are reproduced with good quality down to a rate of 1 bit/pixel. For all of the images from both ensembles, the subjective quality is at most fair when coded with the adaptive DCT at the lower rate of 0.5 bits/pixel.

Adaptive RBC coding of ensemble A produces good quality images at rates down to 1 bit/pixel (even 0.5 bits/pixel for the airplane). The baboon image provides problems as before but the reconstructed image is now blurred rather than blocky. Blurring occurs because the class 4 blocks are reconstructed as bilinear patches and the tile effect is absent because, unlike the constant intensity DCT blocks, the patches are at least continuous in their amplitude from block to block. The stream image loses some texture in the class 4 blocks but it is only noticeable in a side by side comparison with the original. At 0.5 bits/pixel the quality is always at least fair while the airplane and tiffany are judged as very good and good respectively.

When coding ensemble B, the performance obtained with adaptive RBC is considerable better than with DCT and the reconstructed images

TABLE 5.4.1(a). Adaptive coding results for ensemble A.

image	DCT	RBC
aerial	1.5, 1 bits — good, slight blocks 0.5 bits — blocky 0.25 bits — unacceptable	1.5, 1 bits — good, slight blurring 0.5 bits — blurred in smooth regions; but better than DCT 0.25 bits — unacceptable
airplane	1.5, 1 bits — very good 0.5 bits — slightly blocky 0.25 bits — blocky but usable	1.5, 1, 0.5 bits — very good 0.25 bits — patchy but usable
baboon	1.5, 1 bits — blocky 0.5 bits — very blocky 0.25 bits — unacceptable	1.5, 1 bits — good but loss of texture in fur at bottom of image 0.5 bits — patchy, but ok 0.25 bits — unacceptable
buildings	1.5 bits — good, but contours in the background 1 bit — class transitions clearly visible in the background 0.5 bits — extremely blocky 0.25 bits — unacceptable	1.5, 1 bits — good 0.5 bits — loss of detail 0.25 bits — unacceptable
couple	1.5, 1 bits — good, slight blocks 0.5 bits — very blocky 0.25 bits — unacceptable	1.5, 1 bits — very good 0.5 bits — patchy but ok 0.25 bits — unacceptable
stream	1.5, 1 bits — blocky 0.5 bits — very blocky 0.25 bits — unacceptable	1.5, 1 bits — good 0.5 bits — patchy 0.25 bits — unacceptable
tiffany	1.5, 1 bits — good, slight blocks 0.5, 0.25 bits — very blocky	1.5, 1 bits — very good 0.5 bits — good 0.25 bits — patchy

are subjectively equivalent to the originals at 1 bit/pixel in all cases and even at 0.5 bits/pixel for lynda, peppers, and splash. As the rate is lowered to 0.25 bits/pixel the quality drops to fair in most cases but is unacceptable for the sailboat.

Individual Design

We will now consider what performance improvement is possible if we allow more on-line computation so that we can compute the coefficient variances and design the bit maps for each image just prior to coding. The results are for adaptive DCT and RBC coding at a rate of 1 bit/pixel. However the rate would actually be slightly higher in this case since it is now required to transmit the bit maps and coefficient variances to the decoder, and we have not calculated this extra overhead component into the reported rate of 1 bit. Examples are shown in in Fig. 5.4.3 for the more difficult baboon, buildings, and stream images when coded using individual DCT and RBC designs at 1 bit/pixel. Note that the class 4 problems are still present and therefore not a result of the ensemble design.

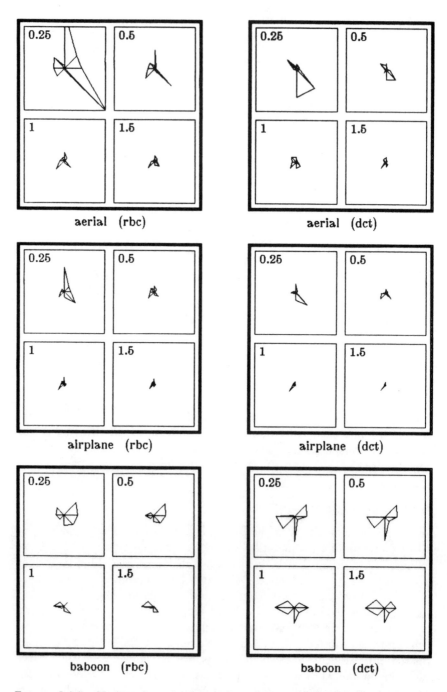

FIGURE 5.4.1. H-plots for adaptive coding at rates of 0.25, 0.5, 1, and 1.5 bits/pixel. RBC plots on the left; DCT plots on the right.

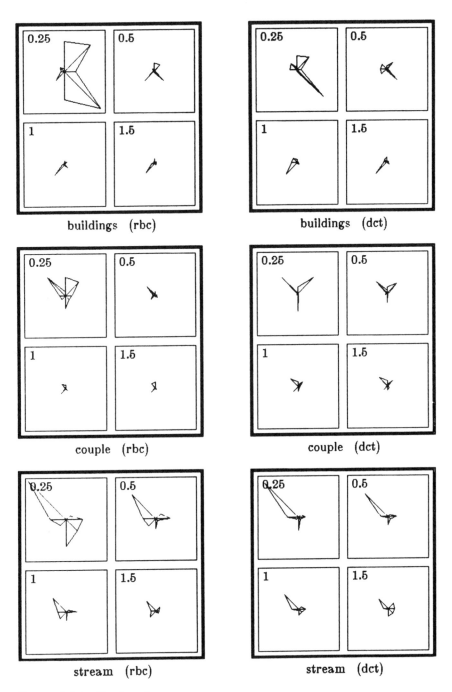

FIGURE 5.4.1. Continued.

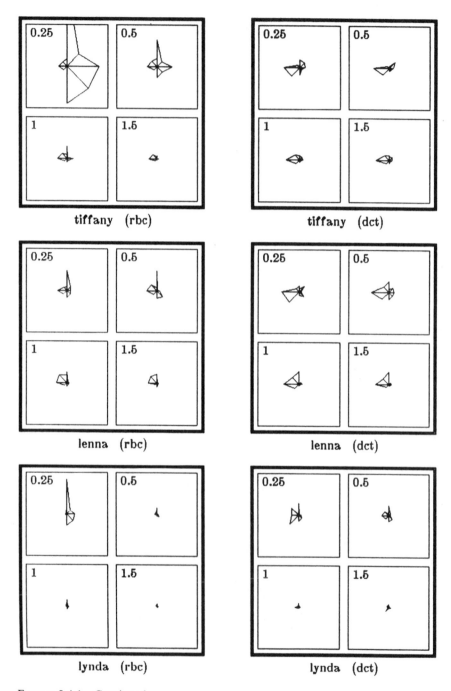

FIGURE 5.4.1. Continued.

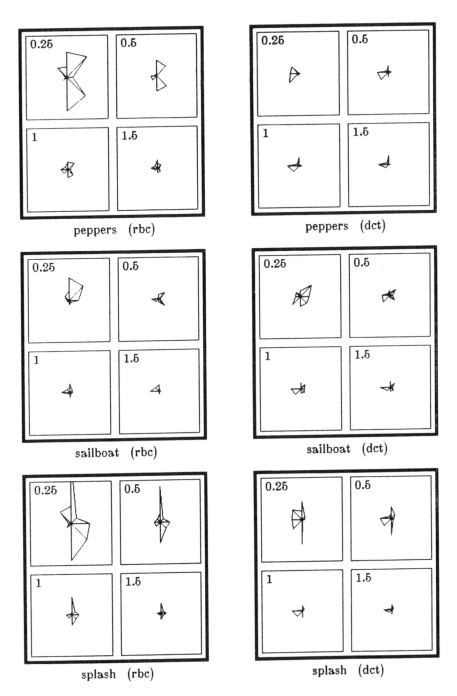

peppers (rbc)   peppers (dct)

sailboat (rbc)   sailboat (dct)

splash (rbc)   splash (dct)

FIGURE 5.4.1. Continued.

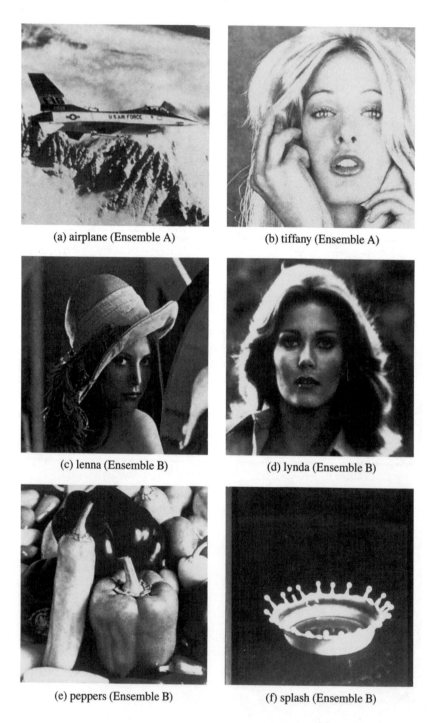

(a) airplane (Ensemble A)

(b) tiffany (Ensemble A)

(c) lenna (Ensemble B)

(d) lynda (Ensemble B)

(e) peppers (Ensemble B)

(f) splash (Ensemble B)

Fig. 5.4.2   Four class adaptive RBC coding results at 0.5 bits/pixel.

TABLE 5.4.1(b). Adaptive coding results for ensemble B.

image	DCT	RBC
lenna	1.5, 1 bits − good, slight blocks in shoulder and forehead 0.5 bits − very blocky 0.25 bits − unacceptable	1.5, 1 bits − perfect 0.5 bits − good, slight loss of detail 0.25 bits − patchy
lynda	1.5, 1 bits − very good, faint blocks in forehead 0.5 bits − very blocky 0.25 bits − unacceptable	1.5, 1, 0.5 bits − perfect 0.25 bits − patchy, but ok
peppers	1.5, 1 bits − good, slight blocks 0.5 bits − blocky 0.25 bits − unacceptable	1.5, 1, 0.5 bits − perfect 0.25 bits − patchy, but ok
sailboat	1.5, 1 bits − blocks in sky and lake 0.5 bits − very blocky 0.25 bits − unacceptable	1.5, 1 bits − very good 0.5 bits − patchy in lake and sky 0.25 bits − unacceptable
splash	1.5, 1 bits − perfect 0.5 bits − very faint blocks and noise in splash 0.25 bits − blocky	1.5, 1, 0.5 bits − perfect 0.25 bits − patchy, but ok

When DCT coding the A ensemble there is very little, if any, perceptible difference for the majority of the images. However, for the smooth images (airplane, tiffany) the results are actually worse because there are now more blocks visible, while buildings is visibly improved by the individual design because of a reduction in the noise level.

When we code the B ensemble with the DCT there is no perceptible difference except for lynda which is improved by the elimination of blocks on her forehead.

The individual designs for the images in ensemble A all lead to no active ac coefficients in class 4, so there is no change here and the observed differences are explained by comparing the bit maps for class 3. The ensemble design allocates 19 ac bits to class 3 at this rate, as shown in Table 5.2.3, while the airplane design leads to no active ac coefficients for class 3, and the tiffany design only allocates 4 bits to the ac coefficients in this class, and this leads to an increased visibility of individual blocks. The only improvement for ensemble B is when coding lynda and this is due to an increase from 0 to 22 in the available ac bits for class 4 which allows more possible patterns for these blocks and the *tile effect* disappears.

The extra flexibility, which is of only limited value for the DCT scheme, offers even less improvement for RBC coding. In particular, the only change for the A ensemble is a noise reduction for both the buildings image, although less so than with DCT coding, and the airplane but here the reduction is only marginal. When coding the B ensemble there is no noticeable improvement for any of the images.

TABLE 5.4.2. MSE and SNR′ figures for adaptive coding.

image	algorithm	MSE				SNR′			
		rate				rate			
		1.5	1.0	0.5	0.25	1.5	1.0	0.5	0.25
aerial	dct	33.2	63.4	159.7	295.3	32.9	30.1	26.1	23.4
	rbc	26.1	50.9	137.0	311.8	33.9	31.1	26.8	23.2
airplane	dct	10.2	18.3	44.5	112.9	38.0	35.5	31.7	27.6
	rbc	7.8	14.0	36.9	118.1	39.2	36.7	32.5	27.4
baboon	dct	108.3	190.0	375.5	567.2	27.8	25.3	22.4	20.6
	rbc	96.7	175.1	380.0	640.9	28.3	25.7	22.3	20.1
buildings	dct	22.2	37.3	95.8	239.4	34.7	32.4	28.3	24.3
	rbc	14.3	25.4	68.3	216.5	36.6	34.1	29.8	24.7
couple	dct	27.2	43.5	92.3	168.8	33.8	31.8	28.5	25.9
	rbc	26.4	42.5	87.0	178.7	33.9	31.9	28.8	25.6
stream	dct	58.4	96.1	190.9	290.8	30.5	28.3	25.3	23.5
	rbc	49.3	85.9	182.6	328.9	31.2	28.8	25.5	23.0
tiffany	dct	17.7	30.2	60.0	109.2	35.7	33.3	30.4	27.8
	rbc	13.6	23.4	49.4	103.3	36.9	34.4	31.3	28.0

(a) Ensemble A

image	algorithm	MSE				SNR′			
		rate				rate			
		1.5	1.0	0.5	0.25	1.5	1.0	0.5	0.25
lenna	dct	11.6	19.2	40.9	91.9	37.5	35.3	32.0	28.5
	rbc	10.1	16.3	35.2	91.8	38.1	36.0	32.6	28.5
lynda	dct	3.9	4.8	11.2	33.4	42.2	41.3	37.7	32.9
	rbc	1.6	2.4	5.4	18.3	46.1	44.2	40.9	35.5
peppers	dct	15.1	25.2	50.3	115.5	36.3	34.1	31.1	27.5
	rbc	13.5	22.4	45.9	113.9	36.8	34.6	31.5	27.6
sailboat	dct	28.7	52.0	112.4	256.0	33.6	31.0	27.6	24.1
	rbc	27.7	48.3	106.7	246.0	33.8	31.3	27.8	24.3
splash	dct	7.9	12.7	26.6	60.7	39.2	37.1	33.9	30.3
	rbc	6.2	10.4	21.6	58.4	40.3	38.0	34.8	30.5

(b) Ensemble B

There is always an improvement in the MSE even though the subjective results are sometimes better, sometimes worse, but usually the same. This is shown in Table 5.4.3 as SNR′ improvements for the individual design over the ensemble design.

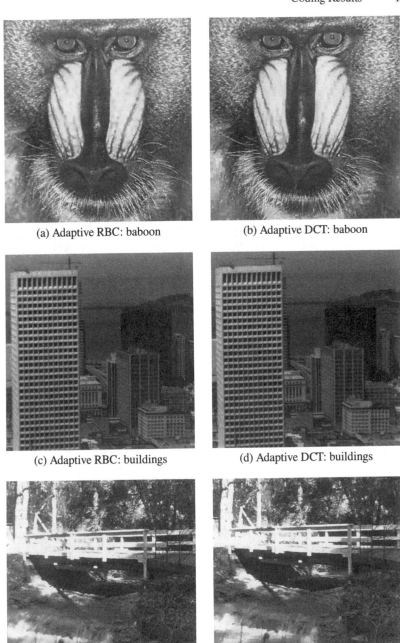

(a) Adaptive RBC: baboon

(b) Adaptive DCT: baboon

(c) Adaptive RBC: buildings

(d) Adaptive DCT: buildings

(e) Adaptive RBC: stream

(f) Adaptive DCT: stream

Fig. 5.4.3   Even when using the individual design there are class four problems
with adaptive coding at 1 bit/pixel.

TABLE 5.4.3. SNR′ improvements (dB) for the individual design at 1 bit/pixel.

image	DCT	RBC	image	DCT	RBC
aerial	0.3	0.2	airplane	1.9	1.2
baboon	0.7	0.5	buildings	4.8	3.7
couple	0.5	0.7	stream	0.3	0.3
tiffany	1.0	0.7	lenna	0.5	0.4
lynda	3.8	1.8	peppers	0.6	0.5
sailboat	0.2	0.2	splash	0.6	0.4

5.5   Conclusions

We have shown that the RBC results are improved when we allow adaptation. That is, at a given rate, the image quality is superior to that obtained using zonal RBC and the *tile effect* is still not visible. For DCT, the adaptively coded results are sometimes better in terms of overall fidelity but the block structured artifacts remain. This is to be expected since there has been no fundamental change in the coding technique which addresses this problem. In fact, the artifact is sometimes worse as can be seen with the buildings image where the background contains clusters of class 3 and class 4 blocks which are clearly identifiable when coded at 1 bit/pixel. Here adjacent blocks from different classes are intentionally coded differently and the *tile effect* is enhanced because the blocks are clustered and provide a much larger effective block size leading to a clear boundary between the two regions.

The RBC results for ensemble B are excellent, however, some of the ensemble A images suffer from perceptible blurring within class 4 blocks. If we study the distribution of bits between the four classes presented in Table 5.3.3 we see that, even at the highest rate of 1.5 bits/pixel, class 4 is allocated no bits. As seen in Table 5.2.3, the same is true for DCT coding. For DCT coding this means that the smooth regions belonging to class 4 are reconstructed as blocks of constant intensity which makes the individual blocks clearly visible in all but the smoothest regions. This problem is less marked with adaptive RBC because if a class 4 core has boundaries from other classes then the prediction, which is also the reconstruction in this case, might be acceptable and at worst even when surrounded by class 4 boundaries these regions are reproduced as a series of bilinear patches which are still continuous from block to block. Consequently the blocks from class 4 are reproduced as smooth surfaces which may be appropriate in many cases and not produce any noticeable artifacts. However, if the class 4 blocks contain any texture, for example with the baboon and stream, then this will amount to blurring of the image and the texture in these blocks will be lost. We will now investigate the bit allocations in more detail and suggest how to avoid this class 4 problem.

If we compare our bit allocations with those reported by Chen [51] and Clarke [75, pp. 197-202], who also uses Chen's technique but with different images, we see that their distribution of bits between the various classes is markedly different from ours and this is most clearly seen when comparing the allocations for class 4. Chen uses a block size of 16 while we have presented results for a block size of 8, but when we apply our design technique to this larger block size there are still very few bits allocated to the fourth class. In particular, at a rate of 1 bit/pixel an ensemble design with $N = 16$ produces an ac bit distribution of (503, 334, 149, 3) for ensemble A which is considerably different from Chen's (366, 341, 212, 51) for an aerial image which would be classified as an A ensemble image. The ensemble B ac allocation is (452, 354, 193, 0) which is unlike Clarke's (381, 281, 184, 104) for a head and shoulders image which is a typical ensemble B image.

This discrepancy is attributable to the different assumptions made in deriving the bit allocation. Chen assumes a Gaussian distribution for the ac coefficients and uses the allocation formula (3.3.13) based on an approximation to the Lloyd-Max rd function for a Gaussian variable first proposed by Huang and Schultheiss [46]. It is interesting to note that this is exactly the theoretical Shannon bit allocation (3.3.9) assuming that θ is sufficiently small so that $n_k = \frac{1}{2}\log_2\frac{\sigma_k^2}{\theta}$. As we have already discussed, the Shannon bit allocation tends to produce an allocation with a

TABLE 5.5.1. Design and achieved MSE values at 1 bit/pixel, $N = 8$.

image	design MSE	class MSE				average MSE
		Class 1	Class 2	Class 3	Class 4	
aerial	66.5	66.6	67.1	66.3	35.3	58.8
airplane	15.5	15.7	15.5	12.8	3.3	11.8
baboon	194.1	186.4	187.6	189.1	88.8	163.0
buildings	13.8	14.0	13.9	14.8	6.8	12.4
couple	34.7	67.2	37.5	36.0	14.6	38.8
stream	93.9	91.7	90.0	92.0	87.3	90.2
tiffany	25.8	30.2	27.0	25.9	12.9	24.0

(a) Ensemble A

image	design MSE	class MSE				average MSE
		Class 1	Class 2	Class 3	Class 4	
lenna	17.8	19.2	18.6	17.9	12.0	16.9
lynda	1.5	2.2	2.1	1.9	1.9	2.0
peppers	24.6	26.3	24.0	24.2	12.9	21.8
sailboat	60.9	59.7	58.4	61.5	19.0	49.6
splash	10.8	13.3	10.5	10.8	9.7	11.0

(b) Ensemble B

large proportion of 1-bit quantizers and the majority of the bits assigned to class 4 by Chen are indeed for 1-bit quantizers. In contrast, we used the practical Lloyd-Max quantizer rd function and assumed a Laplacian pdf for the ac coefficients. To verify the correctness of our design we compared the distortion level predicted by the design with the values achieved by actual coding using the individual design at 1 bit/pixel with $N = 8$ and the results are listed in Table 5.5.1. It should be noted that the design MSE only refers to the error in those classes which are allocated any bits. In other words, if the ac energy of a particular class is less than the design MSE then no bits are allocated, the ac transform coefficients are set to zero and the MSE for this class will simply be equal to the ac energy for this class. For all of the images except lynda the design produces no bits for class 4 at an average rate of 1 bit/pixel with $N = 8$. This explains why the average MSE is less than the design MSE but if we compare the individual class MSE values then it is seen that there is very good agreement between the design MSE and the individual error levels for classes 1, 2, and 3 (and also 4 for lynda). This shows that the bit allocations are consistent with our design goal of equal distortion in each class. It also indicates that using the Lloyd-Max quantizer distortion function and modeling the ac coefficients as having Laplacian pdf's provides an accurate model for the practical performance curve for transform coding at the design stage without actually coding the image.

So we have shown that we did achieve our design goal with class 4 distortion actually being less than average even when allocated no bits. Chen's design criterion was also equal class distortion but he actually obtained non-equal class distortions because of invalid assumptions in the design process but this provided better results than we achieved using 4 class adaptive DCT coding. It should be stressed however that the blocking problem is still present with Chen's design.

Future Work

We have shown that equal distortion for each class is an inferior design criterion. Consequently we now suggest a modification to the pure MSE design to allow for the psychovisual property that we are more sensitive to distortion in smooth regions than we are in high activity regions. That is we modify the design to produce a class dependent distortion which decreases for the smoother classes. Our design is readily adapted to crudely model the human visual system in this way by weighting the performance curve for each class before combining them and this modified overall characteristic is then used to derive the individual bit rates for each class as before. The weighting function would increase the class 4 curve relative to the class 1 curve and would be determined experimentally but would be of the form (1.0, w(2), w(3), w(4)) where the weights would be larger than one in general. In this way, bits would be redistributed from the higher activity blocks to the lower activity classes.

Further work should be able to provide simplifications which still maintain the improved RBC performance. One possibility would be to only classify the boundaries based on the observation that zonal RBC coding produced a distinct texture, which was actually visible boundaries, as the rate was lowered. Coding the boundaries more accurately may be sufficient to remove this texture which we have eliminated using the fully adaptive scheme here.

If we allow the rate to vary from image to image, then fixing the class transition thresholds, in addition to the allocations, for each ensemble would greatly simplify the coding process. It would also have the advantage of not forcing equal occupation levels. This would allow higher fidelity for the baboon which doesn't intrinsically contain any class 4 blocks as they are defined here for ensemble A.

6

Adaptive Coding Based on Quad Tree Segmentation

6.1   Introduction

In the last chapter we saw one adaptive coding method which classifies each block and then, depending on which class the block belongs to, uses an appropriate set of quantizers. In this and the following chapter we will discuss a second adaptation technique which varies the block size, rather than the quantizers, according to image activity. In this way it will be possible to ensure that the prediction is only made over regions which are relatively smooth and so avoid the large prediction errors which can occur when a block contains a sharp edge. This will then provide a residual which will be a much better candidate for a stationary source. In section 6.2 we will discuss adaptive segmentation in general, and then in section 6.3 we will describe the specific quad tree approach which leads to unequal block sizes. We will complete the segmentation topic in section 6.4 with ways to minimize the overhead incurred by the adaptivity, and in section 6.5 we will discuss modifications to the reconstruction made possible because of the unequal block sizes. We will then turn, in section 6.6, to the second half of the algorithm—coding the residual, and conclude with some results in section 6.7 and conclusions in section 6.8.

Early results from this chapter were presented in [76] and [77].

6.2   Adaptive Segmentation

In traditional RBC, we segment the image into overlapping blocks of a fixed size, and then use the overlapped boundaries to predict the rest of the image and block code the resulting residual using the DST. The RBC theory assumes that the input sequence is stationary, although this is clearly not the case when a block contains an edge. In practice this means that the residual image has a small amplitude except where there are edges, and then the residual takes on large positive and negative values. The residual is easier to code than the original image but it would be even more so if these large transitions could be avoided.

One way to improve the prediction and give a smoother residual, is to segment the image into suitable smooth regions depending on the image content rather than a regular matrix of fixed size blocks. This improved prediction is available at some cost however, since the segmentation itself must now be transmitted or stored for the decoder.

We could adaptively segment the image along arbitrary contours obtained from some edge detection scheme which guarantees closed contours, but this has a high overhead since we must now code a general edge map in addition to the data samples necessary to form the prediction. Alternatively we could constrain the geometric form of our regions and then describe the segmentation in terms of a few parameters such as size and perhaps shape which would require a lower data rate. However, the edge map segmentation may require much fewer data samples than the constrained method to obtain a good prediction, thus outweighing the higher segmentation overhead. At this time we do not know which approach would lead to the more efficient coding technique and in this work we chose to constrain the regions to be variable size squares generated via quad tree segmentation.

6.3   The Quad Tree Approach

Quad tree segmentation is achieved by associating the whole image with the root of a tree and then quartering the image to form four equal sized subimages which are then associated with the four child nodes in the *quad tree*, as shown in Fig. 6.3.1. The decision whether or not to subdivide is based on some uniformity criterion and typically, when used to segment a binary image, this is simply whether the block is constant containing pixels only from the object (black) or the background (white). If the uniformity criterion is not met, then the block is subdivided and by repeating this process as necessary we will finally be left with a series of unequal size blocks which are all uniform. An example is shown in Fig. 6.3.2 where (a) shows the original binary image, (b) shows the segmented image, and (c) shows the corresponding quad tree.

We have just described the classical quad tree segmentation technique used in computer graphics [78, p. 105] where the size of the original image and all of the segmented blocks is a power of 2 and, if necessary, the process can be continued down to the *pixel level* when blocks contain only a single pixel. The quad tree segmentation required for RBC differs in two ways. Firstly, we are interested in the uniformity of the residual rather than the original image and secondly, when subdividing we need

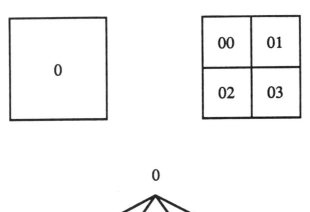

FIGURE 6.3.1. Quad tree representation.

to generate overlapping blocks with common boundaries which can then be used for prediction as before.

Residual

During segmentation we must first form the residual for the block under consideration and then measure the uniformity of this residual to decide whether or not to subdivide further.

Overlapping Blocks

To generate overlapping blocks we must modify the original algorithm and use an original square image with sides of size $2^n + 1$ which can then be subdivided into four overlapping blocks whose size is also a power of 2 plus 1, as shown in Fig. 6.3.3.

We are very accustomed to thinking in terms of powers of two and the sequence: 16, 8, 4, 2, 1 seems very natural. In comparison: 17, 9, 5, 3, 2 is not such an obvious progression and so we will still refer to the block size as being 2^n although in actuality this corresponds to an overlapped block of size $2^n + 1$. The smallest block size which maintains the overlapping is 2 (3) and any further subdivision leads directly to the pixel level. Consequently for Fig. 6.3.3 the possible block sizes are: 16, 8, 4, 2, and 1.

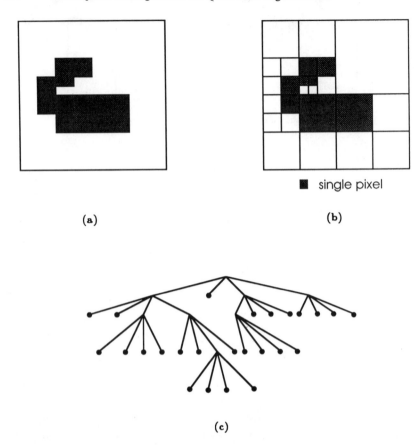

FIGURE 6.3.2. Example of quad tree segmentation: (a) highly magnified sub image; (b) segmented image; (c) corresponding quad tree.

Predictor

Since we must predict the core at each subdivision there will be many predictions per pixel, on the average, and so to limit the complexity we use the simple bilinear predictor. As discussed in chapter two, this prediction is worse than the statistical predictor prescribed by RBC theory [24] and given in equation (2.10.4), but since we are allowing a variable block size, then it should be good enough after subdivision when the block is sufficiently predictable. This means that the data samples needed to form the prediction are simply the shared corner points shown in black in Fig. 6.3.3.

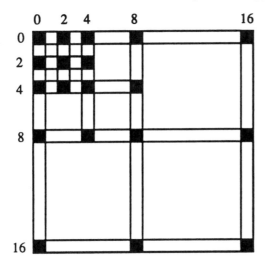

FIGURE 6.3.3. Overlapping blocks.

Uniformity

The unformity criterion involves a threshold since it is impractical to sub-divide a gray scale image until the residual is zero as in the simple binary case discussed above since for many practical images this would result in subdividing the vast majority of the image down to the pixel level. There is no unique uniformity measure and two possibilities are: the maximum absolute value, and the mean energy of the block residual, which we could then compare against some threshold. The magnitude measure involves less computation but is more susceptible to noise while the more complex energy measure is more robust and will not trigger subdivision in response to a single noise spike. In this study we have used the mean residual energy as the uniformity measure.

Mean Residual Energy

To compute the mean residual energy we first form the bilinear predic-tion for the block of size $N(=2^n)$ using the four corner points. We sub-tract the prediction to give the residual $y(i,j)$ where $i,j = 0,...,N$. Ignor-ing the four corner points we compute the mean residual energy as

$$E[y^2(i,j)] = \frac{\sum y^2(i,j)}{(N+1)^2 - 4}. \tag{6.3.1}$$

If the mean residual energy is less than some threshold then the block is uniform according to this criterion.

Unfortunately, even with this simple predictor, it is not possible to use the energy measures for each of the sibling blocks to compute the residual energy for the parent block as we could in the classic case and we must compute the energy directly each time a uniformity decision must be made.

Segmentation

Conceptually we could assign the whole image to the root of the tree and investigate its uniformity, dividing the image into four pieces to generate the next level of the quad tree if it is not uniform. Each of these pieces would then be examined and subdivided as necessary until the image has been segmented into a series of blocks which are all uniform according to the chosen criterion: uniformity measure and threshold.

However we first subdivide the image to some fixed block size to avoid the unnecessary computations which would be required to typically subdivide five or six times to get to the average final block size and, as we shall see later, this also reduces the overhead required to encode the segmentation. We then examine blocks with the same parent in the tree and test for uniformity of the parent block. Where possible we merge the four children and replace them by their parent. We repeat this process until the whole image has been merged into a single block or there are no more candidate blocks to merge and then we complete the segmentation by examining any blocks that were not merged. We continue to subdivide these blocks until we have met the uniformity criterion for each block, or some minimum block size, which could be the pixel level, has been reached. This is Algorithm 6.3.1 which is described in more detail in section 6.4 during the discussion on how to code the segmentation.

Choosing the Segmentation Parameters

The uniformity threshold τ, controls the quality of the predicted image directly since assuming that we allow subdivision to continue right to the pixel level we are guaranteed that the residual energy, or prediction MSE, will be at most τ. However as τ is made smaller then the number of data points needed for the prediction increases rapidly as more regions subdivide to the pixel level. The choice of the threshold value depends on whether we will encode the residual or simply use the prediction as our final image. If we are to code the residual then a relatively high threshold will be appropriate so that the prediction rate is kept low and only the high contrast edges are preserved in the prediction with the low amplitude texture passing to the residual. For a given threshold value τ, the prediction reduces the MSE to τ and then the residual coder reduces the MSE from τ to the final value. To determine the optimal threshold from a MS standpoint, we should calculate the rd function for the residual image, add the prediction rate and plot this characteristic for various threshold values. We have not yet discussed how we will code the

ALGORITHM 6.3.1. Quad Tree Segmentation.

Algorithm 6.3.1

(1) segment the image to the initial level
 	
(2) **while**(there are candidate blocks to merge)
begin
 	
     (3) **if**(parent block is uniform) **then** merge(4 children)
 	
     (4) **else** mark 4 children to prevent further merge attempts
 	
end
 	
(5) **while**(there are blocks to split)
begin
 	
     (6) **if**(block size > minimum size **and** the block is not uniform) **then** split(block)
 	
     (7) **else** mark this block to avoid further split attempts
 	
end

residual but assuming a transform coder, say, then these plots could be derived. This discussion will be continued in section 6.6 after we have presented the residual coder.

A second parameter which controls the prediction data rate is the minimum allowable block size. This has a marked effect since allowing subdivision to the pixel level is potentially very costly leading to the generation of many data points, each requiring PCM coding. By limiting the minimum size we control the data rate but at some cost. The problem comes when a block subdivision is not allowed because of the minimum block size constraint although the residual energy exceeds the threshold. For a reasonable threshold, these blocks will contain edges and when we interpolate across an edge, as shown in Fig. 6.3.4 for a minimum block size of 2, this will cause blurring at a vertical (or horizontal) edge but will be worse for a diagonal edge leading to a staircase effect. In addition to the staircase in the prediction, the residual is difficult to code in a zonal scheme since it now contains the same diagonal edge at an amplitude which is still 75% of the original and contains high frequency transform coefficients. As a result, this staircase remains until the residual rate becomes sufficiently large that the high frequency coefficients along the diagonal are transmitted and then the savings in the prediction rate is more than offset by the increased rate needed to code the residual so that the final image has acceptable quality.

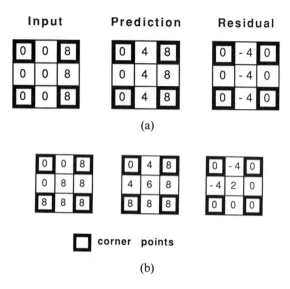

FIGURE 6.3.4. Interpolation across an edge: (a) vertical edge; (b) diagonal edge.

The final parameter which controls the prediction data rate is the number of bits used to PCM code the data points and we have used five bits in this work based on our earlier conclusions in chapter four that at least four bits must be used for the corner points to avoid them being clearly discernible. This allows us to reduce the prediction data rate by a factor of 8/5 with no noticeable degradation.

6.4 Coding the Segmentation

We must encode the quad tree segmentation so that the receiver will be able to locate the corner points which are transmitted by raster scanning the input image and sending each point as it is encountered. This could be done by sending the leaf node labels, e.g. 0013, but this is redundant and if we specify a search order for the tree then the level of each leaf node is sufficient to construct the segmentation as shown in the detailed example of Fig. 6.4.1. This means that for a tree with up to 8 levels to allow block sizes 1,2,...,128 would require a 3-bit code per block. We could exploit the correlation in block size of neighboring blocks and use a differential technique but this would require a variable length Huffman [79, 80] coder.

Alternatively we could use an algorithmic approach and transmit the *split-and-merge* information and let the decoder reconstruct the segmentation given the initial block size, the image size and the minimum allowed block size. The decoder does not have to make all of the

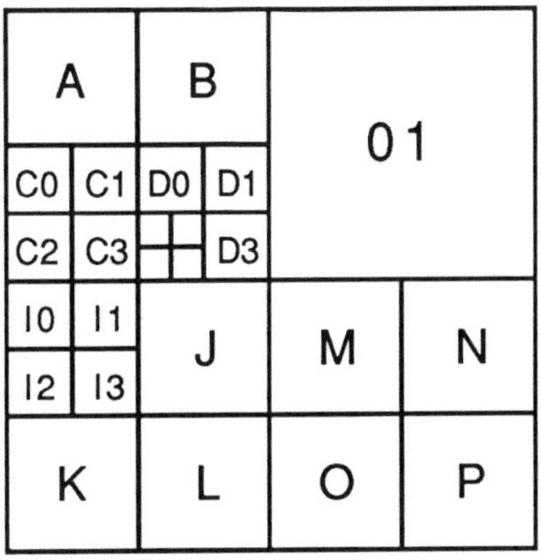

symbol	label	level	change
A	000	2	-
B	001	2	0
C0	0020	3	1
C1	0021	3	0
C2	0022	3	0
C3	0023	3	0
D0	0030	3	0
D1	0031	3	0
	00320	4	1
	00321	4	0
	00322	4	0
	00323	4	0
D3	0033	3	- 1
	01	1	- 2
I0	0200	3	2
I1	0201	3	0
I2	0202	3	0
I3	0203	3	0
J	021	2	- 1
K	022	2	0
L	023	2	0
M	030	2	0
N	031	2	0
O	032	2	0
P	033	2	0

FIGURE 6.4.1. Different ways to code a quad tree segmentation: label, level, and change in level.

predictions that were necessary during the segmentation but rather builds the segmentation map from the transmitted information so that it knows the location of the corner points that will be transmitted. In this way the overhead is reduced since we only need to transmit one bit for each attempted split or merge operation with a 1 signifying that the split or merge was carried out and a 0 otherwise.

As the segmentation is being built, both at the encoder and decoder, a number of rules must be used to decide which blocks are candidates to be merged, and then which should be considered for splitting. It is then possible to send a series of 1s and 0s to represent the whole segmentation process without any need to send an *end of merge* message since the decoder will know when it has finished merging and should start splitting. To illustrate this technique we will now describe, in Fig. 6.4.2, the example from Fig. 6.4.1.

000 A	001 B	010 E	011 F
002 C	003 D	012 G	013 H
020 I	021 J	030 M	031 N
022 K	023 L	032 O	033 P

(a)

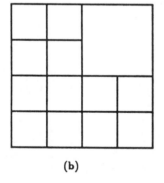

(b)

A	B	\multicolumn 01	
CO	C1	D0	D1
C2	C3		D3
I0 I1 I2 I3		J	M	N
K	L	O	P

(c)

FIGURE 6.4.2. Split and merge codes: (a) initial segmentation; (b) after merging: 0, 1, 0, 0; (c) after splitting: (A)0, (B)0, (C)1, 0, 0, 0, 0, (D)1, 0, 0, (D2)1, (D3)0, (I)1, 0, 0, 0, 0, (J)0, (K)0, (L)0, (M)0, (N)0, (O)0, (P)0. Note that the split codes are simply the 1s and 0s while the letters in ( ) are used to locate the position where the split test was made and the code generated.

Generating Split and Merge Information

For this small example we have chosen an image whose size is 17 x 17 so that the image block size is 16 (it should always be understood that the number of pixels is actually one more but we will continue to use the binary numbers to refer to the block size), and we intend to start with a block size of 4 and subdivide down to the pixel level. These three numbers: 16, 4, 1 must be transmitted to the decoder in addition to the split and merge information. We will now discuss in detail how to generate the split and merge information.

Split and Merge Bits for Fig. 6.4.2

(a)   Subdivide down to fixed 4×4 blocks.

(b)   Examine the uniformity of the first group of four siblings: 000, 001, 002, and 003 marked A, B, C, and D in Fig. 6.4.2(a).

(c)   Not uniform so do not merge—0.

(d)   Move to the next group of siblings: E, F, G, and H which are uniform so merge—1.

(e)   Repeat for I, J, K, and L which are not uniform—0.

(f)   M, N, O, and P are also not uniform—0.

(g)   This leads us to the segmentation in Fig. 6.4.2(b) and at this stage there are no more candidate blocks to merge since there are not four sibling 8×8 blocks and so we now turn to splitting. Notice that the decoder is also able to make this decision and no *end of merge* message is required.

(h)   Examine the uniformity of A, it is uniform so do not split—0.

(i)   Similarly for B—0.

(j)   C is not uniform so split to give C0, C1, C2, and C3—1.

(k)   We now continue down the tree and examine C0, C1, C2, and C3 and any of their children should they be split before moving to D.

(l)   C0 is uniform—0.

(m)   Similarly for C1, C2, and C3—0,0,0.

(n)   D is split—1.

(o)   D0 and D1 are uniform—0,0.

(p)   D2 is split—1.

(q) The children of D2 are single pixels and so the splitting stops and we move to D3. This decision can also be made at the decoder without any additional code words being sent and in general the splitting would stop at the minimum block size which is one of the three segmentation parameters and could be greater than 1.

(r) D3 is uniform—0.

(s) 01 is a merged block and so we do not even consider it during the split stage.

(t) We then split I—1.

(u) The four children I0, I1, I2, and I3 are all uniform—0,0,0,0.

(v) The remaining blocks J, K, L, M, N, O, and P are all uniform—0,0,0,0,0,0,0.

(w) The segmentation is now complete and is shown in Fig. 6.4.2(c).

This example shows most of the possibilities which could arise during segmentation however it does not illustrate the case when there are multiple merges at different block sizes. The order that we use for attempting the merges is to first perform all of the merges which are possible with blocks of size N say. We then repeat the process and merge all blocks of size $2N$ where possible and continue until there are no more candidate blocks to merge or the block size has reached the image size.

Note that we traverse the tree differently for the merge and split steps. During the merge we do a breadth first traversal and iterate upwards until there are no more blocks to merge while the split stage employs a depth first traversal.

For this segmentation there are 28 attempted split and merge operations resulting in an overhead of 28 bits while the direct technique of sending the level for each leaf node (block) requires $25 \times 3 = 75$ bits.

For a more typical segmentation of the 513×513 image lenna at a threshold of 512 with a minimum block size of 1 which results in 9613 blocks and 9680 attempted splits and merges the labeling technique would require $(9613 \times 3)/513^2 = 0.11$ bits per pixel while the algorithmic approach needs only $9680/513^2 = 0.037$ bits per pixel—a threefold reduction.

Prediction Rate

The complete prediction rate consists of the segmentation parameters, the split and merge information and the quantized corner points. The segmentation parameters are the image size, initial block size, and minimum block size, which together constitute a minimal overhead and will be ignored. The split and merge rate is simply the number of attempted split and merge operations divided by the number of pixels, and the data rate for the corner points is the number of such points times the number of bits used to code them also divided by the number of pixels. Mathematically the prediction rate is

$$rate_{pred} = \frac{sam + (q \times n_{cnr})}{N^2} \qquad (6.4.1)$$

where *sam* is the number of split and merge attempts, q is the number of bits used to code the n_{cnr} corner points, and N is the size of the square image. For the lenna example used above $sam = 9680$, $n_{cnr} = 12446$, $q = 5$, and so

$$rate_{pred} = \frac{9680 + (5 \times 12446)}{513^2} = 0.273 \text{ bits/pixel.}$$

6.5   Reconstruction

During reconstruction the transmitted 5 bit PCM coded data points are used to form the boundary response although, for simplicity, the initial segmentation was based on perfect corner points.

If all neighboring blocks are of equal size then each corner point is shared by four adjacent blocks and we use these points to form a bilinear interpolation for each block. However, there are many blocks whose neighbors are either larger or smaller as shown in Fig. 6.4.1. This means that for the larger blocks, in addition to the four corner points there are a number of additional boundary points present, located at the corners of smaller adjacent blocks. It is clearly advantageous to make use of these additional points when reconstructing the block.

We will first describe a fast technique for evaluating the bilinear prediction and then modify this algorithm to include these extra boundary points.

Fast Linear Interpolation for N a Power of 2

Linear interpolation over $N+1$ samples, where N is a power of two, can be implemented by a subdivision technique. The linear interpolation problem is split into two similar problems but with half the number of points: 0 to $\frac{N}{2}$ and $\frac{N}{2}$ to N. This requires the evaluation of the new endpoint $x(\frac{N}{2})$, which is simply the average of the two original endpoints $x(0)$ and $x(N)$. Mathematically we have

$$x(k) = \frac{(N-k)x(0) + k\,x(N)}{N} ; \quad k = 0,...,N \qquad (6.5.1)$$

so

$$x\left(\frac{N}{2}\right) = \frac{x(0) + x(N)}{2} \tag{6.5.2}$$

and manipulating (6.5.1) we obtain

$$x(k) = \frac{\left(\frac{N}{2} - k\right)x(0) + k\, x\left(\frac{N}{2}\right)}{\frac{N}{2}} \; ; \quad k = 0, \ldots, \frac{N}{2} \tag{6.5.3}$$

and

$$x\left(\frac{N}{2} + k\right) = \frac{\left(\frac{N}{2} - k\right)x\left(\frac{N}{2}\right) + k\, x(N)}{\frac{N}{2}} \; ; \quad k = 0, \ldots, \frac{N}{2}. \tag{6.5.4}$$

This is then repeated for the two smaller blocks until all of the pixel values have been determined. Since each subdivision only requires the average of two values this provides a fast implementation for the interpolation which only involves shift and add operations.

Fast Bilinear Interpolation

Bilinear interpolation is a separable operation that can be achieved by linear interpolation in each direction so it can also be evaluated via the fast subdivision algorithm.

The bilinear interpolation equation for the diagram in Fig. 6.5.1 is

$$x(i,j) = \frac{A(N-i)(N-j) + B(N-i)j + Ci(N-j) + Dij}{N^2} \tag{6.5.5}$$

which can be re-written as

$$x(i,j) = \frac{(N-i)\left\{\dfrac{A(N-j) + Bj}{N}\right\} + i\left\{\dfrac{C(N-j) + Dj}{N}\right\}}{N}$$

$$= \frac{(N-i)\,x(0,j) + i\,x(N,j)}{N} \tag{6.5.6}$$

which shows that the bilinear interpolation is separable and can be achieved by first interpolating horizontally to get the values for the jth column: $x(0,j)$ and $x(N,j)$, and then linearly interpolating these values vertically to get $x(i,j)$.

Consequently the problem of bilinearly predicting the block ABCD is subdivided into four similar problems, each of one quarter the area,

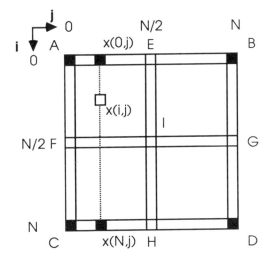

FIGURE 6.5.1. Bilinear interpolation.

namely predicting: AEFI, EBIG, FICH, and IGHD after we have evaluated the values at the midpoints: E, F, G, H, and I as

horizontal: $E = \dfrac{A+B}{2}; \quad H = \dfrac{C+D}{2}$

vertical: $F = \dfrac{A+C}{2}; \quad I = \dfrac{E+H}{2}; \quad G = \dfrac{B+D}{2}.$ (6.5.7)

The center point I can actually be written in many equivalent ways, viz.,

$$I = \frac{E+H}{2} = \frac{A+B+C+D}{4} = \frac{E+F+G+H}{4} = \frac{F+G}{2}. \quad (6.5.8)$$

Modified Interpolation

To account for the extra boundary points, Algorithm 6.5.1 modifies the subdivision algorithm so that the midpoints E, F, G, H, and I are only evaluated if they are not already known. This straightforward modification uses all of the available data points to improve the prediction over standard bilinear interpolation and is illustrated step by step in Fig. 6.5.2 for the example in Fig. 6.4.1.

Of the many ways to compute I we choose

$$I = \frac{E+F+G+H}{4} \quad (6.5.9)$$

since if a large block has smaller neighbors, then one or more of E,F,G,H will contain accurate data which will then be used in the

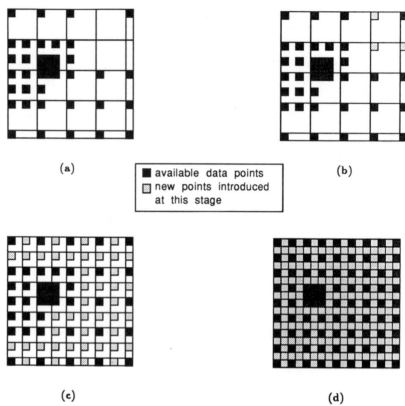

FIGURE 6.5.2. Example of the modified interpolation: (a) original corner points, maximum block size = 8; (b) spacing = 8; (c) spacing = 4; (d) spacing = 2;

prediction of I. If all adjacent blocks are the same size or larger than this block, all forms of evaluation will be equivalent.

Examples of Reconstructed Images

The twelve images from the two ensembles were reconstructed, using this modified interpolation, from segmentations made at six thresholds: 64, 128, 256, 512, 1024, and 2048. The images were then viewed by starting with the best image ($\tau = 64$) and raising the threshold until the image was considered to just still be a good reconstruction of the original. At this threshold value, the major difference between the reconstructed image and the original is the loss of low amplitude texture and so the image now looks somewhat cleaner or smoother in these areas but the edges are preserved and so the image is still *essentially the same*.

As the threshold is raised, more and more texture is lost but the dominant edges are still preserved and the original image can still be

ALGORITHM 6.5.1. Reconstruction After Quad Tree Segmentation.

Algorithm 6.5.1

(1) Using split and merge information, construct the segmentation and record the maximum block size, *max_size* [8 in Fig. 6.5.2(a)].

(2) Set the pixel intensity at the corner points using the transmitted prediction data as shown in Fig. 6.5.2(a).

(3) Set the *spacing* to be *max_size*

(4) **while**(*spacing* > 1)

begin

   (5) consider all pixels at this *spacing* and execute steps 6-10. (Each set of four pixels constitute a hypothetical block with corner values A,B,C,D which have been determined from transmitted data or the previous iteration.)

   (6) **if**(E has not been set) **then** set
   $$E = \frac{A+B}{2}.$$

   (7) **if**(F has not been set) **then** set
   $$F = \frac{A+C}{2}.$$

   (8) **if**(G has not been set) **then** set
   $$G = \frac{B+D}{2}.$$

   (9) **if**(H has not been set) **then** set
   $$H = \frac{C+D}{2}.$$

   (10) **if**(I has not been set) **then** set
   $$I = \frac{E+F+G+H}{4}.$$

   (11) *spacing* ← *spacing*/2

end

recognized from these major features. However, there comes a point at which the reconstruction no longer maintains the characteristic image features and the threshold level just below this corresponds to a *just acceptable* image. Such an image may be useful in applications where the goal is to differentiate images using a low rate reconstruction such as recognizing a person's face. The threshold values, corresponding rate,

TABLE 6.5.1. Limits for acceptable images from the prediction alone.

image	essentially the same			just acceptable		
	τ	$rate_{pred}$	residual energy	τ	$rate_{pred}$	residual energy
aerial	128	2.24	27.8	512	0.90	173.0
airplane	256	0.71	51.3	1024	0.22	224.6
baboon	256	2.99	60.6	1024	1.19	378.0
buildings	256	0.85	63.2	1024	0.27	361.4
couple	128	1.21	39.1	256	0.68	84.4
stream	256	2.00	81.8	512	1.03	203.7
tiffany	128	0.98	43.8	512	0.25	155.5
lenna	128	0.84	41.1	1024	0.12	282.5
lynda	128	0.15	37.5	1024	0.03	356.2
peppers	512	0.37	108.5	2048	0.11	441.8
sailboat	256	1.37	74.3	1024	0.37	286.5
splash	256	0.33	68.5	2048	0.09	362.6

and residual energy which is also the MSE in this case, are tabulated in Table 6.5.1 for the twelve images at these two image qualities.

This data compression algorithm, where the residual is discarded, has also been reported by Spriggs and Nightingale [81] at the PCS in Tokyo, 1986 in the same session as we first presented our results [76]. This is no coincidence since the original idea was conceived during a discussion with Dr. Charles Nightingale in 1983 when we were colleagues at British Telecom Research Labs. (BTRL), in Martlesham Heath, England. However, neither group was aware that the other had decided to investigate this idea further.

As can be seen from the table, this compression scheme produces *essentially the same* images over a considerable range from a low of 0.15 bits/pixel for lynda to a high of 2.99 bits/pixel for the baboon. This leads us to conclude that while this is an excellent technique for some images, most notably lynda, peppers, and splash, it is rather expensive in the case of the baboon, aerial, stream, sailboat, and couple images. This is presumably in agreement with the BTRL group who chose to only report results for images with characteristics similar to the former set. Examples are shown in Fig. 6.5.3 for the six images which are most efficiently represented using this technique.

If used for recognition purposes, or a first pass in a multipass transmission scheme, the rate varies from 0.03 to 1.19 bits/pixel and again the same five detailed images are the cause of the higher rates. The remaining images are easily recognized at rates below 0.27 bits/pixel and the three least detailed images: lynda, peppers, and splash at rates below 0.11 bits/pixel.

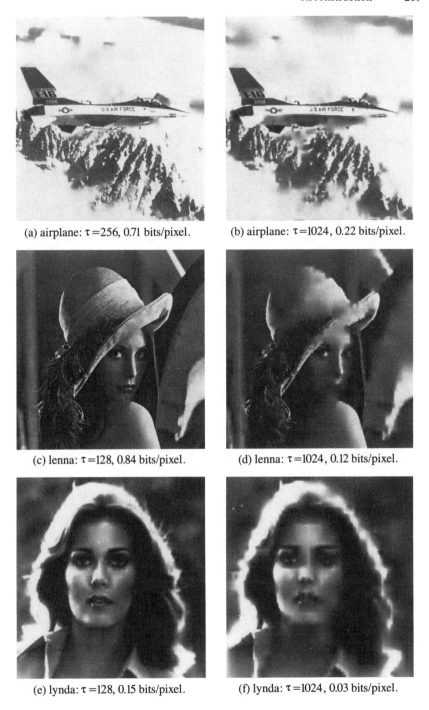

(a) airplane: $\tau = 256$, 0.71 bits/pixel.

(b) airplane: $\tau = 1024$, 0.22 bits/pixel.

(c) lenna: $\tau = 128$, 0.84 bits/pixel.

(d) lenna: $\tau = 1024$, 0.12 bits/pixel.

(e) lynda: $\tau = 128$, 0.15 bits/pixel.

(f) lynda: $\tau = 1024$, 0.03 bits/pixel.

Fig. 6.5.3   Quad tree prediction images which are essentially the same as the originals in (a), (c), and (e); and retain the significant features in (b), (d), and (f).

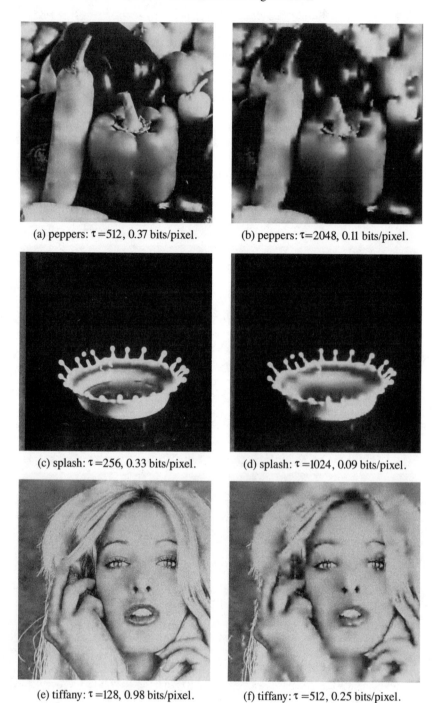

(a) peppers: τ=512, 0.37 bits/pixel.

(b) peppers: τ=2048, 0.11 bits/pixel.

(c) splash: τ=256, 0.33 bits/pixel.

(d) splash: τ=1024, 0.09 bits/pixel.

(e) tiffany: τ=128, 0.98 bits/pixel.

(f) tiffany: τ=512, 0.25 bits/pixel.

Fig. 6.5.3 contd.   Quad tree prediction images which are essentially the same as the originals
in (a), (c), and (e); and retain the significant features in (b), (d), and (f).

6.6   Coding the Residual

Having formed the boundary response we now subtract this from the original to get the residual image. Unlike traditional RBC, where the block size is fixed and we first code the boundaries using 1d RBC and then the core residual using the 2d DST, we are now faced with a problem because of the unequal block sizes. We could employ a number of DST coders of different sizes to code the boundaries and cores of each block but this would result in a fairly complex implementation although it is certainly feasible. In actuality we chose the simpler approach of including the coding error at the corner points (remember they are coded using only 5 bit PCM) into the residual so that the residual image is now square and of the same size as the input. We then treat this just as we would any other image and design a custom transform coder, that is we choose a block size and transform matrix. We could code this residual image in other ways and we will consider vector quantization in the next chapter.

Choice of Transform

RBC theory determines that the DST is the optimal residual transform matrix, but now we have no model for the residual statistics and hence no theory to determine the desired transform. So to investigate their relative performances we generated the rd functions for each of the seven commonly used fast discrete transforms: the DCT [7], Haar (Hr) [10], Hartley [82-84], DST [8], Slant (SWT) [11, 12], Slant-Haar (SHT) [13], and Walsh-Hadamard (WHT) [9]. For this study we selected a threshold of 512 (see *choice of threshold* below) and formed the residual image for the twelve images from the two ensembles allowing subdivision down to the pixel level. We then transformed each residual image using all of the transforms with a block size of 16×16, computed the transform domain variances and made an integer bit allocation at 1.5 bits to give the rd functions.

The seven residual rd functions for each image are grouped very closely together as shown for a typical case in Fig. 6.6.1 where the residual is taken from the lenna image predicted at a rate of 0.273 bits/pixel. At an overall rate of 1 bit/pixel the highest MSE is 27.5 for the Haar transform and the smallest is 21.8 for the DCT which is a range of 1.01 dB ($10 \log_{10} \frac{MSE1}{MSE2}$) while for normal transform coding, also with a block size of 16×16, the spread at 1 bit is from 47.9 for the Haar transform to 24.3 for the DCT, a range of 2.94 dB as shown in Fig. 6.6.2. Although the difference in performance of the seven transforms is greatly reduced for this quad tree based coding, the overall performance ranking is much the same as that obtained for traditional transform coding with the exception of the DST and Hartley which are now better than the slant transforms and comparable to the DCT.

With the exception of the lynda image, the ranking at an arbitrary reference residual rate of 0.5 bits/pixel is generally: (DST or DCT), (DCT or DST), Hartley, (SWT or SHT), (SHT or SWT), WHT, and then Haar. Discounting lynda, the performance spread at this rate for the remaining eleven images which follow the trend is between 0.41 and 1.05 dB which shows a consistently small MSE difference in performance for the various transforms. The three sinusoidal transforms: DST, DCT, and Hartley perform extremely similarly and are consistently the best three with a maximum spread of 0.28 dB also at the reference 0.5 bits/pixel residual rate.

As we saw in chapter two, the DST is the KLT for the RBC residual under suitable assumptions. The DCT however, is not a good approximation as shown in Fig. 6.6.3 where the rd plots for the 2d core lenna image are shown. The core was formed using perfect boundaries, transformed using each of the seven transforms and the transform domain variances then used to drive a standard integer bit allocation algorithm to compute the rd plot. For this example the core size is not 7 as in chapter four, but 8 since the SHT, Haar, and WHT transforms are only defined if the block size is a power of two. At a core residual rate of 0.5 bits/pixel the ranking of the transforms is the same as with the quad tree residual except that the sinusoidal transforms are now ranked DST,

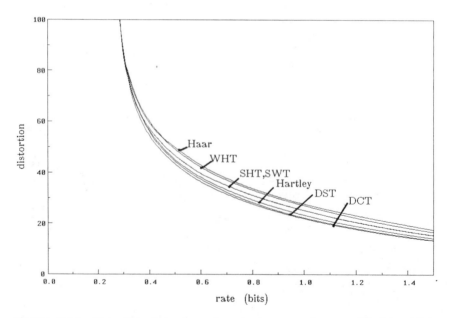

FIGURE 6.6.1. Rate-distortion plots when the lenna quad tree residual is coded using seven fast transforms. The prediction rate is 0.273 bits/pixel.

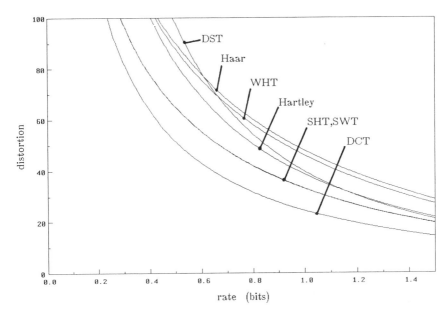

FIGURE 6.6.2. Rate-distortion plots for transform coding the original lenna image using seven fast transforms.

Hartley, DCT instead of DCT, DST, Hartley. At the reference rate there is a spread of 0.96 dB between the DST and DCT and yet here, with a variable block size, the performance of the DST and DCT is very similar (0.09 dB) but they may or may not be a good approximation to the actual residual KLT.

All of the transforms are complete in the sense that they can represent any signal and so the issue is not whether or not the residual can be reproduced but how efficiently this can be done. A good transform is one which can reproduce the residual with a small number of basis vectors, where this small set does not vary too much from block to block, that is we are looking for a transform which packs the residual energy into a few fixed basis vectors. To understand why the sinusoidal transforms now perform similarly let us examine their basis vectors.

With the fixed block size we argued intuitively that Ψ_1, the first basis vector of the DST, which tends to zero at the block extremes works well with a prediction which, on the average, will be at its best at these locations and worst in the center of the block where Ψ_1 has maximum energy. Consequently the DST performs well in this case but now we have a varying block size and the synchronization between good prediction, small amplitude basis vector and bad prediction, large amplitude vector is lost.

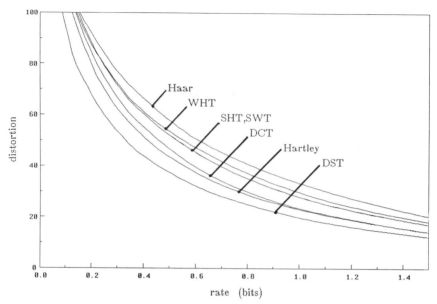

FIGURE 6.6.3. Rate-distortion plots for transform coding the lenna RBC residual using seven fast transforms.

When the block size b, is smaller than the transform size T, Ψ_1 is no longer the fundamental basis vector and if $b = \dfrac{T}{2}$, Ψ_2 becomes a good choice and so may contain a large proportion of the residual energy. However Ψ_2 is not as flexible as using a smaller transform size, equal to the block size, when the same function is served by the smaller Ψ_1s which can now have coefficients in adjacent blocks with either the same or opposite sign as illustrated in Fig. 6.6.4.

When the block size is larger than the transform size the problems are worse and lead to visual artifacts rather than just the loss in possible performance described above for the smaller blocks. This is because both low and high frequency DST basis vectors tend to zero at the extremes, as shown in Fig. 2.7.5, which means that many basis vectors are needed to reproduce non-zero boundary values. This has been observed when using the DST to code natural images at reasonable rates when the low amplitude boundaries produce a *venetian blind* artifact [40] in 1d coding, and black block borders, especially towards the corners, [41] in 2d coding. This is related to the fact that a constant input activates all of the odd DST harmonics as shown in Appendix B and typically the high frequency coefficients are not transmitted. When coding RBC residuals this is not a problem since we want to reproduce only small values at the boundaries. However with the larger blocks in the quad tree segmentation the transform boundaries are now right in the middle of the block

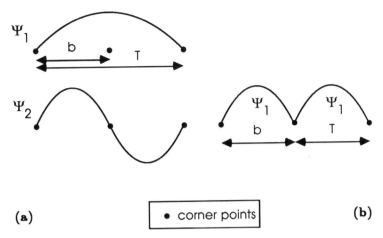

FIGURE 6.6.4. Fundamental basis vectors for different block sizes: (a) Ψ_2 when $b = \dfrac{T}{2}$; (b) Ψ_1 when $b = T$.

where we need to reproduce arbitrary values. The resulting distortion appears as boundary breakthrough in some of the larger blocks as shown in Fig. 6.6.5 where in (a) the lynda quad tree residual is coded using the DST with a transform size of 16, and as shown in (b) lynda has many blocks whose size is 32 or more. This breakthrough is also observed with the Hartley transform but in both cases the problem can be alleviated by using a large transform size which is at least as large as the largest block in the segmentation. However this may be as much as 64 and although we could limit the maximum block size during segmentation to 32 without sacrificing much efficiency the block size is still large which may be an issue in a practical system.

Let us now consider the DCT. Even when the transform and block sizes are equal, the DCT is 90° out of phase with the boundary conditions and so more than one basis vector is needed to meet these conditions and the energy is spread through more of the basis vectors resulting in a loss in performance. However when $b > T$ this is not a problem for the DCT which is quite able to reconstruct the values at the middle of the block.

Having seen how the variable block size prediction limits the available compression with a fixed transform size in different ways for the sinusoidal transforms it is perhaps easier to accept that they perform so similarly. To visually determine which transform is the best for this algorithm we compared the DCT with a block size of 16 and the DST with a larger block size of 64 to avoid the *boundary breakthrough*. We coded all of the image residuals at three rates: 0.25, 0.5, and 1.0 bits/pixel and found that the DST was slightly better since the DCT images contained the *tile effect* and a noisy texture but this was only noticeable at the

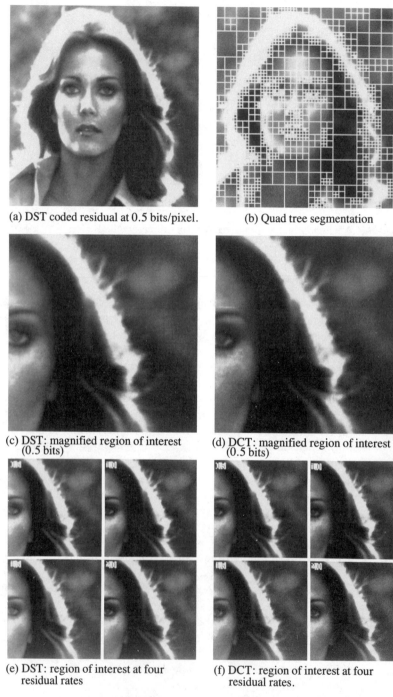

(a) DST coded residual at 0.5 bits/pixel.

(b) Quad tree segmentation

(c) DST: magnified region of interest (0.5 bits)

(d) DCT: magnified region of interest (0.5 bits)

(e) DST: region of interest at four residual rates

(f) DCT: region of interest at four residual rates.

Fig. 6.6.5   Boundary breakthrough distortion with the DST when the transform block size (16) is smaller than the quad tree blocks. Notice how the breakthrough in (a) is coincident with the larger blocks in (b).

lowest residual rate when the images are really not acceptable. So we chose to use the DCT with a block size of 16 and used zero level quantizers, discussed earlier in chapter three, to reduce the texture.

Choice of Threshold

Having fixed the transform, the next stage is to choose the threshold value for segmentation. There is a breakpoint at which it is more productive to allocate bits to the residual rather than the prediction and this depends both on the image and desired quality or equivalently the available total coding rate. To investigate this we limited ourselves to the 16×16 DCT coder and calculated the rd characteristics using the integer bit allocation as before but for each image at six threshold values: 64, 128, 256, 512, 1024, and 2048. We show a typical plot for lenna in Fig. 6.6.6 where it is seen that 128 is the best choice for a rate above 1.0 bit/pixel while 256 is better for $0.65 - 1.0$ bits/pixel and then 512 is better for even lower rates. In other cases, a small threshold is too expensive and the buildings image is shown as an example in Fig. 6.6.7.

If we concentrate on total rates between 0.5 and 1.0 bits/pixel which will give good images in most cases then the optimal choice of threshold for each image is listed below in Table 6.6.1. For the smoother images a choice of 256 seems appropriate while for the more detailed images a

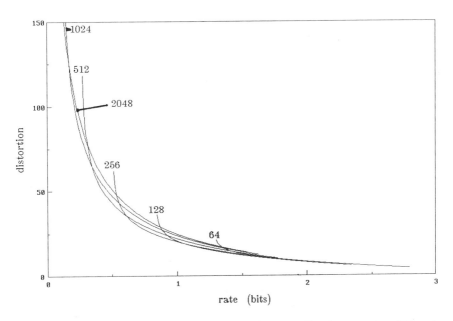

FIGURE 6.6.6. Rate-Distortion plots for quad tree coding lenna using different segmentation thresholds.

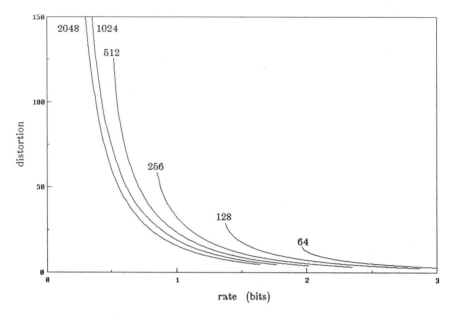

FIGURE 6.6.7. Rate-distortion plots for quad tree coding the buildings using different segmentation thresholds.

TABLE 6.6.1. Threshold preferences at an overall rate of 0.5-1.0 bits/pixel.

Ensemble A		Ensemble B	
image	τ	image	τ
aerial	∞	lenna	256,512
airplane	256,512	lynda	all $\approx$ same
baboon	∞	peppers	256,512
buildings	∞	sailboat	∞
couple	512 $\approx$ 1024 $\approx$ 2048	splash	256
stream	∞		
tiffany	256,512		

higher threshold possibly even infinite, indicating a fixed block size (traditional RBC), should be used. To accommodate both of these extremes a value of 512 was used for all of the images. In practice the threshold could be determined subjectively during closed-loop operation prior to transmission and varied for each image.

6.7   Results

The statistics arising from segmentation to the pixel level with $\tau = 512$ are given in Table 6.7.1.

The percentage of the image p_b, segmented into blocks of a particular size b is tabulated and is calculated from n_b, the number of blocks, via

$$p_b = \frac{n_b b^2}{N^2} \tag{6.7.1}$$

where N is the image size. The total number of data points n_{cnr}, the number of attempted split and merge operations (starting from an initial block size of 8) sam, the corresponding prediction rate $rate_{pred}$, and the resulting prediction error, or residual energy, are also shown.

In almost all cases $n_{cnr} > sam$ and we have $0.8 < \dfrac{n_{cnr}}{sam} < 2.4$ so that the segmentation overhead as a fraction of the total prediction rate given in (6.4.1) is

$$\frac{sam}{sam + (q \times n_{cnr})} = \frac{1}{1 + 5\dfrac{n_{cnr}}{sam}} \tag{6.7.2}$$

TABLE 6.7.1.   Segmentation statistics when $\tau = 512$.

name	final block size distribution (%)							n_{cnr}	sam	$rate_{pred}$ [Eqn. (6.4.1)]	residual energy
	1	2	4	8	16	32	64				
aerial	7	16	21	22	23	11	2	42453	25765	0.904	173.0
airplane	2	9	14	15	18	18	23	20120	14611	0.438	98.6
baboon	29	19	13	12	14	13	0	105699	45173	2.180	146.9
buildings	1	17	28	15	18	17	3	22475	23007	0.514	136.6
couple	2	5	10	20	29	30	5	14246	9580	0.307	180.6
stream	9	16	22	22	19	7	5	48891	27549	1.034	203.7
tiffany	2	3	6	15	33	38	5	11609	6975	0.247	155.5

(a) Ensemble A

name	final block size distribution (%)								n_{cnr}	sam	$rate_{pred}$ [Eqn. (6.4.1)]	residual energy
	1	2	4	8	16	32	64	128				
lenna	1	5	10	17	32	28	6	0	12446	9680	0.273	140.8
lynda	0	0	3	18	33	33	13	0	2432	2786	0.057	144.0
peppers	2	5	12	21	28	30	2	0	17302	11118	0.371	108.5
sailboat	5	14	20	20	21	13	6	0	35834	23061	0.768	140.8
splash	1	4	7	14	15	28	19	13	10446	7665	0.228	105.7

(b) Ensemble B

which is largest for lynda but still less than 20%. Consequently it is the data points that constitute the majority of $rate_{pred}$ as one might expect and there is little point in varying the initial block size to try and minimize the overhead due to *sam*. The prediction rate for fixed blocks using bilinear interpolation is $\frac{q}{b^2}$ and so for $q = 5$ we have Table 6.7.2 showing how the rate rises exponentially as the block size decreases. In fact subdivision causes a fourfold increase in the prediction rate so that subdividing large regions to the pixel level (29% with the baboon) is very expensive and at least the images with the four highest prediction rates: baboon, stream, aerial, and sailboat also have the greatest percentage of single pixel blocks. For the remaining images the prediction rate is less than 0.52 bits/pixel and the high contrast edges are all preserved.

In the extreme case of the baboon with a prediction rate of 2.18 bits, 0.29 x 5 = 1.45 bits, are needed for the single pixel blocks and if the minimum block size were raised to two, then there would be a savings of 0.75 x 1.45 = 1.09 bits plus a reduction in *sam* and the prediction rate would be more than cut in half! However we have noted earlier that this leads to jaggies on diagonal edges and for lenna only 1% of the image subdivides to the pixel level which is a very cost effective way to prevent the jaggies on the hat brim.

Zero Level Quantizers

As mentioned earlier we used zero level quantizers in the residual transform coder. The software implementation of the integer bit allocation algorithm can only produce bit allocations for a given rate assuming that *normal* 2^n level quantizers will be used. Consequently if we require a rate of p bits/pixel using zero level quantizers we must design for a higher rate so that when the 1 bit quantizers are removed and the n bit quantizers replaced with $\log_2(2^n - 1)$ bit quantizers the rate is actually the desired p bits/pixel. Instead of doing this we elected to use nominal residual rates of 0.5, 1.0, 1.5, and 2.0 bits/pixel and then the true rate is just whatever it happens to be.

The number of n-bit quantizers k_n, produced by the integer bit allocation for DCT coding with a block size of 16, again using the transform domain statistics for the whole ensemble, is given in Table 6.7.3 for each non zero k_n. The nominal rate is $\frac{1}{256} \sum_{n=1}^{7} k_n n$ while the actual rate is

TABLE 6.7.2. Prediction rate for different block sizes when $q = 5$.

b	1	2	4	8	16
$rate_{pred}$	5.00	1.25	0.31	0.08	0.02

TABLE 6.7.3. Distribution of n bit quantizers for DCT coding the residual.

nominal	actual	n bit quantizers							
rate	rate	0	1	2	3	4	5	6	7
0.5	0.324	186	35	16	16	2	1	0	0
1.0	0.690	125	61	27	33	8	2	0	0
1.5	1.072	68	84	34	52	15	2	1	0
2.0	1.522	24	87	48	68	21	7	1	0

(a) Ensemble A

nominal	actual	n bit quantizers							
rate	rate	0	1	2	3	4	5	6	7
0.5	0.328	188	36	12	14	5	0	1	0
1.0	0.607	111	85	23	27	7	2	1	0
1.5	0.929	41	121	40	40	8	5	1	0
2.0	1.406	0	113	63	58	15	4	2	1

(b) Ensemble B

$\dfrac{1}{256} \displaystyle\sum_{n=2}^{7} k_n \log_2(2^n - 1)$ bits/pixel and for example in ensemble A this is 0.324 bits/pixel when the nominal rate is 0.5 bits/pixel.

The subjective results are given in Table 6.7.4 where the rate refers to the total rate needed to code both the prediction and the residual. The residual rates are the actual rates from Table 6.7.3 and are therefore the same for all of the images from a single ensemble. However, the prediction rates given in Table 6.7.1 are different for each image and this variation is reflected in the total rate.

The MSE results are presented in Table 6.7.5 for reference.

6.8   Conclusions

The reconstruction alone is a useful recognition tool or compression scheme especially for images which are characterized by relatively simple scenes containing large areas belonging to the same object rather than busy scenes. To further understand the two image classes one might imagine taking a photograph of a busy street or a full auditorium with a wide angle lens which would produce a busy scene with lots of small objects and low intensity transitions which would be an inappropriate source for this technique. However if the focal length of the lens were lengthened to produce a smaller field of view, the number of individual objects would decrease and each would occupy a larger percentage of the photograph and then such a scene would be well suited to such a compression method. Of the twelve images in the two ensembles this method

TABLE 6.7.4. Quad tree coding results.

image	rate (bits)	description
aerial	2.4,2.0	− excellent
	1.6	− good
	1.2	− bad: blocky, patchy
airplane	2.0,1.5,1.1	− excellent
	0.8	− good: slight blocks
baboon	3.7,3.3,2.9	− excellent
	2.5	− good: slight blocks
buildings	2.0,1.6,1.2	− excellent
	0.8	− good
couple	1.8,1.4	− excellent
	1.0	− ok: still loss of texture
	0.6	− bad: very blocky
stream	2.6,2.1	− excellent
	1.7	− good
	1.4	− ok: slight blocks
tiffany	1.8,1.3,0.9	− excellent
	0.6	− bad: blocky, blurred

(a) Ensemble A

image	rate (bits)	description
lenna	1.7,1.2	− very good: just loss of texture in hat
	0.9	− ok: very slight blocks in hat
	0.6	− blocky
lynda	1.5,1.0	− excellent
	0.7	− very good: just loss of texture in shirt
	0.4	− ok: slight blocks
peppers	1.8,1.3,1.0	− excellent
	0.7	− good: very slight blocks
sailboat	2.2,1.7,1.4	− excellent
	1.1	− ok: blocky
splash	1.6,1.2,0.8	− excellent
	0.6	− good: slightly blocky

(b) Ensemble B

is inappropriate for the baboon, aerial, stream, sailboat, and couple images. The best result for the other seven images is lynda which when coded at 0.15 bits/pixel produces a good quality image with no annoying artifacts.

When we also code the residual, this technique produces high quality images at a residual rate of 1 bit/pixel or less. The overall rate is then

TABLE 6.7.5. MSE and SNR' figures for quad tree coding.

image	rd	nominal residual rate			
		2.0	1.5	1.0	0.5
aerial	rate	2.43	1.98	1.59	1.23
	MSE (SNR')	18.1 (35.6)	29.0 (33.5)	43.8 (31.7)	73.3 (29.5)
airplane	rate	1.96	1.51	1.13	0.76
	MSE (SNR')	7.9 (39.2)	12.7 (37.1)	19.7 (35.2)	32.7 (33.0)
baboon	rate	3.70	3.25	2.87	2.50
	MSE (SNR')	30.3 (33.3)	43.0 (31.8)	57.2 (30.6)	78.5 (29.2)
building	rate	2.04	1.59	1.20	0.84
	MSE (SNR')	5.9 (40.5)	9.7 (38.3)	18.0 (35.6)	37.8 (32.4)
couple	rate	1.83	1.38	1.00	0.63
	MSE (SNR')	12.0 (37.4)	18.7 (35.4)	29.3 (33.5)	51.0 (31.1)
stream	rate	2.56	2.11	1.72	1.36
	MSE (SNR')	30.5 (33.3)	45.4 (31.6)	63.5 (30.1)	93.7 (28.4)
tiffany	rate	1.77	1.32	0.94	0.57
	MSE (SNR')	18.4 (35.5)	25.5 (34.1)	34.2 (32.8)	48.5 (31.3)

(a) Ensemble A

image	rd	nominal residual rate			
		2.0	1.5	1.0	0.5
lenna	rate	1.68	1.20	0.88	0.60
	MSE (SNR')	14.7 (36.5)	21.5 (34.8)	28.6 (33.6)	39.3 (32.2)
lynda	rate	1.46	0.99	0.66	0.38
	MSE (SNR')	2.5 (44.1)	3.3 (42.9)	4.4 (41.7)	7.3 (39.5)
peppers	rate	1.78	1.30	0.98	0.70
	MSE (SNR')	14.8 (36.4)	21.3 (34.9)	27.3 (33.8)	35.3 (32.7)
sailboat	rate	2.17	1.70	1.38	1.10
	MSE (SNR')	27.6 (33.7)	40.0 (32.1)	52.5 (30.9)	69.2 (29.7)
splash	rate	1.63	1.16	0.84	0.56
	MSE (SNR')	8.0 (39.1)	12.1 (37.3)	16.4 (36.0)	23.1 (34.5)

(b) Ensemble B

between 2 and 3 bits/pixel for the baboon, stream, and aerial images; 1 and 1.5 bits/pixel for the couple, sailboat, buildings, lenna, and airplane images; and below 1 bit/pixel for lynda, peppers, tiffany, and splash. If we ignore the three most detailed images which should probably be coded in some other way, then this algorithm provides excellent quality images at rates below 1.5 bits/pixel.

It should be noted that lynda needs at least 0.7 bits/pixel to give a high quality image when both the prediction and the residual are coded based on a segmention at $\tau = 512$, while a reasonable picture was obtained from the segmentation alone with $\tau = 128$ at a rate of 0.15

bits/pixel. This illustrates how the choice of threshold can influence the outcome and by fixing the threshold at 512 for all twelve images these results must be considered conservative with improvement possible by determining an appropriate threshold for each image.

There is also potential for improvement if we relax the highly structured positioning of blocks so that uniform rectangular regions, which were not aligned with the quad tree structure and were therefore subdivided, could be rejoined into a single region by applying an affine transformation. This could be done after segmentation when larger uniform regions would be grown at the expense of increased segmentation overhead but with the advantage of a reduced number of transmitted corner points. Alternatively, a single pass could be used if the subdivision criterion were modified to allow an inherently more flexible segmentation. Given these possibilities an even more efficient coding strategy based on adaptive segmentation seems likely.

7

QVQ—Vector Quantization of the Quad Tree Residual

7.1 Introduction

In the last chapter we developed an adaptive RBC algorithm using unequal block sizes and used the DCT to code the resulting residual image. We will now consider a simple variation of this algorithm which uses the same quad tree prediction but replaces the transform coder with a vector quantizer (VQ). We shall use the notation VQ to refer to both the encoding method: vector quantization and also the encoder: a vector quantizer, where the actual meaning will be evident from the context.

In section 7.2 we will introduce standard memoryless VQ and discuss the codebook design and implementation of the coder. We refer the reader to the excellent tutorial article [85] by Gray for a discussion of the many variations on the basic VQ theme.

In section 7.3 we will present the differential and interpolative forms of VQ and show commonality between this latter variation and RBC. VQ of the quad tree residual will then be discussed in section 7.4. The results will be given in section 7.5 and conclusions drawn in section 7.6.

7.2 Vector Quantization

What is vector quantization or VQ? Simply put, VQ is the process of mapping an input set of k-dimensional vectors into an output set of k-dimensional vectors, such that the selected output vector is closest to the input vector according to the selected distortion measure. Each output vector is called a codeword and the set of all codewords comprises the codebook. If the input vectors are represented by b bits per coordinate, then the number of possible input vectors is 2^{kb} and to achieve an output rate of p bits per coordinate, or kp bits/vector, there are 2^{kp} codewords in the codebook. If, as is usual, $p < b$, then the number of codewords is less than the number of input vectors, and the quantization produces data compression.

When VQ coding a 1d sequence such as speech we first split the incoming samples into groups of k samples which then form the input vector for VQ. With multidimensional sources such as images, we must first segment the input into smaller multidimensional regions which we can then scan to again obtain a k-dimensional input vector. In the case of single image frames, this requires segmenting the 2d image into a series of tessellating regions of a fixed shape as shown in Fig. 7.2.1. Notice that the regions need not be rectilinear although they often are. The regions are then scanned to form the input vector so that each coordinate corresponds to one pixel.

To make the discussion concrete, imagine we wish to code 4×4 image blocks so that the vector dimension $k = 16$ and if each pixel is represented by 8 bits then a compression ratio of 16:1 would make $p = 0.5$ and the codebook would contain $2^{(16)(0.5)} = 256$ codewords. Notice that the number of codewords increases exponentially with the output rate p, and when $p = 1$ the codebook contains 65,536 entries or 1,048,576 pixels—the equivalent of four 512×512 images! For examples at different rates and dimensions, see Table 7.4.1 below.

Advantages of VQ Over Scalar Quantization

There are theoretical reasons why VQ always performs better than scalar quantization [15] even when each coordinate of the vector, that is the pixels, are independent. This means that VQ could be usefully applied to the transform coefficients which have only a low residual correlation and are truly uncorrelated in the case of the ideal KLT. Despite these advantages, VQ was not used until recently because there were no practical

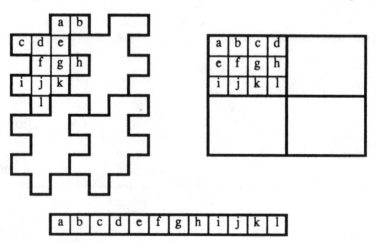

FIGURE 7.2.1. Forming a vector for VQ.

methods available to construct VQ codebooks and even now VQ is limited to small dimensions and/or low rates to avoid ridiculously large codebooks.

Vector Methods: Transform Coding and VQ

Transform methods code blocks or vectors rather than scalars and for this reason outperform PCM, especially at low rates. For example, an image coded at 1 bit/pixel using transform techniques is quite acceptable, whereas a PCM coded image at this rate has just two output levels and the quality is in no way comparable. Although we jointly encode a vector in transform coding, each transform domain coefficient is actually quantized as a scalar so the algorithm is inherently suboptimal in a theoretical sense. The formal name for such a code, where the codeword for the vector is simply the concatenation of the individual codewords for each coordinate of the vector, is a product code [85] and the dimension of the product code is the sum of the dimensions of each constituent code.

Consider the simple 2d product code where there are only two active transform coefficients: u_1 which is allocated two bits, and u_2 with only one bit. These three bits provide eight possible output vectors, or codewords, and assuming symmetric scalar quantizers they are $(\pm a, \pm c)$ and $(\pm b, \pm c)$ as shown in Fig. 7.2.2(a). Further assuming an optimum quantizer and the MSE distortion measure, decision levels are midway between the output levels so the quantizer rule partitions the two dimensional space into eight rectangular regions.

However a general 2d VQ at the same rate could place the eight codewords anywhere in the 2d plane so as to minimize the distortion. Fig. 7.2.2(b) shows how the partitioning of the plane can now be much more complex and the regions no longer rectilinear. Given an input vector, the VQ output is the closest codeword and so to minimize distortion the input region for each output codeword is the set of all points which are closer to that codeword than any other codeword. Therefore the codeword is the centroid of that input region and if the distortion measure is the MSE, which we shall use, then the centroid is simply the Euclidean centroid or arithmetic average. The input regions are constructed by perpendicularly bisecting the vector joining neighboring codewords as shown in Fig. 7.2.2(c).

In the above example, VQ was applied in the transform domain. However it can equally well be applied directly in the spatial domain, with the same results, thus avoiding the need for transformation before and after VQ. It should be noted that a VQ codebook designed in the transform domain for some training sequence will have the same structure as the spatial domain codebook for the same training data. The two codebooks will simply be related by a fixed k-dimensional rotation

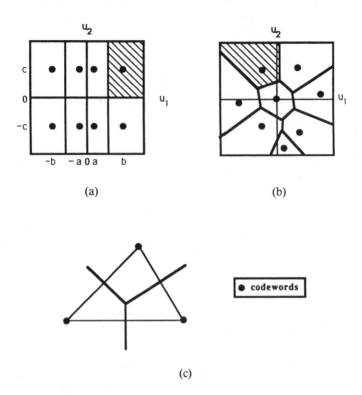

(a)

(b)

(c)

FIGURE 7.2.2. Partitioning 2d space: (a) product code; (b) general 2d VQ; (c) constructing codeword regions for (b).

because unitary transformation is nothing more than a rotation of the coordinate system [86]. Alternatively the corresponding codewords will be related by the transform so that given a transform domain codeword $\hat{c}_j$, inverse transformation will produce the corresponding spatial domain codeword c_j.

So, in summary, we observe that transform coding is a constrained VQ and in fact is a product code.

VQ Design

So how do you design a codebook? The breakthrough came in the late 1970s according to Gray [85] when it was realized that the Lloyd algorithm [48] used to design scalar quantizers was amenable to VQ design for a variety of distortion measures and this generalized Lloyd algorithm (GLA), published in 1980 by Linde, Buzo, and Gray [87], has come to be known as the LBG algorithm. We will use a training sequence based design following the lead of most workers in this field since there is no universally accepted probability distributions for image data, and we have even less knowledge of the distribution of a quad tree residual which we shall VQ code later in this chapter.

We observe that this may be a good reason to design the codebook in the transform domain since, as we have noted earlier, at least the ac coefficients are well modeled using a Laplacian pdf and the codebook could then be transformed back into the spatial domain for actual VQ.

The basic training sequence design technique is outlined in Algorithm 7.2.1.

This iterative algorithm still requires an initial codebook and there are two basic approaches: we can start with some simple codebook of the correct size, or recursively construct larger ones from an initial small codebook. This second approach has the advantage that as a byproduct of the design process the optimal codebook for each of the smaller sizes is produced. We chose this approach since it was the one used by Lookabaugh [88] who kindly provided the software to allow us to investigate VQ coding the RBC residual. We made no modifications to the software except to integrate it into our own simulation system and add the facility to save the intermediate codebooks.

Splitting Codewords

We will now describe, in Algorithm 7.2.2, the recursive codebook generation scheme which is based on a (split, optimize) cycle, that is we take an optimized codebook, split the codewords to generate a larger codebook which we then optimize and continue until we have an optimized codebook of the correct size.

ALGORITHM 7.2.1. LBG Algorithm

Algorithm 7.2.1
(1) Given a training sequence, an initial codebook, and a distortion measure.
(2) Map all training vectors into the closest codeword and compute the associated distortion.
(3) Replace each codeword with the centroid of all those training vectors which are closest to it.
(4) **if(** not the first pass **and** distortion reduction small enough **)** **then** quit
(5) **else** go to step 2

ALGORITHM 7.2.2. Recursive Codebook Generation

Algorithm 7.2.2
(1) Generate the initial codebook with one entry: the centroid of the entire training sequence.   (2) Split each codeword into two codewords: the original and a perturbed version [Eqn. (7.2.1)].   (3) Using Algorithm 7.2.1, optimize the codebook.   (4) **if**(the codebook is large enough) **then** quit   (5) **else** go to step 2

Lookabaugh splits each coordinate of the k-dimensional vector independently using the same technique. If the coordinate being split is x then the perturbed coordinate y is derived via

$$y = x + r\epsilon \qquad (7.2.1)$$

where r is a random variable in the range $[0,1]$ and ϵ depends on the magnitude of x, viz.,

$$\epsilon = \begin{cases} \epsilon_1 & \text{if } x = 0, \\ \epsilon_1 \ \text{sign}(x) & \text{if } |x| < 0.9\epsilon_1, \\ \epsilon_2 x & \text{otherwise.} \end{cases} \qquad (7.2.2)$$

The new coordinates are now x and y and by repeating for each dimension, two new codewords are produced. Gray [85] notes that by keeping the original codeword as one of the new pair it is ensured that the distortion will not increase at the next iteration.

A problem with splitting is that it is possible to generate a codeword which will not be a nearest neighbor to any of the training vectors. If this happens, then this codeword is discarded and the codeword representing the most training vectors is split and step 2 of the LBG algorithm is repeated which will hopefully eliminate the *empty cell*. If more than one cell is empty, the second and subsequent most populous cells are also split as necessary before repeating step 2 of the LBG algorithm. If the empty cell persists after splitting the more populous cells then the split is repeated with a smaller perturbation which will reduce the possibility of the split being poor again.

This algorithm worked well and during our experiments we never needed to split cells more than twice for any codebook size with $\epsilon_1 = \epsilon_2 = 0.01$.

VQ Coding

Having designed the codebook, the coding and decoding are conceptually straightforward and illustrated in Fig. 7.2.3. When coding, the input vector $\mathbf{x}$ is compared against all codewords $\{\mathbf{c}_i\}$ and the distortion d_i, which would occur when reproducing $\mathbf{x}$ as $\mathbf{c}_i$, is computed via

$$d_i = \sum_{n=1}^{k} [x(n) - c_i(n)]^2 \qquad (7.2.3)$$

and the index j is output where d_j is the smallest distortion, viz.,

$$d_j \le d_i \quad \text{for all } i. \qquad (7.2.4)$$

The decoding is even simpler and is achieved by a simple table look up: given the index j output the codeword $\mathbf{c}_j$.

Performance Considerations

The decoding process is so simple to implement that it deserves no further discussion. The design and encoding however, though conceptually simple, require a great deal of computation. For example, when coding with a modest 4×4 VQ coder operating at 0.5 bits/pixel, there are 256 codewords and so for each input vector there are 256 distortion

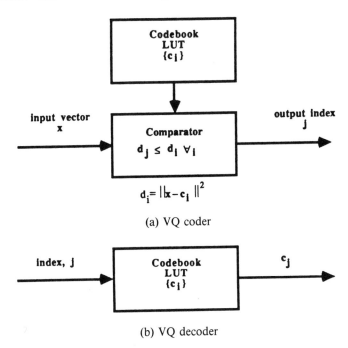

(a) VQ coder

(b) VQ decoder

FIGURE 7.2.3. Vector quantization.

computations each requiring 16 subtractions, 16 multiplications, and 15 additions. As the codebook size increases due to an increased vector dimension or coding rate the number of computations increases exponentially. To ease the computational burden of full-search techniques *tree codebooks* have been used.

To create the simplest tree codebook, a binary tree codebook, one first generates two centroids for the training sequence, using the first two steps of the LBG algorithm for example, and then the training sequence is coded using these two centroids splitting the original training sequence into two smaller sequences. This process is then repeated for each of the two new training sequences and a binary tree is built with two centroid vectors stored at each node. When coding, the vector is compared against the two centroids at the root of the tree and if it is closest to the first a 0 is output and the process continues at the left child node, say, and otherwise a 1 is output and we move to the right. When a leaf node is reached the final binary decision is made, coding is complete and the string of 1s and 0s make up the codeword index. The search time is reduced from $O(N)$ to $O(\log_2 N)$ but since two vectors are stored at each node, the storage requirements are doubled. A further disadvantage is that the codebook generated by this algorithm is suboptimal, and using the same tree search for the encoding results in a suboptimal search of this suboptimal codebook.

Despite the tremendous computational requirement for VQ, there is a great deal of regularity which allows an implementation using a systolic architecture. Tao [18] has proposed an LSI implementation based on two distinct processors, a number of which can then be flexibly combined to achieve full-search or tree-search VQ, while Ramamoorthy [17] has designed a VLSI implementation of full-search VQ.

Equitz [89], noting that the LBG algorithm is clearly a clustering algorithm, introduced some new VQ algorithms borrowing ideas from classical clustering methods used in pattern recognition. He first showed that the LBG algorithm is actually the *k-means* algorithm [90] and then improved on the standard techniques in two ways. The first improvement speeds the exhaustive search by storing the codewords in a multidimensional tree structure: k-dimensional, or $k-d$, trees originally developed by Bentley [91] which then allows rapid access to codewords within a localized neighborhood in k-dimensional space. Consequently, when looking for the closest match, only a small number of codewords usually need to be considered to achieve a true exhaustive search resulting in logarithmic expected time. While the first improvement is an efficient data structure which improves both expensive aspects of VQ: the design and coding stages, the other improvement is specific to the design stage and is based on replacing the LBG algorithm by a nearest neighbor (NN) clustering algorithm which is much quicker and produces codebooks which are neither clearly better nor worse than the LBG codes in a MSE sense.

This emphasizes the fact that the LBG algorithm is only guaranteed to converge to a *local* minimum in the MSE surface. If desired, the NN codes could be used as a good initialization for the LBG algorithm.

For this study we elected to avoid the suboptimal tree codebooks and stay with the standard inefficient exhaustive search strategy since it would require some time to implement Equitz's algorithms and the results would be unchanged.

It is worth stressing just how time consuming VQ can be. The VQ design and coding times are shown in Table 7.2.1 where the times are real elapsed times on an unloaded Sun-3 workstation equipped with a floating point accelerator board (FPA) which produces 315 double precision KFLOPS in the Linpack benchmark [92] as compared to 100 double precision KFLOPS obtained with the standard configuration of the Motorola MC68881 floating point coprocessor chip on the mother board. All times refer to 4×4 VQ coding of 512×512 quad tree residual images and the number of training vectors used was 28,672 for ensemble A and 20,480 for ensemble B as discussed below in section 7.4. The coding times are averages: the actual time being image dependent since the full-search algorithm breaks off a distortion computation as soon as it exceeds the current minimum value.

7.3 Differential and Interpolative VQ

Although simple memoryless VQ can theoretically perform very well, in practice it suffers from the tile effect and edges are poorly reproduced. The tile effect is to be expected since the blocks are coded independently and there is no guarantee that two adjacent codewords will match at their common boundary. The second problem may be due to the design process which minimizes the MSE for a training sequence and since the edge pixels are a minority of the total number of pixels they will be given a low weight in the average design even though they convey a large amount of information to the observer.

Ramamurthi and Gersho [93, 94] proposed coding the edges and the smoother texture regions using different codebooks. Another method to improve the edge fidelity is differential VQ (DVQ) [95] where the mean is

TABLE 7.2.1. VQ execution times on a Sun-3 with FPA.

data rate	number of codewords	time to design for ensemble A (hrs:min)	time to design for ensemble B (hrs:min)	time to code (hrs:min)
0.25	16	0:16	0:10	0:03
0.50	256	3:20	2:10	0:15
0.75	4096	45:28	26:31	2:51

first subtracted from the vector and separately encoded and the residual is then coded using VQ. The resulting product code—mean code followed by VQ code—is simply a constrained VQ and should therefore be suboptimal since all possible means together with all residual codewords forms a structured VQ codebook. However after separating out the mean which varies only slowly from block to block it is possible to exploit this interblock redundancy which simple memoryless VQ does not and hence improve the performance. This is achieved by differentially coding the mean using DPCM rather than memoryless PCM. This strategy can be extended to a *normalized* DVQ where the block is further normalized to be a unit variance vector by dividing the residual by the block standard deviation before VQ [96]. Although DVQ techniques produce better images by increasing the edge fidelity, the tile effect is still present.

As discussed before the tile effect is particularly objectionable because of the regular block structure which the eye readily detects resulting in a subjective amplification of these boundary mismatch errors. With reference to Fig. 7.2.1 we see that the blocks do not have to be rectangular, the only requirement being that they fit together and fill the 2d plane. Consequently we suggest that an irregular shape might be sufficient to remove, or at least significantly reduce, the tile effect commonly observed with standard VQ. At this time we have not yet tested this hypothesis.

Hang and Haskell [63] attacked the tiling problem by effectively overlapping blocks and using overlapped corner points to bilinearly predict the block prior to VQ. They code the corner points with a full 8 bits but use a block size of 8×8, which is large for VQ, so that the overhead is only 0.125 bits/pixel. The bilinear interpolation is then subtracted and the residual coded using VQ, hence the name *interpolative* VQ (IVQ). It is at this point that the paths of VQ and RBC cross, or perhaps merge. In fact, if we replace the DST coder by a VQ and use the simpler bilinear predictor, then RBC becomes IVQ. Furthermore, IVQ is also related to the quad tree segmentation which already uses the same bilinear predictor, and if we set an infinite threshold to maintain equal sized blocks the only difference is the residual coder: DCT or VQ.

We will progress down this common path by using VQ to code the quad tree residual which is both an obvious alternative to the DCT coder used in the previous chapter and also an extension of the IVQ algorithm where the blocks are now of variable size.

7.4 VQ of the Quad Tree Residual

We could apply VQ to standard RBC by replacing the transform coders with VQs and designing two codebooks: one for the 1d boundaries and the other for the 2d core. We would then VQ the boundary residuals and using the decoded values predict the core and then VQ the core residual. As an example of combining VQ and RBC however, it is simpler to apply VQ to the quad tree residual since we then only need a single codebook.

When replacing transform coders with VQs we expect to get the smallest improvement when the transform is the KLT, the optimal product code. Consequently, since the DST is the KLT for the RBC residual, while the DCT may or may not be close to the KLT of the quad tree residual, VQ could potentially produce greater improvements with the quad tree algorithm. As a result of these arguments we choose to apply VQ to the quad tree residual for this initial study and we shall refer to this new quad tree VQ as QVQ.

In IVQ the corner point is reconstructed perfectly as shown in Fig. 7.4.1, and the block for VQ is a square with a missing corner so that the vector dimension is 63 for 8×8 blocks. If we were to use such an approach for QVQ then the variable block size would cause problems since we would need a separate codebook for each possible block size, or dimension: 3, 15, 63, 255, 1023, etc. Furthermore our prediction rate would increase by a factor of 8/5 if we were to use perfect corner points. We therefore continue to use 5 bits to code the corner points and then divide the residual image into fixed blocks including the corners as before, but now use a single VQ instead of the 16×16 DCT coder.

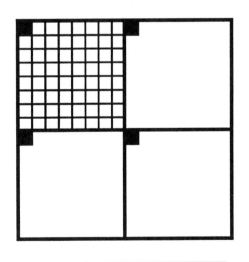
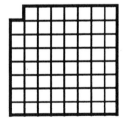

Corner Points

FIGURE 7.4.1. IVQ blocks.

Choosing the Vector Dimension

The vector dimension has to be small enough so that at a reasonable rate the size of the codebook is not too large. A large codebook increases the performance but also the complexity of the encoder and requires many images to form a training sequence which is representative. The relationship between these and other characteristics are presented in Table 7.4.1 for different block sizes. For example, when coding 4×4 blocks at 0.5 bits/pixel the codebook has $2^{(16)(0.5)} = 256$ entries and a single 512×512 image contains $\dfrac{512^2}{4} = 16,384$ vectors so that a single image contains 64 times as many vectors as the codebook. However, if we maintain the same rate but increase the block size to 8×8, then the codebook grows to contain a staggering $2^{(64)(0.5)} = 4,294,967,296$ vectors but a single image now contains only 4096 vectors so the codebook is equivalent to 1,048,576 images which makes it impractical to design a codebook based on a training sequence.

Hang and Haskell [63] used 8×8 blocks but at a lower rate of $10/64 = 0.156$ bits/pixel with a codebook size of 1024. Since we wish to investigate performance over a range of rates comparable to the previous chapter we must use a smaller block size and 4×4 blocks allow us to code the residual at rates of 0.25, 0.5, and 0.75 bits/pixel with codebooks containing 16, 256, and 4096 codewords.

TABLE 7.4.1. VQ parameters for different block sizes assuming a 512×512 image.

block size	dimension k	vectors per image	rate p	codewords	codebooks per image	images per codebook
4×4	16	16,384	0.25	16	1024	–
			0.5	256	64	–
			0.75	4,096	4	–
			1.0	65,536	–	4
6×6	36	7,225	0.25	512	14	–
			0.5	262,144	–	36
			0.75	$1.3 \ 10^8$	–	$1.9 \ 10^4$
			1.0	$6.9 \ 10^{10}$	–	$9.5 \ 10^6$
8×8	64	4,096	0.25	65,536	–	16
			0.5	$4.3 \ 10^9$	–	$1.0 \ 10^6$
			0.75	$2.8 \ 10^{14}$	–	$6.9 \ 10^{10}$
			1.0	$1.8 \ 10^{19}$	–	$4.5 \ 10^{15}$

Choosing the Training Sequence

The training sequence was selected by taking every other block in each direction for all of the images in the ensemble and then using these 4096 training vectors from each image to design two codebooks, one for each ensemble. For ensemble A this resulted in 28,672 training vectors with 20,480 for ensemble B, so there were always at least five times as many training vectors as codewords.

7.5 Coding Results

VQ was applied to the quad tree residual images generated in chapter six so that the overall coding rate for any image is the sum of the prediction rate given in Table 6.7.1 and the VQ rate of 0.25, 0.5, or 0.75 bits/pixel. The subjective results are presented in Table 7.5.1 and the quantitative MSE results are then given in Table 7.5.2.

7.6 Conclusions

When comparing the QVQ results in Tables 7.5.1 and 7.5.2 with the corresponding results for quad tree coding using the DCT given in Tables 6.7.4 and 6.7.5 we conclude that the two approaches give similar results. QVQ seems to have a slight edge in MSE terms but the subjective qualities are comparable. This can be seen by comparing the rates required in each case to achieve excellent or very good quality images. For example, to decode an excellent image the baboon requires 2.9 bits/pixel in each case while the buildings require $(1.3-1.2)=0.1$ bits/pixel more but the stream $(2.1-1.8)=0.3$ bits/pixel less when using VQ.

The best result for VQ is when coding lenna and this is shown in Fig. 7.6.1 where in (a) the residual is VQ coded for a total rate of 1 bit/pixel and in (b) the residual is DCT coded at an overall rate of 1.2 bits/pixel. The hat is shown zoomed by a factor of two in (c) and (d) where it can be seen that the texture, which is lost with the DCT residual coder, is preserved using VQ giving an excellent image while even at 1.2 bits/pixel the DCT coded residual was only judged to be *very good*. This same region, no longer magnified, is then shown in (e) and (f) at different coding rates.

So, in summary, the two residual coders perform similarly with VQ doing a little better but at the expense of more computation. It should also be remembered that the training sequence for the VQ design was simply 25% of the vectors from the images actually coded and we should expect the out of class performance to be somewhat worse. On the plus side however, the VQ coder implemented here is particularly straightforward and could probably be improved.

TABLE 7.5.1. QVQ coding results.

image	rate (bits)	description
aerial	1.7	– very good
	1.4	– good: blocky at transitions
	1.2	– bad: very blocky
airplane	1.2	– excellent
	0.9	– good
	0.7	– bad: very blocky
baboon	2.9	– excellent
	2.7	– very good
	2.4	– ok: slight blocks
buildings	1.3	– excellent
	1.0	– good
	0.8	– bad: very blocky
couple	1.1	– good: appears slightly unclear
	0.8	– ok: still blocky
	0.6	– bad: very blocky
stream	1.8	– excellent
	1.5	– very good
	1.3	– bad: very blocky
tiffany	1.0	– excellent
	0.7	– good: slight blocks at transitions
	0.5	– bad: very blocky

(a) Ensemble A

image	rate (bits)	description
lenna	1.0	– excellent: texture in hat preserved
	0.8	– good: slight blocks at transitions
	0.5	– bad: very blocky
lynda	0.8	– excellent
	0.6	– very good: very slight blocks
	0.3	– bad: very blocky
peppers	1.1	– excellent
	0.9	– very good: very slight blocks
	0.6	– ok: blocky
sailboat	1.5	– excellent
	1.3	– good: slight blocks
	1.0	– bad: very blocky
splash	1.0	– excellent
	0.7	– good: slight blocks
	0.5	– bad: very blocky

(b) Ensemble B

TABLE 7.5.2. MSE and SNR′ figures for QVQ coding.

image	rd	VQ rate		
		0.75	0.5	0.25
aerial	rate	1.65	1.40	1.15
	MSE (SNR′)	30.0 (33.4)	48.8 (31.3)	83.1 (28.9)
airplane	rate	1.19	0.94	0.69
	MSE (SNR′)	14.7 (36.5)	22.9 (34.5)	40.6 (32.0)
baboon	rate	2.93	2.68	2.43
	MSE (SNR′)	36.6 (32.5)	55.9 (30.7)	84.1 (28.9)
building	rate	1.26	1.01	0.76
	MSE (SNR′)	13.6 (36.8)	23.1 (34.5)	48.9 (31.2)
couple	rate	1.06	0.81	0.56
	MSE (SNR′)	23.3 (34.5)	37.4 (32.4)	68.1 (29.8)
stream	rate	1.78	1.53	1.28
	MSE (SNR′)	44.0 (31.7)	67.6 (29.8)	104.7 (27.9)
tiffany	rate	1.00	0.75	0.50
	MSE (SNR′)	25.2 (34.1)	38.3 (32.3)	59.7 (30.4)

(a) Ensemble A

image	rd	VQ rate		
		0.75	0.5	0.25
lenna	rate	1.02	0.77	0.52
	MSE (SNR′)	19.6 (35.2)	29.7 (33.4)	49.4 (31.2)
lynda	rate	0.81	0.56	0.31
	MSE (SNR′)	5.1 (41.0)	8.3 (38.9)	19.2 (35.3)
peppers	rate	1.12	0.87	0.62
	MSE (SNR′)	19.2 (35.3)	29.1 (33.5)	43.2 (31.8)
sailboat	rate	1.52	1.27	1.02
	MSE (SNR′)	34.5 (32.8)	53.3 (30.9)	77.2 (29.3)
splash	rate	0.98	0.73	0.48
	MSE (SNR′)	12.0 (37.4)	18.2 (35.5)	30.9 (33.2)

(b) Ensemble B

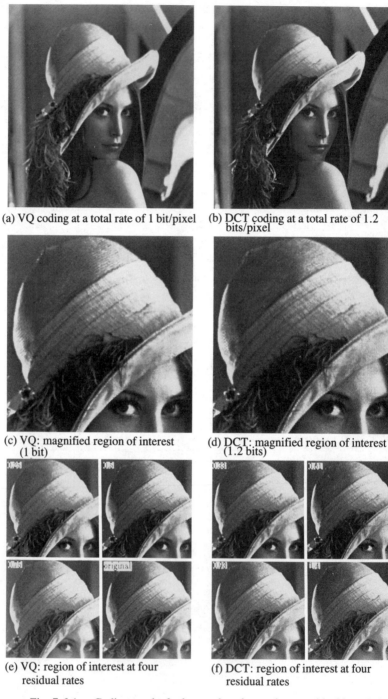

(a) VQ coding at a total rate of 1 bit/pixel

(b) DCT coding at a total rate of 1.2 bits/pixel

(c) VQ: magnified region of interest (1 bit)

(d) DCT: magnified region of interest (1.2 bits)

(e) VQ: region of interest at four residual rates

(f) DCT: region of interest at four residual rates

Fig. 7.6.1   Coding results for lenna when the quad tree residual is coded using VQ and the DCT.

8

Conclusions

8.1 Introduction

In this final chapter we will first summarize the new results, both theoretical and practical, described in detail in this book. We will then draw some overall practical coding conclusions illustrated by examples in the figures 8.1.1, 8.1.2, and 8.1.3. Finally we will indicate those areas where future work is still to be done.

8.2 New Results

We have presented a thorough demonstration of the use of noncausal models for data compression leading to a suppression of block boundary effects. During this exposition the following new results have been presented:

(a) The 1d boundary response for a 1st-order Markov process was shown to be the sum of two hyperbolic sine functions each weighting one of the boundary conditions. The accuracy of the linear approximation used previously [24, 32] has now been clearly demonstrated.

(b) The 2d boundary response has now been interpreted in the spatial domain in addition to the transform domain relationship already reported [24, 32].

(c) The 2d boundary response is the sum of a bilinear patch and a series of residual patches. The first residual patch contains a significant portion of the remaining information allowing an approximation to the 2d boundary response. This is very important since 2d RBC is then no longer *much* more complex than DCT.

(d)   RBC has been shown to completely remove interblock redundancy for the assumed models.

(e)   Even for integer bit allocations, the Lloyd-Max rd function produces significantly different bit distributions from the commonly assumed Shannon rd function, and we therefore recommend that the appropriate practical rd function be used when determining the allocation.

(f)   New closed-form equations for bit allocation have been derived based on piecewise exponential approximations [1] to quantizer rd functions. These are particularly useful when non-integer bit allocations are required, for example using the traditional iterative solution rather than the integer bit allocation algorithm advocated here. They would also be useful for inherently non-integer bit allocations including integer level allocation proposed below in section 8.4.

(g)   We have shown that quantizers with an odd number of levels, or zero level quantizers (ZLQs), reduce granularity in smooth regions of transform coded images.

(h)   We have demonstrated the usefulness of an objective measure, h-plots [30] to help determine subjective image quality.

8.3   Coding Recommendations

After conducting thousands of experiments we feel confident that RBC provides clearly visible suppression of the block boundary artifacts commonly observed with DCT coding. This means that RBC should be used instead of DCT at the lower rates when the *tile effect* is present. In particular this would cover the range of bit rates at and below 1 bit/pixel for a typical adaptive technique. The four class adaptive RBC scheme presented here provides excellent performance for the smoother images in ensemble B at the critical 0.5 bits/pixel rate which would include typical head and shoulder images. It is our belief, that with the modifications suggested at the end of chapter five, this could be extended to the more detailed ensemble A also.

For even lower rates, the quad tree prediction should be used. For smooth images, or reconstructions where there is a possible texture loss, this technique provides good quality images down to 0.15 bits/pixel for at least one head and shoulders image (lynda). To achieve this performance level with other images, the image could first be filtered to remove noise and some texture before applying the segmentation. In any case the segmentation could be modified using suitable affine transformations, as discussed in chapter six, to reduce the number of required data points and hence the rate.

In a progressive transmission system a quad tree technique, such as QVQ, could be used effectively. The data points and segmentation information would be sent first and used to quickly reconstruct the quad tree prediction at the receiver. As transmission continued, the VQ codes would be sent if required, and the residual texture added to further improve the image quality. The standard RBC algorithm could also be used but the initial prediction would not be as good.

If a system required an asymmetric coding/decoding time with the decoding time being much less than the encoding time, then QVQ would be an ideal candidate since VQ is simple table look-up and the quad tree reconstruction involves only shift and add operations as we have already discussed.

For color coding , all of the algorithms that we have discussed could be applied sequentially to each component after making the transformation from R,G,B to Y,U,V space. This is described in section 3.9 where it is suggested that the U and V components are subsampled by two in each direction prior to coding so that the overall rate increase is expected to be 50% when compared to monochrome coding.

Photographic conclusions are presented for coding at 1 bit/pixel in Fig. 8.1.1 for tiffany, a typical ensemble A image, and in Fig. 8.1.2 for lenna which is a typical ensemble B image. In these two figures results are shown for hybrid RBC, 2d RBC, class-adaptive RBC, quad tree segmentation with a DCT coded residual, and finally QVQ. In Fig. 8.1.3, results are presented for the two typical images coded at 0.5 bits/pixel using the three better performing algorithms: class-adaptive RBC, quad tree segmentation with a DCT coded residual, and QVQ.

8.4   Future Work

There are many issues raised in this book which require additional research before conclusions may be drawn and these are listed below.

(a)   The approximation to the 2d boundary response was examined briefly but its applicability should be thoroughly examined since such a simplification provides a significantly simpler 2d RBC algorithm.

(b)   ZLQs were discussed and used to reduce graininess but a more general $(2n+1)$ instead of the (2^n-1) odd level quantizer could be used to improve any transform coder's performance by replacing the integer bit constraint by a more flexible integer level constraint. The new closed form bit allocations could be used in a new integer level allocation algorithm, a generalization of the integer bit allocation used here, which would now involve a tree search to determine the optimal allocation.

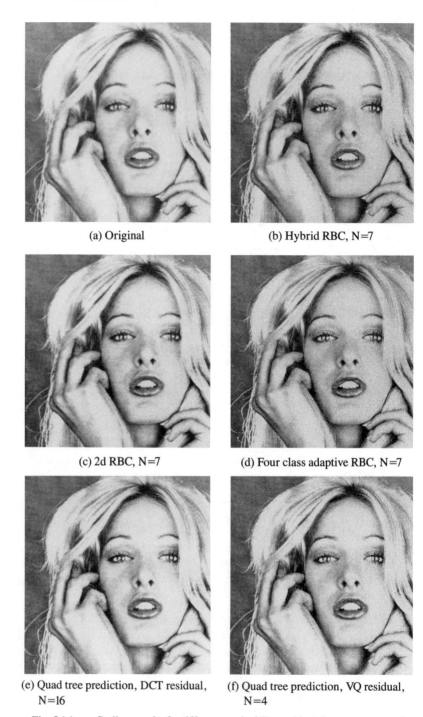

(a) Original

(b) Hybrid RBC, N=7

(c) 2d RBC, N=7

(d) Four class adaptive RBC, N=7

(e) Quad tree prediction, DCT residual,
    N=16

(f) Quad tree prediction, VQ residual,
    N=4

Fig. 8.1.1   Coding results for tiffany, a typical Ensemble A image, at a rate of
1 bit/pixel, except in (e) where the rate is actually 0.9 bits/pixel.

(a) Original

(b) Hybrid RBC, N=7

(c) 2d RBC, N=7

(d) Four class adaptive RBC, N=7

(e) Quad tree prediction, DCT residual, N=16

(f) Quad tree prediction, VQ residual, N=4

Fig. 8.1.2   Coding results for lenna, a typical Ensemble B image, at a rate of 1 bit/pixel, except in (e) where the rate is actually 0.9 bits/pixel.

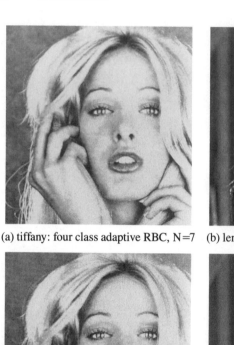

(a) tiffany: four class adaptive RBC, N=7   (b) lenna: four class adaptive RBC, N=7

(c) tiffany: quad tree prediction, DCT
residual, N=16

(d) lenna: quad tree prediction, DCT
residual, N=16

(e) tiffany: quad tree prediction, VQ
residual, N=4

(f) lenna: quad tree prediction, VQ
residual, N=4

Fig. 8.1.3   Coding results for typical images, at a rate of 0.5 bits/pixel, except
in (c) and (d) where the rate is actually 0.6 bits/pixel.

In chapter five we were able to code images from ensemble B using class-adaptive RBC at 0.5 bits/pixel with excellent quality. We also showed that there was room for improvement by modifying the design criterion to incorporate fundamental properties of the human visual system. We feel that the excellent results for one image class together with indications of possible improvements for the more detailed class indicate that this should be investigated further. Threshold coding should also be tried to determine which adaptive technique works best with RBC.

In chapter six we mentioned using arbitrary regions for the segmentation but did not pursue the idea. Marr [97] has used zero crossings to generate closed edge maps which might provide even better results. The problem would be to determine the required data points and functional form for the prediction to provide the boundary response over arbitrarily shaped regions. A simpler alternative would be to maintain the rectilinear structure but, where possible, piece together some of the regions after the quad tree segmentation to provide larger connected areas which were only split because they were not aligned with the quad tree. This could be a very effective means to limit the prediction rate and therefore improve performance.

In chapter seven, we noted the blocking artifacts which arise with VQ. We also mentioned that there was no reason why the VQ blocks had to be rectangular, and in particular the irregular shaped region in Fig. 7.2.1 could be used which should at least suppress these artifacts. This is of course applicable to all block coding techniques but in transform coding the inter-block correlation could change sufficiently to render the DCT no longer such a good candidate for the KLT approximation. With VQ however, this would not be a problem when the design is driven by a training sequence rather than a probabilistic model.

A

Ordinary and Partial Differential and Difference Equations

A.1 Introduction

In this appendix we will present the solution to standard ordinary and partial differential equations and their corresponding difference equations which arise when solving for the boundary response in RBC.

A.2 Second Order Ordinary Differential Equations

We are interested in equations of the type

$$\frac{d^2u}{dt^2} = \pm k^2 u(t) ; \quad 0 \le t \le \tau \qquad (A.2.1)$$

with boundary conditions, $u(0) = A$ and $u(\tau) = B$. The general solution depends on the sign of the right hand side (RHS) of the equation. If we select the positive sign, then the general solution will be

$$u(t) = a\cosh kt + b\sinh kt , \qquad (A.2.2)$$

while the negative sign leads to

$$u(t) = a\cos kt + b\sin kt . \qquad (A.2.3)$$

We solve the full boundary value problem by splitting it into two related problems with boundary values: $\{u(0) = A, \ u(\tau) = 0\}$ and $\{u(0) = 0, \ u(\tau) = B\}$. After solving these two problems we can add the solutions to get the overall solution by calling on the principle of superposition.

We will consider the second set of boundary conditions $\{0,B\}$ in detail and then infer the result for $\{A,0\}$. We use the boundary conditions to determine the unknown coefficients a and b in (A.2.2) and (A.2.3). If we consider the general solution (A.2.2) which contains the hyperbolic functions, we see that the cosh(.) function cannot meet the boundary condition $u(0) = 0$ so $a = 0$ and $b = \dfrac{B}{\sinh k\tau}$ and the solution is

$$u(t) = B\,\frac{\sinh kt}{\sinh k\tau}\ . \qquad (A.2.4)$$

Similarly, with (A.2.3) the cos(.) function must be rejected because of the boundary condition at $t = 0$ and we then have

$$u(t) = B\,\frac{\sin kt}{\sin k\tau}\ . \qquad (A.2.5)$$

By symmetry, the boundary conditions $\{A,0\}$ are met by replacing B with A and t with $\tau - t$ in each case. We then sum the partial solutions to get the overall solution to (A.2.1).

In summary, we have the two equations and their corresponding solutions

$$\frac{d^2u}{dt^2} = k^2u(t)\ ;\quad 0\le t\le\tau,\quad u(0) = A,\quad u(\tau) = B,\quad (A.2.6)$$

$$u(t) = \frac{A\sinh k(\tau-t) + B\sinh kt}{\sinh k\tau}\ , \qquad (A.2.7)$$

and

$$\frac{d^2u}{dt^2} = -k^2u(t)\ ;\quad 0\le t\le\tau,\quad u(0) = A,\quad u(\tau) = B, \quad (A.2.8)$$

$$u(t) = \frac{A\sin k(\tau-t) + B\sin kt}{\sin k\tau}\ . \qquad (A.2.9)$$

A.3   Second Order Ordinary Difference Equations

We can relate the differential equations in section A.2 to analogous difference equations by approximating the second order differential by a second order difference using the Taylor polynomial expansion, viz.,

$$\frac{d^2u}{dt^2} \approx \frac{u(n-1) - 2u(n) + u(n+1)}{h^2} \qquad (A.3.1)$$

where $t = nh$ and $u(n) \triangleq u(nh)$. If we discretize (A.2.1) by setting $\tau = (N+1)h$, we obtain

$$u(n-1) - 2u(n) + u(n+1) = \pm h^2k^2u(n)\ ;\quad 0\le n\le N+1\ . \quad (A.3.2)$$

It can be shown that the general solution of this difference equation has the same functional form as the corresponding differential equation (A.2.1) but the argument is not the *obvious* transformation of $kt \to knh$. Instead the general solution is, for a positive RHS

$$u(n) = a\cosh n\theta + b\sinh n\theta ,\qquad\text{(A.3.3)}$$

and for a negative RHS we have

$$u(n) = a\cos n\theta + b\sin n\theta ,\qquad\text{(A.3.4)}$$

where the parameter θ is determined by substituting the general solution into (A.3.2).

As before the cos(.) and cosh(.) functions are rejected for the boundary value problem with $u(0) = A$ and $u(N+1) = B$, and the general solution is $a\sin n\theta$ or $a\sinh n\theta$, depending on the sign of the RHS of the equation.

Let us consider the negative case with the trigonometric solution and substitute into (A.3.2) to obtain an implicit equation for θ, viz.,

$$\cos\theta = 1 - \frac{h^2 k^2}{2}\qquad\text{(A.3.5)}$$

where we have made use of the identity

$$\sin\alpha + \sin\beta = 2\sin\left(\frac{\alpha+\beta}{2}\right)\cos\left(\frac{\alpha-\beta}{2}\right) .\qquad\text{(A.3.6)}$$

In the hyperbolic case, when we substitute the proposed general solution, we obtain the implicit equation for θ as

$$\cosh\theta = 1 + \frac{h^2 k^2}{2}\qquad\text{(A.3.7)}$$

where we have used the hyperbolic identity

$$\sinh\alpha + \sinh\beta = 2\sinh\left(\frac{\alpha+\beta}{2}\right)\cosh\left(\frac{\alpha-\beta}{2}\right) .\qquad\text{(A.3.8)}$$

More explicitly, we can solve for θ as

$$\theta = \ln\left[\cosh\theta + \sqrt{\cosh^2\theta - 1}\right] .\qquad\text{(A.3.9)}$$

So in conclusion we have the two equations and their solutions, viz.,

$$u(n-1) - 2u(n) + u(n+1) = h^2 k^2 u(n) ;\quad 0\le n\le N+1,$$
$$u(0) = A,\quad u(N+1) = B,\qquad\text{(A.3.10)}$$

with solution

$$u(n) = \frac{A\sinh(N+1-n)\theta + B\sinh n\theta}{\sinh(N+1)\theta} ,\qquad\text{(A.3.11)}$$

where

$$\cosh\theta = 1 + \frac{h^2 k^2}{2} ,\qquad\text{(A.3.7)}$$

and

$$u(n-1) - 2u(n) + u(n+1) = -h^2k^2u(n) ; \quad 0 \leq n \leq N+1,$$

$$u(0) = A, \quad u(N+1) = B, \tag{A.3.12}$$

with solution

$$u(n) = \frac{A\sin(N+1-n)\theta + B\sin n\theta}{\sin(N+1)\theta}, \tag{A.3.13}$$

where

$$\cos\theta = 1 - \frac{h^2k^2}{2}. \tag{A.3.5}$$

In either case as $h \to 0$, if we compare the implicit equations for θ with the series expansions for $\cos\theta$ and $\cosh\theta$ we have $\theta \approx hk$ and then $n\theta \approx nhk = kt$ and the discrete argument, $n\theta$, converges to the continuous kt.

A.4   Second Order Partial Differential Equations

Two dimensional RBC models are boundary value problems in both dimensions and correspond to the elliptic class of partial differential equations (PDEs). We are particularly interested in the Helmholtz equation

$$\frac{\partial^2 u}{\partial x^2} + \frac{\partial^2 u}{dy^2} = \pi^2k^2u(x,y) ; \quad 0 \leq x \leq a, \quad 0 \leq y \leq b. \tag{A.4.1}$$

which is the continuous analogy of the NC1 model. The classical solution to this equation is to propose a separable solution $u(x,y) = X(x)Y(y)$ which results in

$$Y\frac{d^2X}{dx^2} + X\frac{d^2Y}{dy^2} = \pi^2k^2XY. \tag{A.4.2}$$

As in the previous sections we solve this boundary problem by setting the boundary conditions to zero on all but one side and then use superposition to derive the full solution. For example, we specify that the boundary conditions be zero for $u(x, 0)$, $u(x,b)$, and $u(0,y)$ and that $u(a,y) = g(y)$, the true boundary values at $x = a$. We then separate out the PDE into two ordinary differential equations of the form (A.2.1), one in x and the other in y. In order to meet the zero boundary conditions at $y = 0$ and $y = b$ we require a sin(.) function for the y-direction. Hence the RHS is negative for the equation in y and consequently positive for the equation in x and the two equations are

$$\frac{d^2Y}{dy^2} = -\pi^2\gamma^2Y, \tag{A.4.3}$$

$$\frac{d^2X}{dx^2} = \pi^2(\gamma^2 + k^2)X . \tag{A.4.4}$$

Solving for Y we get

$$Y = k_y \sin(\gamma \pi y) \tag{A.4.5}$$

and the boundary condition $u(x,b) = 0$ determines γ as

$$\gamma_p \triangleq \gamma(p) = \frac{p}{b} ; \quad p = 1, 2, \cdots . \tag{A.4.6}$$

The solution for X is

$$X = k_x \sinh(\sqrt{\gamma_p^2 + k^2} \ \pi x) = k_x \sinh(\sqrt{p^2 + b^2 k^2} \ \frac{\pi x}{b}) . \tag{A.4.7}$$

Remembering that $u = XY$ we have the solution

$$u_p(x,y) = c_p \sin(\frac{p \pi y}{b}) \ \frac{\sinh \dfrac{q_b \pi x}{b}}{\sinh \dfrac{q_b \pi a}{b}} \tag{A.4.8}$$

where we have defined $q_b \triangleq \sqrt{p^2 + b^2 k^2}$ and of course there are an infinite number of these solutions so the overall solution is the series

$$u(x,y) = \sum_{p=1}^{\infty} u_p(x,y) \tag{A.4.9}$$

where the $c_p = k_x k_y \sinh \dfrac{q_b \pi a}{b}$ are chosen to meet the boundary condition at $x = a$

$$g(y) = \sum_{p=1}^{\infty} c_p \sin \frac{p \pi y}{b} . \tag{A.4.10}$$

In particular c_p are the coefficients in the Fourier sine series of period $2b$ for $g(y)$ and are given by

$$c_p = \frac{2}{b} \int_0^b g(y) \sin \frac{p \pi y}{b} \, dy . \tag{A.4.11}$$

This is the solution for the boundary conditions at $x = a$ and we must superpose the results for each of the four sides to obtain the complete solution to (A.4.1) as

$$u(x,y) = \sum_{p=1}^{\infty} \frac{a_p\sinh\dfrac{q_b\pi(a-x)}{b} + c_p\sinh\dfrac{q_b\pi x}{b}}{\sinh\dfrac{q_b\pi a}{b}} \sin\frac{p\pi y}{b}$$

$$+ \sum_{p=1}^{\infty} \frac{b_p\sinh\dfrac{q_a\pi(b-y)}{a} + d_p\sinh\dfrac{q_a\pi y}{a}}{\sinh\dfrac{q_a\pi b}{a}} \sin\frac{p\pi x}{a} \qquad (A.4.12)$$

where we have defined $q_a \triangleq \sqrt{p^2 + a^2k^2}$ and a_p, b_p, c_p, and d_p are the pth Fourier sine coefficients of the four boundaries at $x = 0$, $y = 0$, $x = a$, and $y = b$ respectively.

A.5   Second Order Partial Difference Equations

We again approximate the second order differential by a second order difference using the Taylor polynomial expansion. In particular

$$\frac{\partial^2 u}{\partial x^2} + \frac{\partial^2 u}{\partial y^2} \approx \qquad\qquad\qquad\qquad\qquad (A.5.1)$$

$$\frac{u(i-1,j) + u(i,j-1) - 4u(i,j) + u(i+1,j) + u(i,j+1)}{h^2}$$

where $x = ih$, $y = jh$ and $u(i,j) \triangleq u(ih,jh)$. If we discretize (A.4.1) by setting $a = (N+1)h$ and $b = (M+1)h$, we obtain

$$u(i-1,j) + u(i,j-1) - 4u(i,j) + u(i+1,j) + u(i,j+1)$$

$$= \pi^2 h^2 k^2 u(i,j) ; \quad 0 \le i \le N+1 ; \quad 0 \le j \le M+1 . \qquad (A.5.2)$$

The general approach that we take to solve this partial difference equation is analogous to the technique used for the continuous PDE in section A.4 and we propose a separable solution of the form $u(i,j) = X(i)Y(j)$. If we again impose zero boundary conditions on all but the right side at $i = (N+1)$, then we split (A.5.2) into the two discrete counterparts of (A.4.3) and (A.4.4), viz.,

$$Y(j-1) - 2Y(j) + Y(j+1) = -\pi^2\gamma^2 Y(j) \qquad (A.5.3)$$

an ordinary difference equation in j with a trigonometric solution, and

$$X(i-1) - 2X(i) + X(i+1) = \pi^2(\gamma^2 + h^2 k^2) X(i) \qquad (A.5.4)$$

an ordinary difference equation in i with a hyperbolic solution. Solving for Y we get

$$Y = k_y\sin\theta\pi j \qquad (A.5.5)$$

so we have a sin(.) function in the *j-direction* and the argument is again fixed by the boundary condition at $j = (M+1)$ as

$$\theta_p \triangleq \theta(p) = \frac{p}{(M+1)} \; ; \quad p = 1, 2, \cdots, M. \tag{A.5.6}$$

Note that p now only takes M distinct values and so the infinite series solution obtained in the continuous case will now become a finite series and the Fourier sine series will be replaced by the DST as we shall show below.

Now θ_p depends on γ^2 via (A.3.5)

$$\cos \pi\theta_p = 1 - \frac{\pi^2\gamma^2}{2} \tag{A.5.7}$$

so the boundary condition at $j = (M+1)$ effectively balances the two equations (A.5.3) and (A.5.4) by regulating the coupling coefficient γ as

$$\gamma_p^2 \triangleq \gamma^2(p) = \frac{2}{\pi^2}(1 - \cos \pi\theta_p). \tag{A.5.8}$$

As with the ordinary difference equation, the functional form for the PDE is the same in both the continuous and discrete cases but the argument is different. So the solution to the discrete approximation of the Helmholtz equation with one non zero boundary condition at $i = (N+1)$ is the finite series expansion

$$u(i,j) = \sum_{p=1}^{M} c_p \sin(\frac{p\pi j}{M+1}) \frac{\sinh(i\omega_p)}{\sinh(N+1)\omega_p}. \tag{A.5.9}$$

The coefficients c_p are chosen to match the boundary condition at $i = (N+1)$ so

$$u(N+1,j) = \sum_{p=1}^{M} c_p \sin \frac{p\pi j}{M+1} \tag{A.5.10}$$

and c_p are $\sqrt{\dfrac{2}{M+1}}$ times the DST coefficients s_p, of $u(N+1,j)$, viz.,

$$s_p = \sqrt{\frac{2}{M+1}} \sum_{p=1}^{M} u(N+1,j) \sin \frac{p\pi j}{M+1}. \tag{A.5.11}$$

We use (A.3.5) to determine the parameter ω_p as

$$\cosh \omega_p = 1 + \frac{(k^2h^2 + \gamma_p^2)\pi^2}{2}$$

$$= 2 + \frac{k^2h^2\pi^2}{2} - \cos \pi\theta_p \tag{A.5.12}$$

where we have used (A.5.8).

When we solve with the true boundary condition at $j = 0$ or $j = (M+1)$ we must replace M by N and then $\omega_p \to \omega_p'$ which is defined via (A.5.12) with $\theta_p \to \theta_p' \triangleq \dfrac{p}{N+1}$.

We must sum the four partial solutions for each boundary to give the complete solution to (A.5.2) as

$$u(i,j) = \hspace{8cm} \text{(A.5.13)}$$

$$\sum_{p=1}^{M} \left\{ u_{p,a}(i,j) + u_{p,c}(i,j) \right\} + \sum_{q=1}^{N} \left\{ u_{q,b}(i,j) + u_{q,d}(i,j) \right\}$$

where

$$u_{p,a}(i,j) + u_{p,c}(i,j) = \hspace{6cm} \text{(A.5.14)}$$

$$\frac{a_p \sinh(N+1-i)\omega_p + c_p \sinh i\omega_p}{\sinh(N+1)\omega_p} \sin \frac{p\pi j}{M+1}$$

and

$$u_{q,b}(i,j) + u_{q,d}(i,j) = \hspace{6cm} \text{(A.5.15)}$$

$$\frac{b_q \sinh(M+1-j)\omega_q' + d_q \sinh j\omega_q'}{\sinh(M+1)\omega_q'} \sin \frac{q\pi i}{N+1} \ .$$

The coefficients a_p, b_q, c_p, and d_q are, by analogy with (A.5.11), proportional to the pth and qth DST sine coefficients of the four boundaries at $x = 0$, $y = 0$, $x = a$, and $y = b$ respectively. In the special case when $M = N$ we have

$$u(i,j) = \sum_{p=1}^{N} \left\{ \frac{a_p \sinh(N+1-i)\omega_p + c_p \sinh i\omega_p}{\sinh(N+1)\omega_p} \sin \frac{p\pi j}{N+1} \right. \hspace{1.5cm} \text{(A.5.16)}$$

$$\left. + \frac{b_p \sinh(N+1-j)\omega_p + d_p \sinh j\omega_p}{\sinh(N+1)\omega_p} \sin \frac{p\pi i}{N+1} \right\} \ .$$

B

Properties of the Discrete Sine Transform

B.1 Introduction

In this appendix we will introduce the discrete sine transform (DST) and present the DST of the following standard sequences: constant, linear, exponential, sinusoidal and hyperbolic.

Definition

The DST matrix, Ψ is defined as

$$\Psi(i,j) = \sqrt{\frac{2}{N+1}} \, \sin \frac{ij\pi}{N+1} \; ; \quad 1 \le i,j \le N . \qquad \text{(B.1.1)}$$

It is a unitary symmetric transform and hence is its own inverse, viz.,

$$\Psi\Psi = I \qquad \text{(B.1.2)}$$

where I is the N x N identity matrix. We refer to the kth column, or row, of the Ψ matrix as $\Psi_k \triangleq \Psi(i,k)$ with components $\{\Psi(1,k), \Psi(2,k), \ldots, \Psi(N,k)\}$.

Notation

We use lower case letters to indicate vectors and upper case for matrices and then denote the corresponding 1d or 2d transformation by $\hat{\;}$ so

$$\hat{x} = \Psi x \qquad \text{(B.1.3)}$$

and

$$\hat{T} = \Psi T \Psi . \qquad \text{(B.1.4)}$$

Tridiagonal Toeplitz Matrices

The columns, Ψ_k are the eigenvectors of a symmetric tridiagonal Toeplitz matrix $\mathbf{T}$, with entries $\{-a, \ 1, \ -a\}$ since $\mathbf{T}\Psi_k = \lambda(k)\Psi_k$ and therefore

$$\Psi\mathbf{T}\Psi = \Lambda \tag{B.1.5}$$

where Λ is a diagonal matrix of eigenvalues $\lambda(k)$, where

$$\lambda(k) = 1 - 2a \cos \frac{k\pi}{N+1} \ ; \quad k = 1,...,N. \tag{B.1.6}$$

B.2 DST Evaluation Technique

To determine the DST of the standard sequences we will study the following vector equation

$$\mathbf{T}\,\mathbf{x} = \mathbf{b} \tag{B.2.1}$$

where $\mathbf{x}$ is the sequence under study, $\mathbf{T}$ is the tridiagonal Toeplitz matrix $\{-a, \ 1, \ -a\}$, and $\mathbf{b}$ contains only two non-zero entries:

$$b(1) = aA = ax(0); \qquad b(N) = aB = ax(N+1) , \tag{B.2.2}$$

so that the sequence is

$$x(n) = a[x(n-1) + x(n+1)] \ ; \quad n = 1,...,N \ ;$$
$$x(0) = A \ ; \qquad x(N+1) = B \ . \tag{B.2.3}$$

Transforming (B.2.1) we get

$$\Psi\mathbf{T}\,\mathbf{x} = \hat{\mathbf{b}} = aA\,\Psi_1 + aB\,\Psi_N \tag{B.2.4}$$

but using (B.1.2) and (B.1.5) we have $\Psi\mathbf{T}\,\mathbf{x} = \Psi\mathbf{T}(\Psi\Psi)\mathbf{x} = \Lambda\hat{\mathbf{x}}$ so

$$\hat{x}(k) = \frac{A\,\Psi_1(k) + B\,\Psi_N(k)}{\lambda(k)/a} \tag{B.2.5}$$

and we can express the DST coefficients as the sum of two weighted sin(.) functions. Let us now use this technique to determine the DSTs of the standard sequences.

B.3   Exponential Sequences

If we consider $x(n) = e^{np}$ then (B.2.3) is satisfied, and we have

$$A = 1; \qquad B = e^{(N+1)p} \tag{B.3.1}$$

and a is given by

$$e^{np} = a \left[e^{(n-1)p} + e^{(n+1)p} \right] \tag{B.3.2}$$

hence dividing by e^{np} we have

$$a = \frac{1}{e^p + e^{-p}} = \frac{1}{2 \cosh p} . \tag{B.3.3}$$

Applying (B.2.5) we obtain the DST coefficients as

$$\boxed{\hat{x}(k) = \frac{\Psi_1(k) + e^{(N+1)p} \Psi_N(k)}{2(\cosh p - \cos \frac{k\pi}{N+1})}} \tag{B.3.4}$$

for the sequence $x(n) = e^{np}$.

B.4   Constant Sequences

If we consider the exponential sequence with $p = 0$ then we get a constant sequence with $x(n) = 1$. Substituting in (B.3.4) we get

$$\hat{x}(k) = \frac{\Psi_1(k) + \Psi_N(k)}{2(1 - \cos \frac{k\pi}{N+1})} \tag{B.4.1}$$

Now $\Psi_N(k) = (-1)^{k-1} \Psi_1(k)$ therefore the even harmonics are all zero and the odd harmonics are

$$\hat{x}(2r + 1) = \sqrt{\frac{2}{N+1}} \frac{\sin \frac{(2r+1)\pi}{N+1}}{\left\{ 1 - \cos \frac{(2r+1)\pi}{N+1} \right\}} . \tag{B.4.2}$$

Now $\frac{\sin 2\theta}{1 - \cos 2\theta} = \cot \theta$ therefore the DST coefficients for $x(n) = 1$ are

$$\boxed{\hat{x}(2r) = 0 ; \quad \hat{x}(2r+1) = \sqrt{\frac{2}{N+1}} \cot \frac{(2r+1)\pi}{2(N+1)} .} \tag{B.4.3}$$

B.5   Linear Sequences

If we consider the series $x(n) = c + rn$ then this also satisfies (B.2.3) with $A = c$ and $B = c + (N+1)r$ and we can easily see that $a = \dfrac{1}{2}$. Hence using (B.2.5) the DST of the linear sequence: $x(n) = c + rn$, is

$$\hat{x}(k) = \frac{A \ \Psi_1(k) + B \ \Psi_N(k)}{2(1 - \cos \dfrac{k\pi}{N+1})} \ . \tag{B.5.1}$$

In the special case $A = 0$ ($c = 0$) this reduces to

$$\hat{x}(k) = \frac{B \ \Psi_N(k)}{2(1 - \cos \dfrac{k\pi}{N+1})} \ . \tag{B.5.2}$$

or if $B = 0$ then

$$\hat{x}(k) = \frac{A \ \Psi_1(k)}{2(1 - \cos \dfrac{k\pi}{N+1})} \ . \tag{B.5.3}$$

B.6   Hyperbolic Sequences

We can get the DST of the hyperbolic functions by combining the DST coefficients for two exponential sequences. Since

$$\sinh np = \frac{e^{np} - e^{-np}}{2} \tag{B.6.1}$$

using equation (B.3.4) we obtain

$$\hat{x}(k) = \frac{\sinh(N+1)p \ \Psi_N(k)}{2(\cosh p - \cos \dfrac{k\pi}{N+1})} \ . \tag{B.6.2}$$

Similarly for the cosh(.) function:

$$\cosh np = \frac{e^{np} + e^{-np}}{2} \qquad \text{(B.6.3)}$$

and therefore

$$\hat{x}(k) = \frac{\Psi_1(k) + \cosh(N+1)p\ \Psi_N(k)}{2(\cosh p - \cos \frac{k\pi}{N+1})} \cdot \qquad \text{(B.6.4)}$$

The DST of $\sinh(N+1-n)p$ is a combination of (B.6.2) and (B.6.4) since

$$\sinh(N+1-n)p = \qquad \text{(B.6.5)}$$

$$\sinh(N+1)p \cosh np - \cosh(N+1)p \sinh np$$

and this leads to

$$\hat{x}(k) = \frac{\sinh(N+1)p\ \Psi_1(k)}{2(\cosh p - \cos \frac{k\pi}{N+1})} \cdot \qquad \text{(B.6.6)}$$

which is the same as (B.6.2) with Ψ_N replaced by Ψ_1. Similarly the DST of $\cosh(N+1-n)p$ is a combination of (B.6.2) and (B.6.4) and it can be shown that

$$\hat{x}(k) = \frac{\cosh(N+1)p\ \Psi_1(k) + \Psi_N(k)}{2(\cosh p - \cos \frac{k\pi}{N+1})} \cdot \qquad \text{(B.6.7)}$$

which is the same as (B.6.4) with Ψ_N and Ψ_1 interchanged.

B.7 Sinusoidal Sequences

We can also get the DST of the trigonometric functions by combining the DST coefficients for two exponential sequences, since

$$\sin np = \frac{e^{inp} - e^{-inp}}{2i} \qquad \text{(B.7.1)}$$

we have

$$\hat{x}(k) = \frac{\Psi_N(k)}{2(\cos p - \cos \frac{k\pi}{N+1})} .$$

(B.7.2)

Similarly for the cos(.) function

$$\cos np = \frac{e^{inp} + e^{-inp}}{2}$$

(B.7.3)

we have

$$\hat{x}(k) = \frac{\Psi_1(k) + \cos(N+1)p \ \Psi_N(k)}{2(\cos p - \cos \frac{k\pi}{N+1})} .$$

(B.7.4)

C

Transform Domain
Variance Distributions

C.1   Introduction

In this appendix we will derive the normalized variance distributions for
RBC and DCT coding of 1st-order Markov processes. We will first consider RBC in section C.2 and then DCT coding in C.3.

C.2   1d RBC

In this section we will show that the normalized variance distribution varies only slowly with ρ while the variance reduction ratio η, varies very
rapidly with ρ.

Normalized Variance Distribution

Assuming a 1st-order Markov process, we have already seen in (2.7.23)
that

$$\mathbf{R}_{\hat{y}} \triangleq E[\hat{\mathbf{y}}\hat{\mathbf{y}}^T] = E[\mathbf{\Psi}\mathbf{y}\mathbf{y}^T\mathbf{\Psi}] = \mathbf{\Psi}\,\mathbf{R}_y\,\mathbf{\Psi} = \beta^2\mathbf{\Lambda}^{-1} \qquad (C.2.1)$$

and so taking the diagonal entries from the matrix we have the variances,
$\sigma_{\hat{y}}^2(k)$, viz.,

$$\sigma_{\hat{y}}^2(k) = \mathbf{R}_{\hat{y}}(k,k) = \frac{\beta^2}{\lambda(k)} ; \qquad k = 1,...,N \qquad (C.2.2)$$

where

$$\beta^2 = \sigma_x^2 \frac{1-\rho^2}{1+\rho^2} ; \qquad (C.2.3)$$

and

$$\lambda(k) = 1 - \frac{2\rho}{1+\rho^2} \cos \frac{k\pi}{N+1} \; ; \quad k = 1, \ldots, N \,. \qquad (C.2.4)$$

The average value for the transform domain variances is $\bar{\sigma}_y^2$, viz.,

$$\bar{\sigma}_y^2 \triangleq \frac{1}{N} \left[\beta^2 \sum_{k=1}^{N} \frac{1}{\lambda(k)} \right] \,. \qquad (C.2.5)$$

We divide the transform domain variances by their average value $\bar{\sigma}_y^2$ to obtain the normalized variance distribution as

$$\boxed{ \frac{\sigma_y^2(k)}{\bar{\sigma}_y^2} = \frac{N}{\lambda(k) \sum\limits_{j=1}^{N} \frac{1}{\lambda(j)}} } \qquad (C.2.6)$$

where $\lambda(k)$ is given in (C.2.4).

If we now consider the special case when $\rho \approx 1$, which is a good approximation for practical images, then

$$\rho \approx 1 = 1 - \epsilon \,, \quad \text{say} \qquad (C.2.7)$$

and

$$\frac{2\rho}{(1+\rho^2)} = \frac{2}{(\rho + \rho^{-1})} = \frac{2}{(1 - \epsilon) + (1 + \epsilon + O(\epsilon^2))}$$

$$= \frac{2}{(2 + O(\epsilon^2))} \qquad (C.2.8)$$

$$= 1 + O(\epsilon^2) \,.$$

So, we then have

$$\lambda(k) \approx 1 - \cos \frac{k\pi}{N+1} \qquad (C.2.9)$$

which is independent of ρ for highly correlated processes and therefore the normalized distribution is

$$\frac{\sigma_y^2(k)}{\bar{\sigma}_y^2} = \frac{N}{\left[1 - \cos \dfrac{k\pi}{N+1} \right] \left[\sum\limits_{j=1}^{N} (1 - \cos \dfrac{j\pi}{N+1})^{-1} \right]} \qquad (C.2.10)$$

which is also independent of ρ. In summary we have shown that ϵ has only a second order effect on the distribution which is therefore approximately constant for small ϵ (large ρ) and varies only slowly as ρ decreases as shown in Fig. C.2.1 for the case $N = 7$ as ρ varies from 0.5 to 0.99.

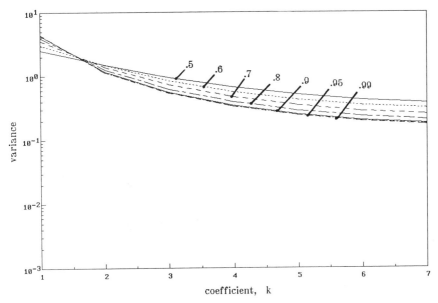

FIGURE C.2.1. Theoretical variance distribution for 1d RBC, $N = 7$, of a 1st-order Markov process for $\rho = 0.5, \cdots, 0.99$.

Variance Reduction Ratio

As we have just shown, the normalized variance distribution is fairly insensitive to changes in ρ, however the variance reduction ratio is very sensitive to such changes as we shall now show.

By definition

$$\eta \overset{\Delta}{=} \frac{\sigma_x^2}{\bar{\sigma}_y^2} = \frac{N\sigma_x^2}{\beta^2 \displaystyle\sum_{k=1}^{N} \frac{1}{\lambda(k)}} \tag{C.2.11}$$

and so from (C.2.3) we have

$$\eta = N \frac{(1+\rho^2)}{(1-\rho^2)} \frac{1}{\displaystyle\sum_{k=1}^{N} \frac{1}{\lambda(k)}} \tag{C.2.12}$$

where as before $\lambda(k)$ is given in (C.2.4).

Again taking the special case when $\rho \approx 1 = (1 - \epsilon)$, $\lambda(k)$ is largely independent of ρ so that

$$\eta \propto \frac{(1+\rho^2)}{(1-\rho^2)} = \frac{1 + (1 - 2\epsilon + O(\epsilon^2))}{1 - (1 - 2\epsilon + O(\epsilon^2))}$$

$$\approx \frac{2 - 2\epsilon}{2\epsilon} \tag{C.2.13}$$

$$= \frac{1}{\epsilon} - 1$$

and so, since $\eta \propto (\frac{1}{\epsilon} - 1)$, $\eta \to \infty$ as $\epsilon \to 0$. For example, $\eta_{.99} \approx \frac{99}{19} \eta_{.95} = 5.2 \, \eta_{.95}$ and $\eta_{.95} \approx \frac{19}{9} \eta_{.9} = 2.1 \, \eta_{.9}$.

Computing η from (C.2.12) for $N = 3, 7, 15$ and $\rho = 0.80, \ldots, 0.995$ we obtain the values shown in Table C.2.1 which closely follow the ratios predicted by the approximate proportional relationship given in (C.2.13). The tabulated results clearly show how very rapidly η increases as ρ approaches unity. Furthermore, as the transform block size N decreases, the prediction improves and η increases.

C.3   1d DCT

In this case since the DCT, although a good approximation, is not the true KLT of the Markov process, there are no simple eigen equations for the transform domain variances and we have

$$\sigma_{\hat{x}}^2(k) = \sigma_x^2 \left[\mathbf{CRC}^T \right] (k,k) \tag{C.3.1}$$

where $\mathbf{C}$ is the DCT matrix and $\mathbf{R}$ is the symmetric Toeplitz image autocorrelation matrix with first row: $[1 \, \rho \, \rho^2 \, \cdots \, \rho^{N-1}]$. We again normalize by the average variance value, $\bar{\sigma}_{\hat{x}}^2$ which is

$$\bar{\sigma}_{\hat{x}}^2 = \frac{1}{N} \sum_{k=1}^{N} \sigma_{\hat{x}}^2(k)$$

$$= \frac{\sigma_x^2}{N} \sum_{k=1}^{N} \left[\mathbf{CRC}^T \right] (k,k) \tag{C.3.2}$$

$$= \frac{\sigma_x^2}{N} \sum_{k=1}^{N} \mathbf{R}(k,k) = \sigma_x^2$$

TABLE C.2.1. Variance reduction ratio, η.

N	.80	.85	.90	.91	.92	.93	.94	.95	.96	.97	.98	.99	.995
15	1.3	1.5	2.0	2.1	2.4	2.6	3.0	3.6	4.4	5.9	8.8	17.6	35.2
7	1.8	2.3	3.3	3.7	4.1	4.7	5.5	6.6	8.2	11.0	16.5	33.2	66.5
3	2.8	3.8	5.8	6.4	7.3	8.3	9.7	11.7	14.7	19.7	29.7	59.7	119.7

where we have made use of the fact that **C** is a unitary transform and so the *trace* of the **R** matrix is unchanged after transformation, that is the sum of the diagonal elements, N in this case, is invariant under unitary transformation. Consequently the normalized variances are simply

$$\frac{\sigma_x^2(k)}{\overline{\sigma_x^2}} = \left[\mathbf{CRC}^T \right](k,k) . \tag{C.3.3}$$

Using (C.3.3), we calculated the normalized transform domain variance distributions for a block size of 8 with ρ varying over the same interval of 0.5 to 0.99 used for RBC. The distributions are plotted in Fig. C.3.1 and as the correlation coefficient varies, the distribution varies much more rapidly than in the case of RBC shown in Fig. C.2.1. These differences are most pronounced as ρ becomes large when the curves are widely spread for the DCT but tightly grouped with RBC.

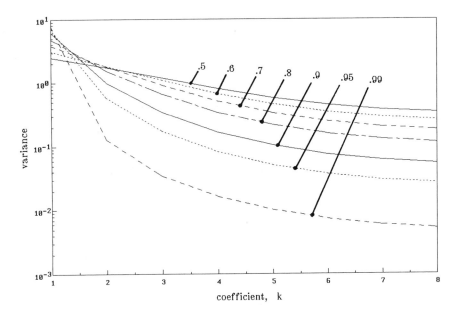

FIGURE C.3.1. Theoretical variance distribution for 1d DCT, $N = 8$, of a 1st-order Markov process for $\rho = 0.5, \cdots , 0.99$.

D

Coding Parameters
for Adaptive Coding
Based on Activity Classes

D.1 Introduction

The normalized variances and resulting bit allocations used for the adaptive coding experiments described in chapter five are given in this appendix. The DCT parameters are given in section D.2 and then the RBC parameters are tabulated in section D.3.

D.2 Adaptive DCT Coding Parameters

The normalized DCT variances for the four activity classes are listed below in Table D.2.1 for ensemble A, and Table D.2.2 for ensemble B. The resulting bit allocations are then given in Tables D.2.3(a)-(d) for ensemble A at the four rates of 1.5, 1.0, 0.5, and 0.25 bits/pixel. The next four tables, D.2.4(a)-(d), are then for ensemble B at these same four data rates.

TABLE D.2.1. Normalized variances for adaptive DCT coding.

Ensemble A

	1	2	3	4	5	6	7	8
1	0.00	17.93	5.31	2.28	1.46	0.82	0.56	0.37
2	11.67	3.48	1.52	0.80	0.50	0.31	0.21	0.16
3	4.02	1.54	0.89	0.53	0.36	0.23	0.16	0.12
4	1.82	0.67	0.48	0.35	0.24	0.16	0.11	0.09
5	0.99	0.36	0.26	0.19	0.15	0.10	0.08	0.06
6	0.53	0.19	0.15	0.12	0.09	0.08	0.06	0.06
7	0.28	0.12	0.10	0.08	0.07	0.06	0.05	0.04
8	0.15	0.09	0.07	0.06	0.05	0.04	0.04	0.03

(i) Class 1 (average ac energy, $\bar{\sigma}_1^2$: 1878.8)

	1	2	3	4	5	6	7	8
1	0.00	11.32	4.74	2.14	1.23	0.72	0.47	0.28
2	11.09	3.91	2.14	1.20	0.74	0.47	0.30	0.23
3	4.56	2.00	1.33	0.79	0.51	0.34	0.24	0.17
4	2.16	1.06	0.75	0.52	0.37	0.26	0.18	0.13
5	1.16	0.62	0.47	0.32	0.26	0.18	0.14	0.10
6	0.62	0.38	0.29	0.23	0.17	0.14	0.10	0.08
7	0.38	0.24	0.20	0.15	0.13	0.11	0.09	0.07
8	0.24	0.18	0.16	0.12	0.10	0.08	0.07	0.06

(ii) Class 2 (average ac energy, $\bar{\sigma}_2^2$: 512.0)

	1	2	3	4	5	6	7	8
1	0.00	11.69	4.75	2.51	1.36	0.75	0.47	0.33
2	9.29	3.55	2.21	1.38	0.85	0.54	0.36	0.29
3	3.73	1.80	1.26	0.89	0.59	0.41	0.30	0.24
4	1.90	1.05	0.74	0.56	0.41	0.31	0.23	0.18
5	1.18	0.61	0.47	0.37	0.30	0.24	0.19	0.15
6	0.69	0.41	0.33	0.26	0.21	0.18	0.15	0.12
7	0.48	0.30	0.25	0.21	0.16	0.16	0.16	0.11
8	0.30	0.23	0.20	0.17	0.14	0.12	0.12	0.09

(iii) Class 3 (average ac energy, $\bar{\sigma}_3^2$: 168.0)

	1	2	3	4	5	6	7	8
1	0.00	8.95	3.81	2.12	1.28	0.83	0.60	0.51
2	7.63	3.40	2.09	1.35	0.93	0.64	0.50	0.40
3	3.30	1.93	1.47	0.98	0.70	0.50	0.41	0.35
4	1.84	1.23	0.97	0.69	0.56	0.41	0.34	0.30
5	1.14	0.80	0.65	0.50	0.43	0.36	0.29	0.26
6	0.75	0.54	0.46	0.39	0.34	0.31	0.26	0.25
7	0.55	0.40	0.35	0.31	0.27	0.28	0.28	0.23
8	0.42	0.33	0.30	0.27	0.23	0.26	0.22	0.52

(iv) Class 4 (average ac energy, $\bar{\sigma}_4^2$: 35.2)

TABLE D.2.2. Normalized variances for adaptive DCT coding.

Ensemble B

	1	2	3	4	5	6	7	8
1	0.00	16.47	3.06	1.16	0.62	0.33	0.16	0.06
2	24.57	3.64	1.19	0.35	0.15	0.07	0.04	0.03
3	4.52	1.28	0.62	0.25	0.10	0.05	0.03	0.02
4	1.67	0.46	0.27	0.13	0.07	0.04	0.02	0.02
5	0.76	0.18	0.13	0.08	0.05	0.03	0.02	0.01
6	0.41	0.09	0.07	0.04	0.03	0.02	0.02	0.02
7	0.18	0.05	0.03	0.03	0.02	0.02	0.03	0.02
8	0.08	0.03	0.02	0.02	0.02	0.02	0.02	0.01

(i) Class 1 (average ac energy, $\bar{\sigma}_1^2$: 1603.4)

	1	2	3	4	5	6	7	8
1	0.00	13.35	3.06	1.39	0.74	0.45	0.28	0.21
2	17.14	4.10	1.62	0.83	0.53	0.32	0.23	0.19
3	3.71	1.62	0.99	0.61	0.41	0.28	0.19	0.16
4	1.50	0.78	0.55	0.43	0.34	0.25	0.18	0.14
5	0.73	0.45	0.35	0.29	0.24	0.18	0.16	0.15
6	0.48	0.28	0.23	0.20	0.17	0.15	0.16	0.13
7	0.30	0.21	0.17	0.22	0.19	0.20	0.26	0.18
8	0.21	0.16	0.14	0.16	0.15	0.14	0.17	0.18

(ii) Class 2 (average ac energy, $\bar{\sigma}_2^2$: 186.4)

	1	2	3	4	5	6	7	8
1	0.00	9.83	2.32	1.24	0.81	0.60	0.48	0.45
2	12.49	2.97	1.34	0.92	0.67	0.54	0.46	0.39
3	3.12	1.48	0.98	0.73	0.59	0.44	0.39	0.35
4	1.50	0.91	0.72	0.58	0.46	0.41	0.38	0.33
5	0.93	0.62	0.54	0.47	0.41	0.35	0.36	0.33
6	0.76	0.50	0.44	0.41	0.36	0.36	0.44	0.40
7	0.54	0.43	0.40	0.41	0.40	0.53	0.78	0.53
8	0.50	0.42	0.35	0.36	0.34	0.37	0.52	0.55

(iii) Class 3 (average ac energy, $\bar{\sigma}_3^2$: 40.6)

	1	2	3	4	5	6	7	8
1	0.00	7.39	2.23	1.24	0.90	0.65	0.57	0.54
2	8.22	2.36	1.26	0.88	0.70	0.59	0.57	0.53
3	2.42	1.24	0.93	0.76	0.62	0.54	0.51	0.48
4	1.32	0.88	0.71	0.62	0.56	0.56	0.53	0.52
5	0.99	0.70	0.63	0.54	0.51	0.45	0.48	0.49
6	0.83	0.64	0.53	0.53	0.48	0.59	0.82	0.88
7	0.64	0.60	0.51	0.58	0.52	0.97	1.74	1.35
8	0.57	0.52	0.46	0.51	0.42	0.66	0.92	1.10

(iv) Class 4 (average ac energy, $\bar{\sigma}_4^2$: 11.5)

TABLE D.2.3(a). Adaptive DCT coding; ensemble A: 1.5 bits/pixel.

```
8  6  5  5  4  4  4  3        8  5  4  4  3  3  2  2
6  5  4  4  3  3  3  3        5  4  4  3  3  3  2  1
5  4  4  3  3  3  3  2        4  4  3  3  3  2  1  1
5  4  3  3  3  3  2  2        4  3  3  3  2  1  1  1
4  3  3  3  3  2  1  1        3  3  2  2  1  1  1  .
3  3  3  2  2  1  1  1        3  2  2  1  1  1  .  .
3  2  2  2  1  1  1  1        2  1  1  1  1  .  .  .
3  2  1  1  1  1  .  .        1  1  1  .  .  .  .  .
```

(i) Class 1: 180 bits   (ii) Class 2: 127 bits

```
8  4  3  3  2  1  1  .        8  .  .  .  .  .  .  .
4  3  3  2  2  1  .  .        .  .  .  .  .  .  .  .
3  3  2  2  1  1  .  .        .  .  .  .  .  .  .  .
3  2  1  1  1  .  .  .        .  .  .  .  .  .  .  .
2  1  1  1  .  .  .  .        .  .  .  .  .  .  .  .
1  1  .  .  .  .  .  .        .  .  .  .  .  .  .  .
1  .  .  .  .  .  .  .        .  .  .  .  .  .  .  .
.  .  .  .  .  .  .  .        .  .  .  .  .  .  .  .
```

(iii) Class 3: 65 bits   (iv) Class 4: 8 bits

TABLE D.2.3(b). Adaptive DCT coding; ensemble A: 1.0 bits/pixel.

```
8  6  5  4  4  3  3  3        8  4  4  3  3  2  1  1
6  4  4  3  3  3  2  2        4  4  3  3  2  1  1  .
5  4  3  3  3  2  2  1        4  3  3  2  1  1  .  .
4  3  3  3  2  2  1  1        3  3  2  1  1  .  .  .
3  3  2  2  1  1  1  .        3  2  1  1  .  .  .  .
3  2  1  1  1  1  .  .        2  1  1  .  .  .  .  .
3  1  1  1  .  .  .  .        1  .  .  .  .  .  .  .
1  1  1  .  .  .  .  .        .  .  .  .  .  .  .  .
```

(i) Class 1: 136 bits   (ii) Class 2: 80 bits

```
8  3  2  1  1  .  .  .        8  .  .  .  .  .  .  .
3  2  1  1  .  .  .  .        .  .  .  .  .  .  .  .
2  1  1  .  .  .  .  .        .  .  .  .  .  .  .  .
1  .  .  .  .  .  .  .        .  .  .  .  .  .  .  .
.  .  .  .  .  .  .  .        .  .  .  .  .  .  .  .
.  .  .  .  .  .  .  .        .  .  .  .  .  .  .  .
.  .  .  .  .  .  .  .        .  .  .  .  .  .  .  .
.  .  .  .  .  .  .  .        .  .  .  .  .  .  .  .
```

(iii) Class 3: 27 bits   (iv) Class 4: 8 bits

TABLE D.2.3(c). Adaptive DCT coding; ensemble A: 0.5 bits/pixel.

```
7  5  4  3  3  3  2  1        7  3  3  1  1  .  .  .
5  4  3  3  2  1  .  .        3  2  1  1  .  .  .  .
4  3  3  2  1  1  .  .        3  1  1  .  .  .  .  .
3  2  2  1  1  .  .  .        1  1  .  .  .  .  .  .
3  1  1  .  .  .  .  .        1  .  .  .  .  .  .  .
2  .  .  .  .  .  .  .        .  .  .  .  .  .  .  .
1  .  .  .  .  .  .  .        .  .  .  .  .  .  .  .
.  .  .  .  .  .  .  .        .  .  .  .  .  .  .  .
```

(i) Class 1: 77 bits   (ii) Class 2: 30 bits

```
7  .  .  .  .  .  .  .        7  .  .  .  .  .  .  .
.  .  .  .  .  .  .  .        .  .  .  .  .  .  .  .
.  .  .  .  .  .  .  .        .  .  .  .  .  .  .  .
.  .  .  .  .  .  .  .        .  .  .  .  .  .  .  .
.  .  .  .  .  .  .  .        .  .  .  .  .  .  .  .
.  .  .  .  .  .  .  .        .  .  .  .  .  .  .  .
.  .  .  .  .  .  .  .        .  .  .  .  .  .  .  .
.  .  .  .  .  .  .  .        .  .  .  .  .  .  .  .
```

(iii) Class 3: 7 bits   (iv) Class 4: 7 bits

TABLE D.2.3(d). Adaptive DCT coding; ensemble A: 0.25 bits/pixel.

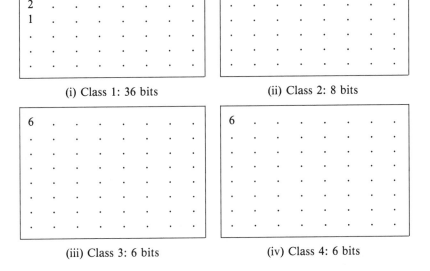

```
6  4  3  2  1  1  .  .        6  1  .  .  .  .  .  .
4  3  2  1  .  .  .  .        1  .  .  .  .  .  .  .
3  2  1  .  .  .  .  .        .  .  .  .  .  .  .  .
2  .  .  .  .  .  .  .        .  .  .  .  .  .  .  .
1  .  .  .  .  .  .  .        .  .  .  .  .  .  .  .
.  .  .  .  .  .  .  .        .  .  .  .  .  .  .  .
.  .  .  .  .  .  .  .        .  .  .  .  .  .  .  .
.  .  .  .  .  .  .  .        .  .  .  .  .  .  .  .
```

(i) Class 1: 36 bits   (ii) Class 2: 8 bits

```
6  .  .  .  .  .  .  .        6  .  .  .  .  .  .  .
.  .  .  .  .  .  .  .        .  .  .  .  .  .  .  .
.  .  .  .  .  .  .  .        .  .  .  .  .  .  .  .
.  .  .  .  .  .  .  .        .  .  .  .  .  .  .  .
.  .  .  .  .  .  .  .        .  .  .  .  .  .  .  .
.  .  .  .  .  .  .  .        .  .  .  .  .  .  .  .
.  .  .  .  .  .  .  .        .  .  .  .  .  .  .  .
.  .  .  .  .  .  .  .        .  .  .  .  .  .  .  .
```

(iii) Class 3: 6 bits   (iv) Class 4: 6 bits

TABLE D.2.4(a). Adaptive DCT coding; ensemble B: 1.5 bits/pixel.

8	7	6	5	4	4	3	3
7	6	5	4	3	3	2	1
6	5	4	4	3	2	1	1
5	4	4	3	3	2	1	1
5	3	3	3	2	1	1	1
4	3	3	2	1	1	1	1
3	2	2	1	1	1	1	1
3	1	1	1	1	1	1	1

(i) Class 1: 177 bits

8	5	4	3	3	3	2	1
6	4	4	3	3	2	1	1
4	4	3	3	2	2	1	1
3	3	3	3	2	2	1	1
3	3	2	2	1	1	1	1
3	2	1	1	1	1	1	1
2	1	1	1	1	1	2	1
1	1	1	1	1	1	1	1

(ii) Class 2: 134 bits

8	4	3	2	1	1	1	1
4	3	2	1	1	1	1	.
3	2	2	1	1	1	.	.
2	1	1	1	1	.	.	.
1	1	1	1	.	.	.	.
1	1	1	.	.	.	1	.
1	1	.	.	.	1	1	1
1	1	.	.	.	1	1	

(iii) Class 3: 67 bits

8	.	.	.	.	.	.	.
.	.	.	.	.	.	.	.
.	.	.	.	.	.	.	.
.	.	.	.	.	.	.	.
.	.	.	.	.	.	.	.
.	.	.	.	.	.	.	.
.	.	.	.	.	.	.	.
.	.	.	.	.	.	.	.

(iv) Class 4: 8 bits

TABLE D.2.4(b). Adaptive DCT coding; ensemble B: 1.0 bits/pixel.

8	6	5	4	4	3	3	2
7	5	4	3	3	2	1	1
6	5	4	3	3	1	1	.
5	4	3	3	2	1	.	.
4	3	3	2	1	1	.	.
4	2	2	1	1	.	.	.
3	1	1	1	.	.	1	.
2	.	.	.	.	.	.	.

(i) Class 1: 135 bits

8	5	4	3	2	2	1	1
5	4	3	3	2	1	1	.
4	3	3	2	1	1	.	.
3	3	2	1	1	1	.	.
2	2	1	1	1	.	.	.
2	1	1	1	.	.	.	.
1	1	.	1	.	1	1	.
1	.	.	.	.	.	.	.

(ii) Class 2: 88 bits

8	3	1	.	.	.	.	.
3	1	.	.	.	.	.	.
2	1	.	.	.	.	.	.
1	.	.	.	.	.	.	.
.	.	.	.	.	.	.	.
.	.	.	.	.	.	.	.
.	.	.	.	.	.	.	.
.	.	.	.	.	.	.	.

(iii) Class 3: 20 bits

8	.	.	.	.	.	.	.
.	.	.	.	.	.	.	.
.	.	.	.	.	.	.	.
.	.	.	.	.	.	.	.
.	.	.	.	.	.	.	.
.	.	.	.	.	.	.	.
.	.	.	.	.	.	.	.
.	.	.	.	.	.	.	.

(iv) Class 4: 8 bits

TABLE D.2.4(c). Adaptive DCT coding; ensemble B: 0.5 bits/pixel.

7	6	4	3	3	3	1	.
6	4	3	3	1	.	.	.
5	4	3	2	1	.	.	.
4	3	2	1	.	.	.	.
3	1	1	.	.	.	.	.
3	1	.	.	.	.	.	.
1	.	.	.	.	.	.	.
.	.	.	.	.	.	.	.

(i) Class 1: 79 bits

7	4	2	1	.	.	.	.
4	3	1	.	.	.	.	.
3	1	1	.	.	.	.	.
1	.	.	.	.	.	.	.
.	.	.	.	.	.	.	.
.	.	.	.	.	.	.	.
.	.	.	.	.	.	.	.
.	.	.	.	.	.	.	.

(ii) Class 2: 28 bits

7	.	.	.	.	.	.	.
.	.	.	.	.	.	.	.
.	.	.	.	.	.	.	.
.	.	.	.	.	.	.	.
.	.	.	.	.	.	.	.
.	.	.	.	.	.	.	.
.	.	.	.	.	.	.	.
.	.	.	.	.	.	.	.

(iii) Class 3: 7 bits

7	.	.	.	.	.	.	.
.	.	.	.	.	.	.	.
.	.	.	.	.	.	.	.
.	.	.	.	.	.	.	.
.	.	.	.	.	.	.	.
.	.	.	.	.	.	.	.
.	.	.	.	.	.	.	.
.	.	.	.	.	.	.	.

(iv) Class 4: 7 bits

TABLE D.2.4(d). Adaptive DCT coding; ensemble B: 0.25 bits/pixel.

6	4	3	2	1	.	.	.
5	3	2	.	.	.	.	.
3	2	1	.	.	.	.	.
3	1	.	.	.	.	.	.
1	.	.	.	.	.	.	.
.	.	.	.	.	.	.	.
.	.	.	.	.	.	.	.
.	.	.	.	.	.	.	.

(i) Class 1: 37 bits

6	.	.	.	.	.	.	.
.	.	.	.	.	.	.	.
.	.	.	.	.	.	.	.
.	.	.	.	.	.	.	.
.	.	.	.	.	.	.	.
.	.	.	.	.	.	.	.
.	.	.	.	.	.	.	.
.	.	.	.	.	.	.	.

(ii) Class 2: 6 bits

6	.	.	.	.	.	.	.
.	.	.	.	.	.	.	.
.	.	.	.	.	.	.	.
.	.	.	.	.	.	.	.
.	.	.	.	.	.	.	.
.	.	.	.	.	.	.	.
.	.	.	.	.	.	.	.
.	.	.	.	.	.	.	.

(iii) Class 3: 6 bits

6	.	.	.	.	.	.	.
.	.	.	.	.	.	.	.
.	.	.	.	.	.	.	.
.	.	.	.	.	.	.	.
.	.	.	.	.	.	.	.
.	.	.	.	.	.	.	.
.	.	.	.	.	.	.	.
.	.	.	.	.	.	.	.

(iv) Class 4: 6 bits

D.3   Adaptive RBC Coding Parameters

The normalized RBC variances for the four activity classes are listed below in Table D.3.1 for ensemble A, and Table D.3.2 for ensemble B. The resulting bit allocations are then given in Tables D.3.3(a)-(d) for ensemble A at the four rates of 1.5, 1.0, 0.5, and 0.25 bits/pixel. The next four tables, D.3.4(a)-(d), are then for ensemble B at these same four data rates.

TABLE D.3.1. Normalized variances for adaptive RBC coding.

Ensemble A

	0	1	2	3	4	5	6	7
0	0.000	4.697	1.210	0.534	0.266	0.138	0.085	0.065
1	4.589	17.466	4.943	2.573	1.346	0.704	0.598	0.414
2	1.111	5.669	1.851	1.055	0.617	0.408	0.282	0.211
3	0.572	2.369	0.927	0.668	0.421	0.271	0.195	0.151
4	0.309	1.086	0.509	0.381	0.243	0.177	0.131	0.113
5	0.176	0.564	0.275	0.216	0.163	0.126	0.103	0.084
6	0.137	0.308	0.168	0.140	0.113	0.087	0.073	0.061
7	0.101	0.215	0.136	0.113	0.082	0.070	0.057	0.047

(i) Class 1 [average residual energies − (row:1896.1, column:2005.4, core:1160.1)]

0	0.000	3.511	1.522	0.781	0.487	0.316	0.218	0.164
1	3.460	12.631	5.377	2.572	1.346	0.811	0.491	0.368
2	1.536	5.053	2.613	1.420	0.850	0.545	0.351	0.268
3	0.783	2.361	1.248	0.856	0.551	0.381	0.258	0.196
4	0.508	1.257	0.718	0.509	0.363	0.270	0.189	0.142
5	0.320	0.699	0.460	0.351	0.261	0.200	0.150	0.113
6	0.222	0.456	0.318	0.237	0.187	0.155	0.126	0.097
7	0.171	0.326	0.230	0.184	0.151	0.115	0.099	0.079

(ii) Class 2 [average residual energies − (row:300.4, column:377.3, core:338.9)]

0	0.000	3.131	1.489	0.854	0.561	0.394	0.313	0.257
1	2.999	11.085	5.124	2.670	1.510	0.852	0.558	0.435
2	1.539	4.500	2.265	1.445	0.905	0.625	0.434	0.370
3	0.878	2.183	1.240	0.889	0.625	0.456	0.326	0.263
4	0.576	1.272	0.753	0.598	0.442	0.340	0.272	0.214
5	0.420	0.788	0.483	0.397	0.322	0.273	0.217	0.167
6	0.317	0.606	0.340	0.308	0.236	0.224	0.216	0.152
7	0.270	0.407	0.285	0.239	0.201	0.179	0.166	0.141

(iii) Class 3 [average residual energies − (row:82.8, column:101.5, core:114.5)]

0	0.000	2.469	1.454	0.939	0.710	0.554	0.445	0.429
1	2.454	9.580	4.054	2.180	1.398	0.885	0.669	0.574
2	1.419	4.178	2.274	1.470	0.978	0.691	0.511	0.418
3	0.959	2.172	1.396	0.978	0.726	0.533	0.413	0.359
4	0.697	1.128	0.848	0.675	0.536	0.426	0.347	0.296
5	0.568	0.818	0.581	0.506	0.415	0.363	0.291	0.290
6	0.467	0.583	0.430	0.368	0.327	0.308	0.292	0.259
7	0.435	0.439	0.340	0.321	0.277	0.281	0.246	0.573

(iv) Class 4 [average residual energies − (row:16.7, column:19.3, core:25.1)]

TABLE D.3.2. Normalized variances for adaptive RBC coding.

Ensemble B

	0	1	2	3	4	5	6	7
0	0.000	5.380	0.984	0.340	0.142	0.074	0.047	0.027
1	5.334	25.108	4.834	1.506	0.586	0.263	0.131	0.067
2	1.008	6.376	1.805	0.681	0.265	0.134	0.067	0.049
3	0.350	2.202	0.750	0.396	0.184	0.099	0.054	0.038
4	0.152	0.885	0.322	0.207	0.111	0.064	0.042	0.031
5	0.075	0.424	0.152	0.115	0.068	0.048	0.042	0.035
6	0.044	0.188	0.082	0.068	0.050	0.049	0.062	0.038
7	0.033	0.089	0.050	0.045	0.033	0.032	0.035	0.030

(i) Class 1 [average residual energies − (row:1294.0, column:1136.8, core:750.2)]

	0	1	2	3	4	5	6	7
0	0.000	3.631	1.311	0.658	0.428	0.334	0.350	0.288
1	3.508	15.092	3.977	1.708	0.926	0.568	0.399	0.335
2	1.212	4.573	2.033	1.131	0.738	0.502	0.357	0.287
3	0.707	1.899	1.092	0.772	0.607	0.417	0.323	0.269
4	0.503	0.927	0.634	0.503	0.437	0.317	0.323	0.259
5	0.383	0.700	0.422	0.363	0.312	0.285	0.294	0.265
6	0.354	0.424	0.293	0.388	0.374	0.372	0.483	0.323
7	0.333	0.362	0.262	0.295	0.275	0.272	0.335	0.494

(ii) Class 2 [average residual energies − (row:105.3, column:88.5, core:101.2)]

	0	1	2	3	4	5	6	7
0	0.000	2.659	1.226	0.779	0.611	0.560	0.611	0.553
1	2.522	9.493	2.951	1.471	0.976	0.718	0.589	0.568
2	1.213	3.493	1.655	1.115	0.811	0.651	0.545	0.494
3	0.829	1.679	1.191	0.836	0.684	0.564	0.499	0.458
4	0.643	1.121	0.808	0.661	0.599	0.496	0.468	0.448
5	0.566	0.829	0.639	0.593	0.502	0.504	0.549	0.543
6	0.617	0.660	0.553	0.561	0.515	0.636	0.937	0.678
7	0.610	0.589	0.512	0.463	0.439	0.530	0.658	1.065

(iii) Class 3 [average residual energies − (row:30.3, column:27.2, core:29.8)]

	0	1	2	3	4	5	6	7
0	0.000	2.063	1.151	0.824	0.742	0.683	0.822	0.716
1	2.020	7.596	2.653	1.305	0.907	0.676	0.592	0.591
2	1.144	2.925	1.380	0.981	0.741	0.634	0.524	0.518
3	0.832	1.539	1.148	0.789	0.624	0.592	0.553	0.551
4	0.733	1.203	0.780	0.660	0.574	0.526	0.520	0.516
5	0.713	0.846	0.650	0.589	0.519	0.640	0.898	0.920
6	0.756	0.613	0.552	0.594	0.546	1.011	1.628	1.369
7	0.803	0.579	0.486	0.492	0.459	0.697	0.962	1.350

(iv) Class 4 [average residual energies − (row:7.4, column:7.1, core:9.2)]

TABLE D.3.3(a). Adaptive RBC coding; ensemble A: 1.5 bits/pixel.

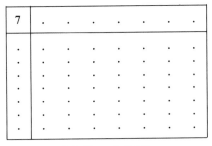

7	5	4	4	3	3	2	1
5	6	5	4	4	3	3	3
4	5	4	4	3	3	3	3
4	4	4	3	3	3	2	2
3	4	3	3	3	2	2	1
3	3	3	3	2	2	1	1
3	3	2	2	1	1	1	1
2	3	2	1	1	1	1	.

(i) Class 1: 180 bits

7	4	3	3	2	1	1	.
4	5	4	4	3	3	2	1
3	4	4	3	3	2	1	1
3	3	3	3	2	2	1	1
2	3	3	2	2	1	1	.
2	3	2	1	1	1	.	.
1	2	1	1	1	.	.	.
1	1	1	1	.	.	.	.

(ii) Class 2: 120 bits

7	3	1	1	.	.	.	.
3	4	3	3	2	1	1	.
2	3	3	2	1	1	.	.
1	3	2	1	1	1	.	.
1	2	1	1	.	.	.	.
.	1	1	.	.	.	.	.
.	1	.	.	.	.	.	.
.	.	.	.	.	.	.	.

(iii) Class 3: 58 bits

7	.	.	.	.	.	.	.
.	.	.	.	.	.	.	.
.	.	.	.	.	.	.	.
.	.	.	.	.	.	.	.
.	.	.	.	.	.	.	.
.	.	.	.	.	.	.	.
.	.	.	.	.	.	.	.
.	.	.	.	.	.	.	.

(iv) Class 4: 7 bits

TABLE D.3.3(b). Adaptive RBC coding; ensemble A: 1.0 bits/pixel.

6	5	4	3	3	1	1	1
5	6	4	4	3	3	3	3
4	5	4	3	3	3	2	1
3	4	3	3	3	2	1	1
3	3	3	2	2	1	1	1
2	3	2	1	1	1	.	.
1	2	1	1	1	.	.	.
1	1	1	1	.	.	.	.

(i) Class 1: 136 bits

6	3	3	1	1	.	.	.
3	4	4	3	3	2	1	1
3	3	3	3	2	1	1	.
2	3	2	2	1	1	.	.
1	2	1	1	1	.	.	.
1	1	1	1	.	.	.	.
.	1	.	.	.	.	.	.
.	.	.	.	.	.	.	.

(ii) Class 2: 73 bits

6	1	.	.	.	.	.	.
1	3	2	1	1	.	.	.
1	2	1	.	.	.	.	.
.	1	.	.	.	.	.	.
.	.	.	.	.	.	.	.
.	.	.	.	.	.	.	.
.	.	.	.	.	.	.	.
.	.	.	.	.	.	.	.

(iii) Class 3: 20 bits

6	.	.	.	.	.	.	.
.	.	.	.	.	.	.	.
.	.	.	.	.	.	.	.
.	.	.	.	.	.	.	.
.	.	.	.	.	.	.	.
.	.	.	.	.	.	.	.
.	.	.	.	.	.	.	.
.	.	.	.	.	.	.	.

(iv) Class 4: 6 bits

TABLE D.3.3(c). Adaptive RBC coding; ensemble A: 0.5 bits/pixel.

5	4	3	2	1	.	.	.
4	5	4	3	3	2	1	1
3	4	3	2	1	1	1	.
3	3	2	2	1	.	.	.
1	3	1	1	.	.	.	.
1	1	.	.	.	.	.	.
.	1	.	.	.	.	.	.
.	.	.	.	.	.	.	.

(i) Class 1: 73 bits

5	2	.	.	.	.	.	.
3	3	2	1	.	.	.	.
1	2	1	.	.	.	.	.
.	1	.	.	.	.	.	.
.	.	.	.	.	.	.	.
.	.	.	.	.	.	.	.
.	.	.	.	.	.	.	.
.	.	.	.	.	.	.	.

(ii) Class 2: 21 bits

5	.	.	.	.	.	.	.
.	.	.	.	.	.	.	.
.	.	.	.	.	.	.	.
.	.	.	.	.	.	.	.
.	.	.	.	.	.	.	.
.	.	.	.	.	.	.	.
.	.	.	.	.	.	.	.
.	.	.	.	.	.	.	.

(iii) Class 3: 5 bits

5	.	.	.	.	.	.	.
.	.	.	.	.	.	.	.
.	.	.	.	.	.	.	.
.	.	.	.	.	.	.	.
.	.	.	.	.	.	.	.
.	.	.	.	.	.	.	.
.	.	.	.	.	.	.	.
.	.	.	.	.	.	.	.

(iv) Class 4: 5 bits

TABLE D.3.3(d). Adaptive RBC coding; ensemble A: 0.25 bits/pixel.

4	3	2	.	.	.	.	.
3	3	3	1	1	.	.	.
2	3	1	.	.	.	.	.
1	1	.	.	.	.	.	.
.	.	.	.	.	.	.	.
.	.	.	.	.	.	.	.
.	.	.	.	.	.	.	.
.	.	.	.	.	.	.	.

(i) Class 1: 28 bits

4	.	.	.	.	.	.	.
.	.	.	.	.	.	.	.
.	.	.	.	.	.	.	.
.	.	.	.	.	.	.	.
.	.	.	.	.	.	.	.
.	.	.	.	.	.	.	.
.	.	.	.	.	.	.	.
.	.	.	.	.	.	.	.

(ii) Class 2: 4 bits

4	.	.	.	.	.	.	.
.	.	.	.	.	.	.	.
.	.	.	.	.	.	.	.
.	.	.	.	.	.	.	.
.	.	.	.	.	.	.	.
.	.	.	.	.	.	.	.
.	.	.	.	.	.	.	.
.	.	.	.	.	.	.	.

(iii) Class 3: 4 bits

4	.	.	.	.	.	.	.
.	.	.	.	.	.	.	.
.	.	.	.	.	.	.	.
.	.	.	.	.	.	.	.
.	.	.	.	.	.	.	.
.	.	.	.	.	.	.	.
.	.	.	.	.	.	.	.
.	.	.	.	.	.	.	.

(iv) Class 4: 4 bits

TABLE D.3.4(a). Adaptive RBC coding; ensemble B: 1.5 bits/pixel.

7	4	3	2	2	1	1	1
4	5	4	3	3	2	1	1
3	4	3	3	3	2	1	1
2	3	3	3	2	1	1	1
2	3	2	2	2	1	1	1
1	2	2	1	1	1	1	1
1	2	1	1	1	1	2	1
1	1	1	1	1	1	1	2

(i) Class 1: 171 bits

7	4	3	2	2	1	1	1
4	5	4	3	3	2	1	1
3	4	3	3	3	2	1	1
2	3	3	3	2	1	1	1
2	3	2	2	2	1	1	1
1	2	2	1	1	1	1	1
1	2	1	1	1	1	2	1
1	1	1	1	1	1	1	2

(ii) Class 2: 123 bits

7	3	1	1	1	.	1	.
3	4	3	2	1	1	1	1
1	3	2	1	1	1	.	.
1	2	2	1	1	1	.	.
1	1	1	1	1	.	.	.
.	1	1	1	.	.	.	.
1	1	.	.	.	1	1	1
.	1	.	.	.	.	1	1

(iii) Class 3: 63 bits

7	.	.	.	.	.	.	.
.	.	.	.	.	.	.	.
.	.	.	.	.	.	.	.
.	.	.	.	.	.	.	.
.	.	.	.	.	.	.	.
.	.	.	.	.	.	.	.
.	.	.	.	.	.	.	.
.	.	.	.	.	.	.	.

(iv) Class 4: 7 bits

TABLE D.3.4(b). Adaptive RBC coding; ensemble B: 1.0 bits/pixel.

6	6	4	3	3	2	1	.
6	6	5	4	3	3	2	1
4	5	4	3	3	2	1	1
3	4	4	3	2	1	1	.
3	4	3	3	2	1	.	.
1	3	2	2	1	.	.	.
1	2	1	1	1	1	1	.
.	1	1	.	.	.	.	.

(i) Class 1: 131 bits

6	3	3	1	1	1	1	.
3	4	3	3	2	1	1	1
2	3	3	2	2	1	1	.
1	3	2	2	1	1	1	.
1	2	1	1	1	1	1	.
1	1	1	1	.	.	.	.
1	1	.	1	1	1	1	.
.	1	.	.	.	.	1	1

(ii) Class 2: 80 bits

6	1	1	.	.	.	.	.
1	3	1	.	.	.	.	.
1	2	1	.	.	.	.	.
.	1	.	.	.	.	.	.
.	.	.	.	.	.	.	.
.	.	.	.	.	.	.	.
.	.	.	.	.	.	.	.
.	.	.	.	.	.	.	.

(iii) Class 3: 18 bits

6	.	.	.	.	.	.	.
.	.	.	.	.	.	.	.
.	.	.	.	.	.	.	.
.	.	.	.	.	.	.	.
.	.	.	.	.	.	.	.
.	.	.	.	.	.	.	.
.	.	.	.	.	.	.	.
.	.	.	.	.	.	.	.

(iv) Class 4: 6 bits

TABLE D.3.4(c). Adaptive RBC coding; ensemble B: 0.5 bits/pixel.

5	5	3	3	1	1	.	.
5	6	4	3	2	1	.	.
3	4	3	3	1	.	.	.
3	3	3	2	1	.	.	.
1	3	1	1	.	.	.	.
.	2	.	.	.	.	.	.
.	1	.	.	.	.	.	.
.	.	.	.	.	.	.	.

(i) Class 1: 74 bits

5	2	1	.	.	.	.	.
2	3	2	.	.	.	.	.
1	2	1	.	.	.	.	.
.	1	.	.	.	.	.	.
.	.	.	.	.	.	.	.
.	.	.	.	.	.	.	.
.	.	.	.	.	.	.	.

(ii) Class 2: 20 bits

5	.	.	.	.	.	.	.
.	.	.	.	.	.	.	.
.	.	.	.	.	.	.	.
.	.	.	.	.	.	.	.
.	.	.	.	.	.	.	.
.	.	.	.	.	.	.	.
.	.	.	.	.	.	.	.
.	.	.	.	.	.	.	.

(iii) Class 3: 5 bits

5	.	.	.	.	.	.	.
.	.	.	.	.	.	.	.
.	.	.	.	.	.	.	.
.	.	.	.	.	.	.	.
.	.	.	.	.	.	.	.
.	.	.	.	.	.	.	.
.	.	.	.	.	.	.	.
.	.	.	.	.	.	.	.

(iv) Class 4: 5 bits

TABLE D.3.4(d). Adaptive RBC coding; ensemble B: 0.25 bits/pixel.

4	4	2	.	.	.	.	.
4	4	2	1	.	.	.	.
2	3	1	.	.	.	.	.
.	1	.	.	.	.	.	.
.	.	.	.	.	.	.	.
.	.	.	.	.	.	.	.
.	.	.	.	.	.	.	.

(i) Class 1: 28 bits

4	.	.	.	.	.	.	.
.	.	.	.	.	.	.	.
.	.	.	.	.	.	.	.
.	.	.	.	.	.	.	.
.	.	.	.	.	.	.	.
.	.	.	.	.	.	.	.
.	.	.	.	.	.	.	.

(ii) Class 2: 4 bits

4	.	.	.	.	.	.	.
.	.	.	.	.	.	.	.
.	.	.	.	.	.	.	.
.	.	.	.	.	.	.	.
.	.	.	.	.	.	.	.
.	.	.	.	.	.	.	.
.	.	.	.	.	.	.	.
.	.	.	.	.	.	.	.

(iii) Class 3: 4 bits

4	.	.	.	.	.	.	.
.	.	.	.	.	.	.	.
.	.	.	.	.	.	.	.
.	.	.	.	.	.	.	.
.	.	.	.	.	.	.	.
.	.	.	.	.	.	.	.
.	.	.	.	.	.	.	.
.	.	.	.	.	.	.	.

(iv) Class 4: 4 bits

References

1. Jain, A. K., *Fundamentals of Digital Image Processing*, Prentice-Hall, Englewood Cliffs, NJ, 1989.

2. Algazi, V. R. and Jain, A. K., *Noise analysis and measurement and data compression study for a digital x-ray system*, Signal and Image Processing Laboratory, U. C. Davis, Davis, CA, Nov. 1981.

3. Jain, A. K., Farrelle, P. M., and Algazi, V. R., "Image Data Compression," in *Digital Image Processing Techniques*, ed. M. Ekstrom, Prentice-Hall, Englewood Cliffs, NJ, 1984.

4. Jain, A. K., "Image data compresion: A review," *Proc. IEEE*, vol. 69, 349-389, March 1981.

5. Netravali, A. N. and Limb, J. O., "Picture coding: A review," *Proc. IEEE*, vol. 68, 366-406, March 1980.

6. Cooley, J. W. and Tukey, J. W., "An algorithm for the machine calculation of complex Fourier series," *Math. of Comput.*, vol. 19, 297-301, 1965.

7. Ahmed, N., Natarajan, T., and Rao, K. R., "Discrete cosine transform," *IEEE Trans. Comput.*, vol. C-23, 90-93, Jan. 1974.

8. Jain, A. K., "A fast Karhunen-Loève transform for a class of stochastic processes," *IEEE Trans. Commun.*, vol. COM-24, 1023-1029, Sept. 1976.

9. Harmuth, H. F., *Transmission of Information by Orthogonal Functions*, Springer Verlag, New York, 1972.

10. Andrews, H. C., *Computer Techniques in Image Processing*, Academic Press, New York, 1970.

11. Enomoto, H. and Shibata, K., "Orthogonal transform coding system for television signals," *IEEE Trans. Electromagnetic Compatibility*, vol. EMC-13, 11-17, Aug. 1971.

12. Pratt, W. K., Chen, W. H., and Welch, L. R., "Slant transform image coding," *IEEE Trans. Commun.*, vol. COM-22, 1075-1093, Aug. 1974.

13. Fino, B. J. and Algazi, V. R., "Slant-Haar transform," *Proc. IEEE*, vol. 62, 653-654, May 1974.

14. Habibi, A., "Hybrid coding of pictorial data," *IEEE Trans. Commun.*, vol. COM-22, 614-624, May 1974.

15. Shannon, C. E., "A mathematical theory of communication," *BSTJ*, vol. 27, 379-423, 623-656, 1948.

16. Shannon, C. E., "Coding theorems for a discrete source with a fidelity criterion," *IRE Nat. Conv. Rec., Part 4*, 142-163, 1959.

17. Ramamoorthy, P. A. and Tran, T., "A systolic architecture for real-time composite video image coding," *MILCOM 86*, 49.6.1-49.6.4, Monterey, CA, Oct. 1986.

18. Tao, B. P., Abut, H., and Mehran, F., "LSI architecture for VQ systolic array systems," *MILCOM 86*, 49.4.1-49.4.5, Monterey, CA, Oct. 1986.

19. Miyahara, M. and Kotani, K., "Block distortion in orthogonal transform coding – analysis, minimization, and distortion measure," *IEEE Trans. Commun.*, vol. COM-33, 90-96, Jan. 1985.

20. Reeve, H. C. and Lim, J. S., "Reduction of blocking effect in image coding," *Proc. ICASSP 83*, 1212-1215, Boston, 1983.

21. Nakagawa, M. and Miyahara, M., "Generalized Karhunen-Loève transformation I (theoretical consideration)," *IEEE Trans. Commun.*, vol. COM-35, 215-223, Feb. 1987.

22. Meiri, A. Z. and Yudilevich, E., "A pinned sine transform image coder," *IEEE Trans. Commun.*, vol. COM-29, 1728-1735, Dec. 1981.

23. Jain, A. K., "Partial differential equations and finite difference methods in image processing, Part I: Image representation," *J. Optimiz. Theory Appl.*, vol. 23, 65-91, Sept. 1977.

24. Farrelle, P. M. and Jain, A. K., "Recursive block coding – a new approach to transform coding," *IEEE Trans. Commun.*, vol. COM-34, 161-179, Feb. 1986.

25. Faux, I. D. and Pratt, M. J., *Computational Geometry for Design and Manufacture*, Ellis Horwood Ltd., Chichester, England, 1983.

26. Schreiber, W. F. and Knapp, C. F., "TV bandwidth reduction by digital coding," *IRE Nat. Conv. Rec., Part 4*, vol. 6, 88-89, 1958.

27. Schreiber, W. F., Knapp, C. F., and Kay, N. D., "Synthetic highs: an experimental TV bandwidth reduction system," *J. Soc. Motion Pict. Telev. Eng.*, vol. 68, 525-537, Aug. 1959.

28. Yan, J. K. and Sakrison, D. J., "Encoding of images based on a two-component source model," *IEEE Trans. Commun.*, vol. COM-25, 1315-1322, Nov. 1977.

29. Wang, S. H. and Jain, A. K., "Applications of stochastic models for image data compression," *Signal and Image Processing Lab.*, Dept. Elec. Comput. Eng. Univ. California, Davis, Sept. 1979.

30. Hosaka, K., "A new picture quality evaluation method," *Proc. International Picture Coding Symposium*, Tokyo, Japan, April 1986.

31. Jain, A. K., "Advances in mathematical models for image processing," *Proc. IEEE*, vol. 69, 502-528, May 1981.

32. Farrelle, P. M., "Recursive block coding techniques for data compression," M. S. Thesis, Signal and Image Processing Laboratory, U. C. Davis, Davis, CA, Dec. 1982.

33. Papoulis, A., *Probability, Random Variables, and Stochastic Processes*, McGraw-Hill, Inc., New York, 1965.

34. Ranganath, S. and Jain, A. K., "Two-dimensional linear prediction models, Part I: Spectral factorization and realization," *IEEE Trans. Acoust., Speech, Signal Processing*, vol. ASSP-33, 280-299, Feb. 1985.

35. Berger, T., *Rate Distortion Theory*, Prentice-Hall, Englewood Cliffs, New Jersey, 1971.

36. Ray, W. D. and Driver, R. M., "Further decomposition of the Karhunen-Loève series representation of a stationary random process," *IEEE Trans. Inform. Theory*, vol. IT-16, 663-668, Nov. 1970.

37. Yip, P. and Rao, K. R., "A fast computational algorithm for the discrete sine transform," *IEEE Trans. Commun.*, vol. COM-28, 304-307, Feb. 1980.

38. Wang, Z., "Comments on 'A fast computational algorithm for the discrete sine transform'," *IEEE Trans. Commun.*, vol. COM-34, 204-205, Feb. 1986.

39. Wang, Z., "Fast algorithms for the discrete W transform and for the discrete Fourier transform," *IEEE Trans. Acoust., Speech, Signal Processing*, vol. ASSP-32, 803-816, Aug. 1984.

40. Bisherurwa, E. J. K. and Coakley, F. P., "New fast discrete sine transform with offset," *Electron. Lett.*, vol. 17, 803-805, 15 Oct. 1981.

41. Ahmed, N. and Flickner, M., "Some considerations of the discrete cosine transform," *Proc. 16th Asilomar Conf. Circuits Syst. Comput.*, 295-299, Pacific Grove, CA, Nov. 1982.

42. Jain, A. K., "A sinusoidal family of unitary transforms," *IEEE Trans. Pattern Anal. Mach. Intelligence*, vol. PAMI-1, 356-365, Oct. 1979.

43. Jain, A. K. and Jain, J. R., "Partial differential equations and finite difference methods in image processing, Part II: Image restoration," *IEEE Trans. Automat. Contr.*, vol. AC-23, 817-834, Oct. 1978.

44. Bellman, R., *Introduction to Matrix Analysis*, Tata McGraw-Hill Publishing Co. Ltd., New Delhi, India, 1974.

45. Eggerton, J. D. and Srinath, M. D., "A visually weighted quantization scheme for image bandwidth compression at low data rates," *IEEE Trans. Commun.*, vol. COM-34, 840-847, Aug. 1986.

46. Huang, J. J. Y. and Schultheiss, P. M., "Block quantization of correlated Gaussian random variables," *IEEE Trans. Commun. Syst.*, vol. CS-11, 289-296, Sept. 1963.

47. Max, J., "Quantizing for minimum distortion," *IRE Trans. Inform. Theory*, vol. IT-6, 7-12, March 1960.

48. Lloyd, S. P., "Least squares quantization in PCM," *IEEE Trans. Inform. Theory*, vol. IT-28, 129-137, Mar. 1982. This is nearly a verbatim reproduction of a draft manuscript circulated for comments at Bell Laboratories; the Mathematical Research Dept. log date is July 31,1957.

49. Segall, A., "Bit allocation and encoding for vector sources," *IEEE Trans. Inform. Theory*, vol. IT-22, 162-169, March 1976.

50. Chen, W. H., Smith, C. H., and Fralick, S. C., "A fast computational algorithm for the discrete cosine transform," *IEEE Trans. Commun.*, vol. COM-25, 1004-1009, 1977.

51. Chen, W. H. and Smith, C. H., "Adaptive coding of monochrome and color images," *IEEE Trans. Commun.*, vol. COM-25, 1285-1292, Nov. 1977.

52. Reininger, R. C. and Gibson, J. D., "Distribution of two-dimensional DCT coefficients," *IEEE Trans. Commun.*, vol. COM-31, 835-839, June 1983.

53. Yuan, S. and Yu, K. B., "Zonal sampling and bit allocation of HT coefficients in image data compression," *IEEE Trans. Commun.*, vol. COM-34, 1246-1251, Dec. 1986.

54. Andrews, H. C., "Entropy considerations in the frequency domain," *Proc. IEEE (letters)*, 113-114, Jan. 1968.

55. Wintz, P. A. and Kurtenbach, A. J., "Waveform error control in PCM telemetry," *IEEE Trans. Inform. Theory*, vol. IT-14, 650-661, Sept. 1968.

56. Kurtenbach, A. J. and Wintz, P. A., "Quantizing for noisy channels," *IEEE Trans. Commun. Tech.*, vol. COM-17, 291-302, Apr. 1969.

57. Wood, R. C., "On optimum quantization," *IEEE Trans. Inform. Theory*, vol. IT-15, 248-252, Mar. 1969.

58. Paez, M. D. and Glisson, T. H., "Minimum mean-squared-error quantization in speech PCM and DPCM systems," *IEEE Trans. Commun. (concise papers)*, vol. COM-20, 225-230, Apr. 1972.

59. Adams, W. C. and Giesler, C. E., "Quantizing characteristics for signals having Laplacian amplitude probability density function," *IEEE Trans. Commun.*, vol. COM-26, 1295-1297, Aug. 1978.

60. Fox, B., "Discrete optimization via marginal analysis," *Management Sci.*, vol. 13, 201-216, Nov. 1966.

61. Tzou, K., "A fast computational approach to the design of block quantization," *IEEE Trans. Acoust., Speech, Signal Processing (Corresp.)*, vol. ASSP-35, 235-237, Feb. 1987.

62. Limb, J. O., Rubinstein, C. B., and Thompson, J. E., "Digital coding of color video signals – a review," *IEEE Trans. Commun.*, vol. COM-25, 1349-1385, Nov. 1977.

63. Hang, H. M. and Haskell, B. G., "Interpolative vector quantization of color images," *Proc. International Picture Coding Symposium*, Tokyo, Japan, April 1986.

64. Weber, A. G., "Image Data Base," USC SIPI Report 101, Signal and Image Processing Institute, University of Southern California, Feb. 1986.

65. Kernighan, B. W. and Ritchie, D. M., *The C Programming Language*, Prentice-Hall, Englewood Cliffs, New Jersey, 1978.

66. Anderson, G. and Anderson, P., *The Unix C Shell Field Guide*, Prentice-Hall, Englewood Cliffs, New Jersey, 1986.

67. Jain, A. K. and Wang, S. H., "Stochastic image models and hybrid coding," *Signal and Image Processing Lab.*, Dept. Elec. SUNY, Buffalo, Final Rep., NOSC Contract N00953-77-C-003MJE, Oct. 1977.

68. Tasto, M. and Wintz, P. A., "Image coding by adaptive block quantization," *IEEE Trans. Commun. Tech.*, vol. COM-19, 956-972, Dec. 1971.

69. Algazi, V. R. and Sakrison, D. J., *Computer processing in communications*, Polytechnic Institute of Brooklyn, Brooklyn, NY, 1969.

70. Andrews, H. C. and Tescher, A. G., "The role of adaptive phase coding in 2 and 3 dimensional Fourier and Walsh image compression," *Proc. Walsh Function Symposium*, Washington D.C., March 1974.

71. Narasimhan, M. A., Rao, K. R., and Raghava, V., "Image data processing by hybrid sampling," *SPIE*, vol. 119 Application of Digital Image Processing, 130-136, 1977.

72. Saghri, J. A. and Tescher, A. G., "Adaptive transform coding based on chain coding concepts," *IEEE Trans. Commun.*, vol. COM-34, 112-117, Feb. 1986.

73. Gimlett, J. I., "Use of 'activity' classes in adaptive transform image coding," *IEEE Trans. Commun. (Corresp.)*, vol. COM-23, 785-786, July 1975.

74. Cox, R. V. and Tescher, A. G., "Channel rate equalization techniques for adaptive transform coders," *SPIE*, vol. 87 Advances in Image Transmission Techniques, 239-246, 1976.

75. Clarke, R. J., *Transform Coding of Images*, Academic Press, London, 1985.

76. Farrelle, P. M. and Jain, A. K., "Recursive block coding with a variable block size," *Proc. International Picture Coding Symposium*, Tokyo, Japan, April 1986.

77. Farrelle, P. M. and Jain, A. K., "Quad-tree based two source image coding," *MILCOM 86*, 49.2.1-49.2.5, Monterey, CA, Oct. 1986.

78. Pavlidis, T., *Algorithms for Graphics and Image Processing*, Computer Science Press, Rockville, MD, 1982.

79. Huffman, D. A., "A method for the construction of minimum redundancy codes," *Proc. IRE*, vol. 40, 1098-1101, 1952.

80. Gallager, R. G., "Variations on a theme by Huffman," *IEEE Trans. Inform. Theory*, vol. IT-24, 668-674, Nov. 1978.

81. Spriggs, H. and Nightingale, C., "Recursive binary nesting .. a quad tree approach to image compression," *Proc. International Picture Coding Symposium*, Tokyo, Japan, April 1986.

82. Hartley, R. V. L., "A more symmetrical Fourier analysis applied to transmission problems," *Proc. IRE*, vol. 30, 144-150, 1942.

83. Bracewell, R. N., "Discrete Hartley transform," *J. Opt. Soc. America*, vol. 73, 1832-1835, 1983.

84. Bracewell, R. N., "The fast Hartley transform," *Proc. IEEE*, vol. 72, 1010-1018, 1984.

85. Gray, R. M., "Vector quantization," *IEEE ASSP Magazine*, 4-29, April 1984.

86. Habibi, A. and Wintz, P. A., "Image coding by linear transformation and block quantization," *IEEE Trans. Commun.*, vol. COM-19, 50-62, Feb. 1971.

87. Linde, Y., Buzo, A., and Gray, R. M., "An algorithm for vector quantizer design," *IEEE Trans. Commun.*, vol. COM-28, 84-95, Jan. 1980.

88. Lookabaugh, T., "stdvq.c and stdvqe.c − a vector quantizer package," *Information Systems Laboratory,* Stanford University, Stanford, CA, Jan. 15, 1987. Private communication.

89. Equitz, W. H., "Fast algorithms for vector quantization picture coding," M. S. Thesis, Massachusetts Institute of Technology, June 1984.

90. Hartigan, J. A., *Clustering Algorithms*, Wiley, 1975.

91. Bentley, J. L., "Multidimensional binary search trees used for associative searching," *Communications of the ACM*, vol. 18, 509-517, Sept. 1975.

92. *Floating Point Programmers Guide for the Sun Workstation*, Version A, Sun Microsystems, 23 May 1986.

93. Gersho, A. and Ramamurthi, B., "Image coding using vector quantization," *Proc. ICASSP 82*, 428-431, April 1982.

94. Ramamurthi, B. and Gersho, A., "Image coding using segmented codebooks," *Proc. International Picture Coding Symposium*, Davis, CA, March 1983.

95. Baker, R. L. and Gray, R. M., "Differential vector quantization of achromatic imagery," *Proc. International Picture Coding Symposium*, Davis, CA, March 1983.

96. Murakami, T., Asai, K., and Yamazaki, E., "Vector quantizer for video signals," *Electron. Lett.*, vol. 7, 1005-1006, Nov. 1982.

97. Marr, D., *Vision: a computational investigation into the human representation and processing of visual information*, W. H. Freeman and Co., San Francisco, CA, 1982.

Index